ARISTOTLE

ARISTOTLE

HIS LIFE AND
SCHOOL

CARLO NATALI
EDITED BY D. S. HUTCHINSON

PRINCETON UNIVERSITY PRESS
PRINCETON AND OXFORD

Copyright © 2013 by Princeton University Press
Published by Princeton University Press,
41 William Street, Princeton, New Jersey 08540
In the United Kingdom: Princeton University Press,
6 Oxford Street, Woodstock, Oxfordshire OX20 1TW

press.princeton.edu

Library of Congress Cataloging-in-Publication Data

Natali, Carlo, 1948–
[Bios theoretikos. English]
Aristotle : his life and school / Carlo Natali ; edited by D.S. Hutchinson.
pages cm
Includes bibliographical references and index.
ISBN 978-0-691-09653-7 (alk. paper)
1. Aristotle. 2. Peripatetics. 3. Philosophers, Ancient—Biography.
I. Hutchinson, D. S., 1955– II. Title.
B481.N3813 2013
185—dc23 [B]   2013009174

British Library Cataloging-in-Publication Data is available

The translation of this book has been funded by SEPS

Via Val d'Aposa 7, 40123 Bologna, Italy
Tel: 39 051 271992 Fax: 39 051 265983
seps@seps.it - www.seps.it

This book has been composed in Dante MT Std

Printed on acid-free paper. ∞

Printed in the United States of America

1 3 5 7 9 10 8 6 4 2

CONTENTS

PREFACE (2013)

One of the first books I recall reading, after I learned Italian in my fortieth year, was Carlo Natali's scholarly study on Aristotle's biography and the establishment of the Lyceum, *BIOS THEORETIKOS: la vita di Aristotele e l'organizzazione della sua scuola* (Bologna 1991). I found it to be a masterful demonstration of the skill of marshalling complex information; and a stable and more detailed picture of Aristotle came into focus for me. I thought I was an expert in Aristotle, as I had read many books on Aristotle in the course of my university career; but I had never seen such a quantity of information about who Aristotle really was, some derived from extraordinarily arcane sources, presented with such clarity and such compactness. What I absorbed by reading this one book amply repaid the effort I invested in learning Italian.

It gives me great pleasure to present this translated and updated version of Carlo Natali's book to English readers. I am confident that *Aristotle: His Life and School* will serve as the new modern standard biography of Aristotle, and the essential starting point for all future research on the person of Aristotle and on the intellectual way of life that he pioneered.

Aristotle's thought remains very much alive for us today, despite the great antiquity of his works, and his *Nicomachean Ethics* is the most widely studied book of moral philosophy at present on North American university campuses. Aristotle invented a new way of being an intellectual and his legacy as an institution-builder is profound: he founded an institution dedicated to advancing the life of the mind and the progress of the sciences, a research and teaching institution that is the distant forerunner of modern scientific learned societies. As our modern academic and research institutions continue to evolve in changing times, the life that Aristotle led and the intellectual life of his Lyceum remain topics of fascination and inspiration.

It is no easy matter to assemble all the available information about Aristotle and sort it from the misinformation, so that a complete and coherent biography results. There were two celebrated attempts to do this in the twentieth century, both of which remain classics in the field: Werner Jaeger's *Aristotle* (1923, translated into English in 1934), and Ingemar Düring's *Aristotle in the Ancient Biographical Tradition* (1957). For judicious evaluations of these books, readers are invited to consult Natali's comments on them (these can be located by using the indexed bibliography compiled for this updated English edition). It is not my place to evaluate the contributions made by these two books, but this surely is the place for me to point out to my readers the virtues of Natali's book.

In my view, this book is as comprehensive as Düring 1957, and as insightful as Jaeger 1923; the evidence is as close to hand as in Düring, and the prose is as readable as in Jaeger; Natali's organization is far clearer and more user-friendly than Düring's, and his judicious conclusions are not vitiated by controversial speculations about the supposed development of Aristotle's philosophy, a vice of historiography that represents the main flaw in Jaeger's work. In my personal library, Natali's book has become the standard-setting work, the most outstanding Aristotle biography of the twentieth century.

In the rest of this preface, I will give a brief account of how this revised and updated English edition came about, as well as what is new and what has been improved. But first I wish to reflect briefly on the achievements of the original Italian edition in bringing together a coherent biographical framework with which to control the scattered, exiguous, indirect, and uncertain forms of evidence that presently survive.

In his introduction (1990), Natali reflected on what it would be to succeed at his task, starting from criteria derived from George Steiner. The biography of a philosopher should "seek to make the biographical data correspond with the work of the philosopher, and to draw from this attempt the grounds of its legitimation; and yet completing a project of this sort, with a vision of the connections between life and theory that is both analytic and intuitive, would 'require something like genius' and 'demand formidable authority.' Linking the biographical events of a philosopher with the special characteristics of his thought is therefore an undertaking as difficult as it is fascinating." In some cases, this linkage is possible and has been brilliantly carried out, notably by Maurice Cranston in his magnificent biographies *Jean-Jacques: The Early Life and Work of Jean-Jacques Rousseau, 1712–1754* and *The Noble Savage: Jean-Jacques Rousseau, 1754–1762* (published in 1983 and 1991). These biographies have the rich narrative flow and insightful detail of novels, while being rigorously based only on the most primary evidence, namely archival documents written by Rousseau himself or his correspondents.

But this is precisely where the difference resides between an Aristotle biography and a Rousseau biography. The surviving handwritten archival evidence written by and pertaining to Rousseau is so extensive and so expressive of his personality and thought that Cranston was able to dispense with later scholarly sources, since he had better evidence in the modern archives than had been used by previous Rousseau biographers. With Aristotle, the situation is entirely reversed: not a single archival document survives from the classical period; Aristotle's personality was not morbidly self-expressive in the way that Rousseau's clearly was (I cannot conceive of Aristotle writing a work like Rousseau's *Confessions*); the facts and probabilities about key events need to be puzzled out on the basis of later ancient scholarly sources, all of whose works have themselves been lost in their original forms, except to the extent that there are damaged papyrus fragments remaining, or portions of their work that happen to have survived in one or more medieval manuscripts and have received a modern printed edition. Access to the scattered exiguous information on Aristotle is multiply indirect, and often compromised into uncertainty by the agendas of the ancient (or modern) scholars who transmit it. The brilliance of a successful Aristotle biography such as this one resides primarily in the careful marshaling and judicious assessment of the intermediate sources, as well as the insightful interpretation of passages in Aristotle's own works; the result is a stable and responsible picture of the biography, even though the philosopher is not personally revealed as fully or as intimately as Rousseau.

I became acquainted with Carlo Natali in 1997–98 in Padua, where I was spending the year as a guest of our colleague Enrico Berti. After I had commented on a draft of an English translation of Natali's book *La Saggezza di Aristotele* (published in 2001 as *The Wisdom of Aristotle*), I suggested to him that this book, his *BIOS THEORETIKOS*, needed to be translated into English as well; and when the idea was offered to Princeton University Press in 1998, the publisher was receptive. A contract was later proposed and entered into by PUP, a professional translator was engaged, and funds were sought and found to pay for the translating. Although progress was made, the project got stuck for a number of years, and things seemed hopeless when I learned the unfortunate story from Natali several years ago; but my friend and colleague Monte Johnson, whom I was introducing to Natali that evening, resolved that we should rescue it and bring it to completion ourselves. The next stage of work was done by Monte Johnson, and then the file was handed over to me, and I began to check the accuracy of the Italian translation.

It was at this point that I noticed a systematic problem in the draft of the book, that the original translator had used "standard translations," such as those in the Loeb Classical Library, to render the Greek and Latin passages that form the evidence base, whereas the original Italian translations that Natali had made for the first edition differed sometimes in significant ways. On some occasions the "standard translations" contradicted or undermined the line of thought for which Natali was arguing. To sort all this out, it was in fact necessary to find someone who knew all the relevant languages and who also understood the sometimes subtle historiography of the author; the professional translator needed to be supplemented or replaced by a professor translating.

So I volunteered myself for the job and, in the course of carrying it out, I came to understand at first hand why scholarly books are so rarely published in translation, and I developed a deeper appreciation for the scholar-translators who toiled to render crucial foreign language scholarship into English versions before I was able to read the originals. Indispensable contributions were made by the American scholar Edwin L. Minar Jr. in translating Walter Burkert's book *Lore and Science in Ancient Pythagoreanism* (first German edition 1962, English edition 1972), and by the Oxford philosopher Richard Robinson in translating Werner Jaeger's book *Aristotle: Fundamentals of the History of His Development* (first German edition 1923, English edition 1934, revised 1948).

I set myself the task in the summer of 2012 to retranslate all the passages from ancient sources that were used as evidence in Natali's book, in order to make sure that they were not only accurate but also harmonious with the interpretation he was advancing. To keep myself organized, I developed an index of sources, which I then decided to incorporate into the book. Since twenty years had passed since Natali had done his own translating for the original version of the book, I resolved to find out and make use of the most recent critical editions of the original texts. One effect of these decisions was that I carried out a sort of repetition of Natali's original philological procedures, the classical studies equivalent of repeating a scientific experiment. Every passage from ancient sources was independently translated by me, on the basis of the best critical editions (many of which were not available to Natali twenty years ago), and then confirmed by e-mail with Natali, especially where there were real or apparent differences in construal. This collaborative process resulted in many smaller and a few larger revisions to the primary evidence portions of the book, the more important of which will be mentioned below. But the most important result was deep confirmation: with the exception of one passage only (see below), we agree with each other on the proper construal of every ancient passage, and the ancient portions of the book are in effect doubly translated.

The long passage of time since the first edition made it opportune for the English edition to include a postscript by the author, to take stock of intervening developments in scholarship. The postscript (p. 145) serves to update the reader on several fronts of recent research, but it mostly confirms the stability and solidity of Natali's interpretations of the evidence, which have not been shaken by subsequent studies. His postscript was finalized in July of 2012, but in the intervening six months we have noticed several further contributions relevant to the topics of this book, contributions that I mention at the end of this preface.

Apart from the addition of the postscript and the indexes (a word on these below), in almost all other respects the book is essentially unchanged. Each page is dense with information, including reference to the primary sources and to the main secondary sources. I resisted suggestions to move the references to notes for the sake of "smoother reading," because the provenance of the evidence is always historiographically relevant in a field bedeviled with complexities in sources, and because on my own first reading of the book I appreciated the immediate access to the references back to the primary evidence. Rather than have the ancient citations set off from the body, I decided to highlight them in boldface type, which serves the reader as a visual signal meaning "primary evidence." In the case of papyrus texts, words in bold are translations of words fully legible in Greek, but words that are printed partly in bold are only partly legible in the papyrus; words and parts of words that are not in bold are supplemented wholly or partly by scholars, with more or less reliability; the result of this convention is a mottled effect which gives a visual impression of the varying amount of supplementation of gaps in the document.

Every item of ancient evidence has been indexed in the new index of sources (p. 181), which cross-indexes intermediate lost works as well as surviving texts. In some cases, the train of evidence is remarkably long and complex: for example (p. 36), an epigram hostile to Aristotle composed by Theocritus of Chios was cited in a book by an otherwise unknown person called Bryon, which was exploited in a commentary *On Demosthenes* by Didymus of Alexandria, which is mostly lost except for papyrus fragments recently re-edited by P. Harding; the same epigram of Theocritus was also cited in the lost work *On Philosophy* by Aristocles of Messene (recently re-edited by M. L. Chiesara), of which large excerpts are cited by Eusebius; so there are index entries leading to this epigram on this page under "Theocritus," "Bryon," "Didymus" (with bibliographical details to Harding's edition), "Aristocles" (with bibliographical details to Chiesara's edition), and "Eusebius." As well as providing access from passages to locations in the book, the index of sources also tracks the networks of nested sources.

The bibliographical index is an expansion of the original bibliography of the book, incorporating recent scholarship. Each item is provided with page references, so that the reader whose point of access is a secondary source can be directed to the relevant page. For certain particularly important modern books, such as Jaeger's *Aristotle* and Düring's *Aristotle in the Ancient Biographical Tradition*, I have provided fuller indexes that guide the reader from specific pages in these books to pages in this book. Certain specialized sources, such as the *Vita Marciana* (surviving in Greek in a single damaged manuscript in Venice) and the other ancient *Lives*, are indexed according to the subdivisions printed in Düring's book. I decided to provide the primary references of such texts in terms of Düring's reference system, relegating to the index Gigon's Prussian Academy edition, which has not succeeded in becoming the currently standard edition of this material; but the index provides cross-references to enable those scholars who can afford its high price to work with Gigon's book as well as or instead of Düring's.

Some notes have been supplemented, including these: note 34 to chapter 1 (Aristotle came to Plato's Academy "in the time of Eudoxus"); note 4 to chapter 3 (an extra detail about the Library of Alexandria); note 13 to chapter 3 (more details about the textual crux); note 15 to chapter 4 (more information on Hermippus); and note 23 to chapter 4 (the report by Aristocles about the seventy-five bronze "saucepans" of Aristotle). A few notes have been reduced, including note 63 of chapter 1, because Harding's 2006 edition of the papyrus fragments of Didymus cleared up most of the problems and confusions that made the note necessary.

Some accidentally mistaken or cryptic references have been corrected, or given in more detailed form. Some bibliographical references and cross-references have been provided with more information (never with less). Abbreviations of ancient names have been expanded. I have generally suppressed the ellipses in citations, preferring to cite the whole passage in full, or else to break the citation into two determinate ones. All chapter and section divisions and most paragraph divisions have been preserved, but a few paragraphs have been split or combined when I judged this an improvement. I used my judgment freely in splitting or combining sentences or clauses for the sake of the English version, and in placing reference information within sentences. I am responsible for all the final details of the translation, which I tried to make as literal and precise as possible.

When I made the decision to base the translations of the primary evidence on the most recent and most authoritative critical editions, I had not realized how much progress in philology had been achieved in the previous two decades. For example, from 2005 to 2012 Douglas Olson published a much-needed new edition of Athenaeus with Loeb, in eight volumes; the study of Strabo was put on a new foundation by

Stefan Radt, who published ten substantial volumes from 2002 to 2011, of edition, translation, and commentary; and the *Research on Plants* by Theophrastus was published for Les Belles Lettres in five volumes by Suzanne Amigues from 1988 to 2006. The old edition by Wimmer of the fragments of Theophrastus has now been replaced by eight volumes published since 1991 on *Theophrastus of Eresus: Sources for His Life, Writings, Thought, and Influence*, edited by W. Fortenbaugh, P. Huby, R. Sharples, and D. Gutas. We also benefitted from the new edition of the Theophrastean *On Weather Signs*, edited by D. Sider and C. W. Brunschön, who supplied some new facts related on p. 107. New work to replace Wehrli's *Die Schule des Aristoteles* has brought new light to the study of Dicaearchus, with a 2001 edition of his fragments by D. Mirhady, in W. Fortenbaugh and W. Schütrumpf (eds.), *Dicaearchus of Messana: Text, Translation, and Discussion*. There was also progress on Demetrius of Phalerum, with the 2000 publication of *Demetrius of Phalerum: Text, Translation, and Discussion* (eds. W. Fortenbaugh and E. Schütrumpf), containing a new edition of his fragments by P. Stork, J. M. von Ophuisjen, and T. Dorandi.

When new editions are made of ancient works witnessed by multiple medieval manuscripts, there is generally little change in the text constituted, and most passages will be literally identical in the new edition. Occasionally, however, more careful collations of the MSS will produce changes in the printed reading, and this has happened in a curious corner of this field of evidence, the report from Aristocles of Messene about the seventy-five bronze saucepans allegedly carried by Aristotle on his escape from Athens to Chalcis in 322 (see p. 132). In his original publication, Natali was relying on a nineteenth-century edition of Eusebius, who quotes Aristocles in lengthy excerpts, including his incredulous comment about the "very stupid story" that customs officials in Chalcis had discovered seventy-four bronze frypans on board Aristotle's ship. In her 2001 edition of the fragments of Aristocles, Maria Lorenza Chiesara revised this number to seventy-five, based on new collations of manuscripts of this and a related passage. When working with this evidence, I realized that "frypans" is not the correct translation of the noun in question; it is rather a large collection of "saucepans" that was allegedly discovered (see note 23 to chapter 4). Perhaps it makes no difference whether the hostile story was about seventy-four frypans or seventy-five saucepans; and yet when we reflect that the Greek for "saucepan" is a diminutive of the word meaning "platter" or "plaque," the possibility arises that what was discovered was a priceless archival collection of inscribed bronze plaques. If so, the so-called "stupid" story may well be a sly distortion of an interesting fact, rather than an invention *ex nihilo*.

When an ancient text is transmitted by a single damaged papyrus, improvements can often be brought about by fresh scrutiny of the document with modern techniques, including multispectral imaging. This is currently happening with the works of Philodemus, the Epicurean scholar whose books were discovered in carbonized scrolls in Herculaneum, and we have benefited from the new edition of David Blank of the end of Philodemus' *On Rhetoric* (pp. 27–29). We base our translation of the relevant passages on this new edition, which supersedes what was available to Natali in 1990, including more responsible supplementation of gaps in the document.

Another significant improvement to a papyrus text was brought about by Philip Harding in his 2006 edition of the fragments of Didymus, *On Demosthenes*. This was a major advance relative to the Teubner edition of Pearson and Stephens, which had occasioned much difficulty and uncertainty in the first edition of Natali's book; and our translations of this material are based on the text, and informed by the supplements and the construals, of Harding's edition.

Some works by ancient authors are transmitted by a single medieval manuscript, which makes their text especially vulnerable to error. Until recently, the latest edition of the work of Heraclides "Criticus" was published by Müller in 1848, which I consulted, resulting in this provisional translation of fragment 1, referring to three philosophical *gymnasia* in third-century Athens: "all of them thickly planted with trees and grassy lawns, gardens fully blooming with philosophers of every kind, recreation and pastimes for the soul, many schools, frequent spectacles." I noticed and puzzled a bit over the odd phrase "fully blooming with philosophers." But then when I consulted the most recent edition of this text (A. Arenz 2006) I found that this odd phrase was in fact a philological ghost, and the correctly collated and punctuated reading of xvi • Preface •

the text was less odd and more mundane: "**all of them thickly planted with trees and grassy lawns. Festivals of every kind; recreation and pastimes for the soul from every kind of philosopher; many schools, frequent spectacles.**"

The widely used editions of Diogenes Laertius published in the Loeb Classical Library and in the Oxford Clarendon Texts are both defective in a crucial passage (5.37), concerning Theophrastus on the process of revising and publishing his books (see p. 110 and note 13 of chapter 3). At this point, the MSS transmit different readings, one of which is not even reported by these two editions; but the situation was cleared up in the 2000 Teubner edition of Diogenes Laertius edited by M. Marcovich, who not only reports this variant but also selects it as the correct one. The passage is independently interesting, as it seems to refer to an ancient version of the "pressure to publish," as noted by Robert Sharples in his comments on the book when he was editor of *Phronesis* (vol. 38 (1993), p. 111), the only notice of the original Italian edition of Natali's book that was ever published in English.

On a few occasions we decline to follow the fancy of the latest edition, if the editor decided to "improve" on the transmitted text with one of his own speculations. A particularly egregious example of this, a new conjecture we decline to follow, is in Plato's famous comment about Aristotle, where the manuscripts provide a perfectly sound text, meaning this: "**Aristotle kicked us out, just as colts kick out the mother who gave them birth.**" Without providing a reason, Marcovich, the latest editor of the text of Diogenes Laertius, conjectures the loss of a remarkable adjective, yielding this: "Aristotle kicked us out, just as <*hupoptera* = 'winged' or 'flighty'> colts kick out the mother who gave them birth." But no, Plato's comment is remarkable enough without needing to be embellished by unsupported conjecture.

In a few cases, our revision process resulted in significant alteration in the evidence without there being a new edition of the primary text. At p. 19 and note 34 to chapter 1, Natali had wrestled with the confusing report that Aristotle arrived in Plato's Academy "in the year of Eudoxus." Since this does not provide an archon date (no such archon name is recorded for these years), speculation had arisen that this meant "in the year that Eudoxus was in charge of the Academy," a speculation that caused further puzzles. Natali noted that, in his 1962 edition of the *Vita Marciana*, Gigon had suggested other possibilities, that the list of archons is incomplete or that "Eudoxus" is a mistaken version of the relevant archon name. The problem was in the meantime resolved in 1977 in the first chapter of the publication by H.-J. Waschkies of his Kiel doctoral dissertation as *Von Eudoxos zu Aristoteles: Das Fortwirken der Eudoxischen Proportionentheorie in der Aristotelischen Lehre vom Kontinuum*; the list of archons is in fact complete, and the name "Eudoxus" is a simple textual corruption of the name "Euboulus," who was indeed archon in the relevant year 345 / 344, as many sources attest. I was made aware of Waschkies' solution to the problem by David Sedley several years ago, and we decided to add a postscript to add this information to note 34.

Aristotle personally observed and described a lunar occultation of Mars (p. 24), and in 1609 Johannes Kepler first calculated the date of this event as 357 BCE April 4. There were errors in Kepler's calculation, which was corrected in 1927 by K. Schoch to yield the date of 357 May 4, at 9 pm in Athens. When Monte Johnson, together with his student Cole Macke, looked into this question in connection with revising this book, they found, by using widely available astronomical software, that there were in fact several different possible dates for this observation in Aristotle's lifetime. When they were looking into the question of how to establish this rigorously, they discovered that similar conclusions had recently been reached and published by a professional astronomer (D. Savoie 2003), who calculated the occultations answering to Aristotle's description, at the locality of Athens during his lifetime, as having taken place on three possible evenings: most probable is 357 BCE May 4, from 20:12–21:30 local time; also possible is 361 March 20, 22:48–23:39, and 324 March 16, 23:53–00:15. For four hundred years it was thought that this observation, since it could have taken place on one occasion only, proved that Aristotle was doing astronomy at that specific time, presumably under Plato's leadership; but the establishment of alternative dates of the observation opens up the possibility not only that Aristotle's observation was perhaps even earlier in his first Athenian period but also that it might have taken place in his last Athenian period, and under his own direction, not Plato's.

Professor Natali and I find that we disagree about the construal of the primary evidence in exactly one case, namely the interpretation of a critical comment made by Cephisodorus, a student of the Athenian teacher Isocrates, against Aristotle. In his postscript (p. 148), Natali reports the discussion of the issue in the "Cephisodorus" article in the *Dictionnaire des Philosophes Antiques*, and draws support from the author's reasoning in favor of his construal, in which the accusation is that Aristotle made a collection of proverbs, something which is of no value. Our translation of the passage on p. 25 is neutral as between this interpretation and a different one that I favor, namely that the accusation of Cephisodorus was that Aristotle's arguments (in his lost dialogue *Protrepticus*, to which Cephisodorus was responding) made it not worthwhile to assemble mere collections of proverbs, such as Isocrates had done in his essay *To Demonicus*; proverbs do clearly have value, as Aristotle's own work richly shows, but their value is not realized by the assembly of proverbs into anthologies without explanations, something that Aristotle never did. The Greek sentence is capable of being understood in both ways, and its construal is ultimately a matter of scholarly opinion.

Professor Natali finalized his bibliographical update in July of 2012, but in the six months that have passed while I have been editing the book, we have noticed a handful of relevant publications about which our readers would surely like to be informed.

Our late lamented colleague Robert Sharples produced a volume published posthumously in 2010, an outstanding sourcebook of *Peripatetic Philosophy 200 BC to AD 100*, which delivers far more than what is promised by its modest subtitle: *An Introduction and Collection of Sources in Translation*. This meticulously presented work is the essential resource for the history of the later Peripatetic tradition in the periods following the one discussed in this book.

Andrew Ford's 2011 study *Aristotle as Poet* examines his "Hymn to Hermias" from a variety of perspectives, arguing that this was a significant poem in the history of Greek verse, against the background of Aristotle's alliance with Hermias at Atarneus (see pp. 32–42). Readers of this book are likely to find *Aristotle as Poet* very rewarding, not only for its independent translations and interpretations of the key passages that shed light on this period in Aristotle's life.

The essay by T. Bénatouïl, in T. Bénatouïl and M. Bonazzi (eds.), *Theoria, Praxis, and the Contemplative Life after Plato and Aristotle* (2012), is a fresh exploration of the debate between Theophrastus and Dicaearchus about the value and status of the intellectual life (see p. 117).

Publication of the CNRS *Dictionnaire des Philosophes Antiques* (ed. R. Goulet) has resumed, and the fifth volume was published in 2012, covering philosophers from Paccius to Rutilius Rufus; but neither one of us has yet studied this resource.

Finally, we look forward to the publication, announced for later in 2013, of Tiziano Dorandi's new edition of Diogenes Laertius, in the series Cambridge Classical Texts and Translations.

I am grateful to Prof. Enrico Berti for introducing me to Carlo Natali in Padua and for hosting my stay there in 1997–98. I appreciate the patience shown by Carlo himself in the course of the sometimes frustrating development of this book, as well as the patience and faith of Al Bertrand, our editor with Princeton University Press, and his assistant Hannah Paul and our production editor Natalie Baan. Thanks are due to Monte Johnson for his initiative in rescuing this project and for laboring to complete the first draft. I wish to express thanks as well to all the other supporters of this enterprise for their various contributions: Dimitris Apostolopoulos, David Blank, Alessandro Bonello, Jody Cundy, Sylvia Gaspari, Kasra Koushan, Cole Macke, Martha Perrier, and Anthony Shugaar.

D. S. HUTCHINSON
SAN DIEGO, 2013 JANUARY 30

INTRODUCTION (1990)

This outline of the life of Aristotle is not the work of a professional historian of the ancient world, only the fruit of the reflections of a scholar of the history of ancient philosophy; and it was born out of the need felt by the author to get his ideas clear when he was faced with a quantity of biographical reports, affirmations, and anecdotes often repeated but not always reliable. Historians with expertise in this period will not find much to learn from these pages, but my fellow "philosophers" or, better, "historians of philosophy," may perhaps find it useful to have in hand a brief sketch and a general interpretation of the available historical data about Aristotle. This reconstruction, like any other, is burdened by personal prejudices, historical conditioning, and limitations of every sort. But perhaps it is good that readers have an overall picture in front of them to discuss, and perhaps refute, rather than a series of dubious data and conflicting reports.

At a general level, perhaps, one might wonder whether a reconstruction of this sort does, after all is said and done, serve any useful purpose, or whether it is instead a futile exercise. There are some who have urged this doubt; for example, George Steiner, in the course of reviewing a biography of Wittgenstein (*London Review of Books,* 23 June 1988), wondered why in the world people feel the need to write biographies of philosophers. Husserl, he recalls, "believed that a philosophical argument was worth considering only if it aspired to the universality, to the truth-conditions of the anonymous." And Jonathan Barnes maintained, in his preface to *The Presocratic Philosophers* (1979), that "philosophy lives a supracelestial life, beyond the confines of space and time; and if philosophers are, perforce, small spatio-temporal creatures, a minute attention to their small spatio-temporal concerns will more often obfuscate than illumine their philosophies." To an Italian reader such as myself, these statements appear rather paradoxical, even if their caution is perhaps justified by certain excessively daring historical reconstructions of the lives of ancient philosophers. Located at the other end, both cultural and geographical, are the ideas of those who think it impossible to explain and expound correctly the life of an ancient philosopher such as Aristotle without taking into account the entirety of his life and the dramatic events that make it up (for a Russian example, see Losev and Takho-Godi 1982, p. 11).

Perhaps it is banal to say so, but very probably the truth lies in the middle. A truly serious biography, Steiner maintains, should seek to make the biographical data correspond with the work of the philosopher, and to draw from this attempt the grounds of its legitimation; and yet completing a project of this sort, with a vision of the connections between life and theory that is both analytic and intuitive, would "require something like genius" and "demand formidable authority." Linking the biographical events of a philosopher with the special characteristics of his thought is therefore an undertaking as difficult as it is fascinating.

Where Aristotle is concerned, one illustrious example of an ambitious attempt to produce a biography that connects life and theory is that of Werner Jaeger, in his *Aristoteles* (1923). Jaeger combined an account of Aristotle's life with a description of the evolution of his thought, from time to time halting the narrative of historical events and personal stories in order to provide a panoramic overview of Aristotle's thought in each particular phase of his life and spiritual evolution. The very remarkable allure and the impressive compactness of Jaeger's book, which remains a classic in the field even though many of its hypotheses are no longer accepted, derive from its original structure and from the application to Aristotle's works of the concept of "spiritual evolution," more than from any actual discovery of a strictly historical-biographical nature. But in the case of Jaeger the whole appears to be much more significant than the sum of its parts, and his work, together with that of Düring (which I will discuss later), remains a model to keep in mind.

In general, however, reconstructions of the life of Aristotle do not set themselves such ambitious goals. Speaking in very broad terms, one could say that academic historians are disposed, in general, to believe many of the anecdotal accounts offered us by ancient authors, and their writings tend to accept what is found in sources from Hellenistic and Roman times, such as Plutarch and Aulus Gellius; on the other hand, the studies of philologists and of historians of philosophy, who are more critical and diffident, cast doubt on the greater part of the data and traditional reports. The pictures that result are very different. Moreover, certain aspects of Aristotle's life, such as his relations with Alexander the Great or his link with Hermias, are at times treated by the same author in a contradictory manner, and it sometimes happens that we see attributed to the same historical figure the most contrasting positions.

While I do not set myself the objective of successfully resolving all these problems and these impasses in research, I have sought to make a summary of the situation, get to the bottom of certain doubts, and correct a few misunderstandings. My reconstruction starts off with ambitions far more modest than the requirements set out by Steiner, although it has no intention to be limited to a series of anecdotes and curious stories about the life and the personality of an ancient philosopher.

In my view, the interest to be taken in an investigation into the biography of Aristotle, as with the biography of Plato or of other figures of the ancient world, lies principally in the paradigmatic value of their intellectual experience. With Aristotle, in my view, a new cultural type was born, a model of the wise man different from that of his predecessors, and especially different from the sages who have been called the "Presocratics"; and a new style of philosophical reflection was worked out, the impact of which on European culture in all the centuries that followed would be very difficult to overestimate. What I am interested in doing here is to reconstruct as well as possible the historical features of this new intellectual figure, and to determine its specific characteristics.

In the reconstruction of these historical events I shall not concern myself directly with the content of Aristotle's thought; its birth and its development will be understood in a more global context, by means of a comparison with the philosophical discussions of the school of Plato and the influences of other cultural currents of his time. In this sense my research is lacking and insufficient, but it is impossible to proceed otherwise, given the enormous difficulty and the great complexity of this material. A major contribution to the delineation of the intellectual figure of Aristotle was made by Berti (1989), whose conclusions should be kept in mind, particularly when reading section 10 of chapter 1 of this book.

In working out this endeavor, the results of the work of Ingemar Düring (in particular Düring 1957) have been of precious guidance to me, as he analyzes the general trends, the prejudices, and the assumptions tacitly underlying the various biographical information on Aristotle; today the fruits of his investigations are an essential point of departure, even though, as we shall see, the logic of our endeavor has led me at times to an approach that is rather more constructive.

In the first three chapters of the present work I have started off by going back to the ancient sources, rather than the scholarly *status quaestionis*; and I have instead devoted the whole of chapter 4 of the present study to a delineation of the panorama of biographic research on Aristotle from the time of Zeller to the present. In the first three chapters I have not failed to keep in mind the results of the critical debate, at least of most of it, but I have undertaken first and foremost to re-read the texts, and have attempted to reconstruct a coherent picture of the life and of the intellectual personality of the philosopher by making use of the most reliable facts or, if not those, of the least uncertain ones. In order to give my readers some tools with which to check up on what I am going to be saying, I thought it a good idea to provide for them, in my own Italian translation, most of the data and most of the texts upon which I base my reconstruction.

CARLO NATALI
PADUA, 1990

CHAPTER ONE
THE BIOGRAPHY OF ARISTOTLE:
FACTS, HYPOTHESES, CONJECTURES

1. MANY FACTS, NOT ALL OF EQUAL INTEREST

On the biography of Aristotle we have few certain facts, and there has been much conjecture. We lack information on the most important issues, whereas there is much information about matters that are ultimately of marginal significance. The most recent discussion, from Düring 1957 and onward, is largely focused on the analysis of the sources, in order to identify their standpoint. It is very important to follow this approach, known to philologists by the name *Quellenforschung*, which has historically been the most rigorous and reliable method; when carried to excess, however, it tends to transform itself into the attitude of those who doubt every fact and, faced with any information, ask themselves only what intention was manifested by the ancient author or authors who are its source, without ever reaching a positive reconstruction. This attitude of diffidence is certainly justified by the history of the modern discussion of Aristotle's life (see chapter 4); but it can also lead one to focus too much on the discussion of details and lose sight of the general context.

All things considered, the certain facts that we have about Aristotle's life, though scarce overall, are actually far more numerous than those available for the lives of many other ancient philosophers. So without falling into the errors of ancient biographers, who reconstructed the biography of the philosopher by choosing eclectically from among the various reports and available facts those that best fit with their preconceived image of Aristotle, we can try to make use of the certain facts and the most plausible information to establish, in the most precise method possible, some of the most interesting aspects of his life and of his intellectual personality. It goes without saying, certainly, that today it is no longer possible to clear up all the obscure issues, to the point of giving a complete and exhaustive description of the historical figure of Aristotle. In this sense, the modest approach of Gigon (1961, p. 27), which acknowledges that the portrait of Aristotle "is to this day visible only in indefinite outlines," strikes me as the best one.

2. STAGIRA

"**Aristotle, son of Nicomachus and Phaestis, a Stagirite**" (Diogenes Laertius 5.1). "**Aristotle the philosopher was of the city of Stagira, and Stagira was a *polis* of Thrace, near Olynthus and Methone**" (*Vita Marciana* 1). Aristotle was a citizen of a small Greek *polis*, Stagira, located on the Silean Plain, in the Chalcidian peninsula, a colony of Andros (Herodotus 7.115; Thucydides 4.88.2, 5.6.1), which was an ally and tributary of Athens during the first Athenian league.[1] So Aristotle was not a "Macedonian subject," as some say, confused about his political status.

The history of Stagira is not illustrious: in 480 BCE, the army of Xerxes passed by it while on its way to invade Greece; then, in 424, during the Peloponnesian War, Stagira abandoned Athens and allied itself with Sparta, and for this it was besieged in 422 by Cleon of Athens. In 348, Philip of Macedon invaded the Chalcidian peninsula, conquered Zereia, and destroyed or forced the independent Greek city-states of that region into submitting to him (Demosthenes, *Third Philippic* 26; Diodorus Siculus 16.52.9). He then conquered and destroyed Olynthus, an Athenian ally. An ancient source, the democratic orator Demochares, nephew of Demosthenes, gave a speech in 306, during a trial connected to an attempted closure of all the philosophical schools of Athens,[2] accusing Aristotle of having been a friend of Philip of Macedon and of having played a role in this Macedonian expedition; according to Aristocles, in his *On Philosophy* (fr. 2 Chiesara), Demochares "**says that letters of Aristotle written against the city of the Athenians were intercepted, that he betrayed his home town of Stagira to the Macedonians, and also that, following the destruction of Olynthus, he was Philip's informer, in the place where the booty was being sold, about the wealthiest of the Olynthians**" (excerpted in Eusebius 15.2.6 = *testimonium* 58g Düring). On the basis of the passage quoted above and of the Neoplatonic biographies of Aristotle,[3] modern historians hypothesize that Stagira was destroyed by Philip of Macedon in 348

BCE, and that it was later rebuilt, during the life of Alexander the Great, by the intercession of Aristotle, who is also thought to have dictated the laws for the city.

All the same, we cannot be certain that the events described in the ancient biographies really took place; Demochares does not actually state that Stagira was destroyed; he only says that Aristotle "betrayed" Stagira, his homeland. Given the fragmentary state in which his words have come down to us, this argument from silence may not have much relevance. It is true, though, that the most reliable ancient sources do not list Stagira among the cities destroyed by Philip (see Mulvany 1926, p. 163 and Düring 1957, p. 59). It is therefore likely that the town was not destroyed, since in 322, twenty-six years after the invasion of Philip of Macedon, Aristotle's father's house seems to be still standing. In Aristotle's will, in fact, Aristotle mentions the house of his father in Stagira, directing that, if Herpyllis wishes to live in Stagira, she should be given "**my father's house**."[4] So what are we to say now about these assertions of Demochares?

When an ancient orator, during a trial held in a court in Athens, describes an event or an episode of his time to derive from it arguments in favor of one of his proposals, his method of presenting the facts is not excessively preoccupied with historical veracity. So we do not know whether Aristotle was actually in the camp of Philip of Macedon during the king's expedition. Other sources suggest that, in the period when Philip conquered Olynthus, Aristotle was not on the Chalcidian peninsula at all but elsewhere, perhaps still in Athens or perhaps already in Assos. But this passage from Demochares attests, at least, that in all likelihood something ugly happened in Stagira in 348, and that, toward the end of the fourth century BCE, in Athens at least, Aristotle was generally considered to be a friend of the Macedonians. I shall come back to this point later.

In Aristotle's works Stagira is never mentioned. His father's house, which is mentioned in his will, passed to Theophrastus, who gives directions about it in his own will: "**the estate in Stagira belonging to me I give and bequeath to Callinus**" (Diogenes Laertius 5.52). Theophrastus, in his *Research on Plants* (4.16.3), mentions a "*mouseion* **in Stagira**."[5] The source of our word "museum," the term *mouseion* originally designated a temple dedicated to the Muses, but it was later stretched to mean any place dedicated to cultural pursuits. We do not know whether this *mouseion* of Stagira was a temple of the Muses or Aristotle's own house, converted to a philosophical school and temple of knowledge. In the time of Theophrastus in any case (he died between 288 and 284 BCE), the city does not give the impression of being abandoned. However, by the time of Strabo (first century CE), Stagira had long been little more than a heap of ruins (book 7, fr. 15 Radt).

3. A FAMILY OF NOTABLES

We are well informed about Aristotle's family from the philosopher's will, which gives us much more information than is usual on these matters. All biographers, both ancient and modern, starting with Hermippus[6] (a biographer of the Aristotelian school, third century BCE), have based their works on the facts given in this will, with personal interpretations and additions. Not all the information is very interesting, but the sum of the information serves to delineate some aspects of the philosopher's native environment.

"**Aristotle was the son of Nicomachus and Phaestis, both descended from the family of Machaon, son of Asclepius** [. . .] **Aristotle was born under Diotrephes** [384/383 BCE]" (*Vita Marciana* 1 and 10). "**Aristotle, son of Nicomachus and Phaestis, Stagirite. Nicomachus traced his descent from Nicomachus who was the son of Machaon, who was the son of Asclepius** [. . .] **Apollodorus in his** *Chronicles* **says that he** [Aristotle] **was born in the first year of the 99th Olympiad** [384]" (Diogenes Laertius 5.1 and 5.9). "**Aristotle was the son of Nicomachus, who traced his family and his vocation back to Machaon, the son of Asclepius. His mother Phaestis was descended from one of the leaders of the expedition from Chalcis that colonized Stagira. He was born in the ninety-ninth Olympiad, when Diotrephes was archon at Athens, and so he was three years older than Demosthenes**" (Dionysius of Halicarnassus, *First Letter to Ammaeus* 5.1).

All we know about Aristotle's father is his name. According to several sources, his father died when Aristotle was young, a supposition strengthened by the fact that Neoplatonic biographies speak of his

being assigned a "guardian"; I shall return to this point later. The report
that he was a doctor is not confirmed in the will, where he is never mentioned. This information comes from one of Aristotle's earliest biographers, Hermippus,[7] who claimed that Nicomachus, Aristotle's father,
was a descendant of one of the most illustrious branches of the Asclepi-
ads. The biographers of late antiquity, expanding on this story in order
to honor Aristotle, say that Nicomachus was court physician and friend
of Amyntas, king of Macedonia (Diogenes Laertius 5.1, *Vita Marciana* 2,
Vita Vulgata 1, *Vita Latina* 2).

All of this might seem an invention, and to a great degree perhaps,
it is, but at the end of the fourth century BCE, both Epicurus and
Timaeus accuse Aristotle of being dissolute and of having sold drugs
or practiced medicine. The evidence that stems from Epicurus is
preserved for us in four later sources: Diogenes Laertius, Aristocles,
Athenaeus, and Aelian. In his biography of Epicurus, Diogenes Laertius (10.8) said that Epicurus called Aristotle **"a wastrel, who after
devouring his father's fortune took to soldiering and selling drugs"**
(*testimonium* 59a). In his *On Philosophy*, Aristocles asked, **"how could**
[Aristotle] **have consumed all his father's wealth, and then gone
off to be a soldier, and having failed at this as well, entered the
drug trade, and then joined Plato's Peripatos, which was open to
all comers, as Epicurus says in his letter *On Vocations*?"** (excerpted
in Eusebius 15.2.1 = *testimonium* 58b). One of the erudite speakers in
Athenaeus declares (8, 354b–c), **"I am well aware that Epicurus, who
was very devoted to truth, has said of him, in his letter *On Vocations*, that after he had devoured his father's inheritance he rushed
into the army, and because he was bad at this, he got into selling
drugs. Then, since the peripatos of Plato was open to everybody,
he** [Epicurus] **said, Aristotle presented himself and sat in on the
lectures, not without talent, and gradually got out of that and
into the theoretical** [disposition]**. And I know that Epicurus is the
only one to have said these things against him, not even Eubulides,
nor has even Cephisodorus dared to say that kind of thing against
the Stagirite, although they have published works written against
the man"** (*testimonium* 59b).[8] Aelian also reports, in his *Miscellaneous
Research* (5.9), a short version of the story transmitted by Epicurus, but

without identifying him as his source. "**Aristotle wasted the property he had from his father and rushed into the army. After turning out badly at this, he showed up again as a drug seller. He insinuated himself into the Peripatos and listened to the lectures, and, since he was naturally better than many, he then acquired the disposition that he possessed after this point**" (*testimonium* 59c).

From Timaeus of Tauromenium, historian of the late fourth century BCE, there are some other comments, preserved by Aristocles and by Polybius, that attempt to cast a discreditable light on Aristotle's character and his involvement with medicine. Aristocles protests, "**how can anyone accept what Timaeus of Tauromenium said in his *Histories*, that he** [Aristotle] **locked the doors of a disreputable medical clinic, when he was at a late age in life?**" (excerpted in Eusebius 15.2.2 = *testimonium* 58c). The abuse hurled by Timaeus against Aristotle was evidently too much for Polybius (12.8.1–4), who says, "**let's agree that people are ignorant and raving mad if they treat their neighbors with such enmity and harshness as Timaeus treated Aristotle. He says that he was brash, rash, and reckless, and, furthermore, that he said absolutely outrageous things about the city of Locri, alleging that their colony was a colony of fugitives, servants, adulterers, and slave dealers. And he says that he tells all this with such trustworthiness that he has the air of being the *numero uno* of those who were on campaign and had just now defeated the Persians marshaled at the Cilician gates, by his own strength, and not instead a retarded and insatiable sophist who had just shut down an expensive medical clinic; furthermore, that he used to jump into every house and every tent, and also that he was a glutton and a *chef de cuisine*, always getting carried away in the direction of his mouth**" (*testimonium* 60a; on this passage, see below, section 6.2).

Given the generally rather heavy way of engaging in polemics that is typical of ancient authors, these might even be "subtle" allusions to his father's profession. If so, Hermippus's assertion would appear to be confirmed. Even those who have hypothesized that the hostile tone of these reports should not be thought to go back to Epicurus himself, but rather to the polemical zeal of a former disciple of the Garden, still recognize that these statements are substantially to be attributed to

Epicurus (see Sedley 1976, p. 132). The many passages in which Aristotle speaks about medicine do not give any useful indications on this point.

Aristotle's mother, Thestis or Phaestis, on the other hand, is mentioned in his will, unlike his father.[9] Dionysius of Halicarnassus tells us that Aristotle's mother was a descendant of the Chalcidians who founded Stagira. Thucydides, however, claims that Stagira was founded by colonists from Andros, as we have seen, and not by Chalcidians. In antiquity, to say that someone was descended from the founders of a *polis* was a way of honoring them. However, it is likely that Phaestis was from Chalcis, since Aristotle went to live in that city after having left Athens the second time; and from his will it appears that he owned a house and garden there (Diogenes Laertius 5.14). Both parents were likely of Greek origin.[10] Aristotle also had a brother called Arimnestus,[11] who died before Aristotle, without children, and was mentioned in his will. Aristotle wished to erect a statue in his memory; his executors "**shall set up the bust which has been made of Arimnestus, so as to be a memorial of him, since he died without children**" (Diogenes Laertius 5.15).

As was said earlier, the Neoplatonic *Lives* claim that Proxenus, a citizen of Atarneus,[12] adopted Aristotle on his father's death; "**after being orphaned he was raised by Proxenus of Atarneus**,"[13] and Chroust ventures a date (370–369) for this event. If this report is true, Proxenus must obviously be considered an important figure in the life of Aristotle. If it is true that Proxenus was a citizen of Atarneus, this could explain the close relationship there always was between Aristotle and the tyrant Hermias of Atarneus. Moreover, Usaibia, an Arabic translator of a version of the Neoplatonic biography of Aristotle, claims that Proxenus was a friend of Plato, and that he sent Aristotle to the Academy for that reason; "**Proxenus, the mandatory of his father, handed over the young man to Plato. Some relate that he was entrusted to Plato in compliance with an oracle of God the Lord Almighty in the temple of Pythion. Others say that this so happened only because Proxenus and Plato were friends**" (Usaibia, *Life of Aristotle* 3, tr. Düring 1957; see Gigon 1962, commentary to line 31).

So Proxenus had apparently put Aristotle in contact with several of the people who would count for the most in his life. Of this Proxenus we know almost nothing; but Aristotle in his will had statues dedicated to Proxenus, Nicanor, and Nicanor's mother. He instructed his executors **"to make sure, when the images commissioned to Gryllion are finished, that they be erected, one of Nicanor, and one of Proxenus, which I intended to commission, and one of Nicanor's mother"** (Diogenes Laertius 5.15). It is fairly clear that Proxenus is the father of this Nicanor, who was still alive at that time, and of whom we ought to speak at somewhat greater length.

It seems that this Nicanor was adopted by Aristotle, who was his stepbrother. This report seems to be confirmed beyond doubt by a very fragmentary inscription at Ephesus, published by Heberdey in 1902, in which the privilege of *proxenia* is extended to a **"Nicanor, son of Aristotle of Stagira"** (see *testimonia* 13a–c). In Aristotle's will (Diogenes Laertius 5.12), Nicanor served as a testamentary executor, in second place, after the Macedonian general Antipater,[14] and was supposed to marry Aristotle's daughter **"when the girl has reached the suitable age."** In the will, Nicanor appears to be the oldest male of the family and to serve as its head (see Düring 1957, p. 263); **"if anything should happen to the girl before her marriage (may it not, nor will it), or after she is married but before there are children, Nicanor shall have power to administer, both concerning the child and everything else, in a manner worthy both of him and of us. Nicanor shall be responsible for the girl and the boy Nicomachus in all that concerns them, in such a way that he takes an interest in their affairs as if he were father and brother."** At the time that Aristotle died, Nicanor must have been away on a dangerous journey,[15] perhaps related to his professional obligations as a general (on which see below), since in his will Aristotle makes offerings for his safe return.

Many scholars (Zeller, Wilamowitz, Berve, Plezia, Gigon, and others) believe that this Nicanor, the son of Proxenus, is the same Nicanor who served as a general under Alexander the Great;[16] and if this hypothesis is right, he is certainly one of the most historically intriguing members of the whole family. I also tend to accept it, without being able to give a definitive proof of it, and from this point forward I shall take it as fact. Nicanor of Stagira (see Diodorus Siculus 18.8.3), a general in Alexander's army, was the one who in 324 read an edict at Olympia from

Alexander, in which the Macedonian king demanded that the Greek cities accord him divine tribute and recall those who had been exiled. And then after the death of Alexander, Nicanor fought in the service of Cassander (son of the Macedonian general Antipater), in the war that Cassander waged against Polyperchon (whom Antipater had named as successor instead of Cassander), a war that involved Attica directly (319–318 BCE). In that war, Nicanor was sent to command the Macedonian garrison in Athens, stationed in the port of Munychia by this same Cassander, after the death of his father Antipater (319). According to Plutarch's *Life of Phocion* (31.3), when he was in Athens Nicanor made a political alliance with the moderate politician Phocion, who "**met with Nicanor and conversed with him, making him in general meek and mild and favorably disposed to the Athenians**," and he became a friend of Demetrius of Phalerum, a pupil of Theophrastus.[17]

Nicanor was then drawn into the struggles among the various Athenian parties, which were in turn supported by the several Macedonian factions, and he occupied the entire port of Piraeus, from which he witnessed the condemnation and execution of Phocion (318). Demetrius of Phalerum, condemned *in absentia* from court, may have taken refuge with Nicanor and, through him, come into contact with Cassander.[18] In the same year (318), Nicanor and Antigonus defeated the fleet of Polyperchon in a naval battle, and in 317 the Athenians made peace with Cassander, who set up Demetrius of Phalerum as the governor of the city. Immediately after, Cassander had Nicanor killed, perhaps because he had acquired too much power.

Demetrius of Phalerum did not share his friend's fate, and he remained in power in Athens for ten years, during which time he had a way of favoring the philosophers: he arranged for Theophrastus to be accorded the right to own a landed estate (*enktēsis*) in Athens (Diogenes Laertius 5.39); and he ordered the release of Xenocrates,[19] who had been arrested because he was too poor to be able to pay the tax imposed by the city of Athens on *metics*, that is, on foreigners residing in Athens (Diogenes Laertius, 4.14). He is also said to have intervened in favor of philosophers and people tied to the cultural life of the city, including Theodorus "the Atheist," whom he supposedly saved from judgment before the Areopagus (Diogenes Laertius 2.101), the Cynic Crates, from whom he received little gratitude (Athenaeus 10, 422c–d), and, finally, the descendants of Aristides the Just, for whom he arranged to have a pension (Plutarch, *Life of Aristides*, 27.3–5).

Several of Aristotle's relatives and pupils, then, at the end of the fourth century BCE, appear to us to have been involved in the political affairs of Athens, on the pro-Macedon side, and we can guess at close ties of friendship and acquaintance among them. We shall come back to this point later.

There were two women named Pythia in the family. The first was Aristotle's wife, a relative of Hermias of Atarneus, a friend of Proxenus (the relationship between Hermias and Pythia is unclear: she may have been his daughter, niece, or some other relative; see below, section 6.1). The second was his daughter. Aristotle wished to be buried near his late wife Pythia; "**Wherever my tomb is erected, there the exhumed bones of Pythia shall also be laid, in accordance with her instructions**" (Diogenes Laertius 5.16). The ancients, stimulated by accusations of impiety, created the strangest stories about the couple's conjugal relations. For example, according to Diogenes Laertius (5.3–4), "**Aristippus in the first book of his *On the Luxury of the Ancients* says that Aristotle fell in love with a girl of Hermias. He came to an agreement with him and married her, and, overjoyed with the little woman, he made sacrifice to her in the way the Athenians sacrifice to Demeter of Eleusis.**" And in his *On Philosophy*, Aristocles declared that "**surpassing in foolishness all** [the other accusations] **are what Lyco said, the one who calls himself a 'Pythagorean'; he actually claimed that Aristotle made sacrifice to his late wife, the same sort of sacrifice that the Athenians make to Demeter**" (excerpted in Eusebius 15.2.8 = *testimonium* 58i). There must have been something about Aristotle's character that excited such piquant fantasies; even in the Middle Ages great sport was made of scenes of the great thinker on all fours, straddled by a courtesan.

When Aristotle died in 322 BCE, his daughter seems to have been younger than fourteen, since she was not yet old enough to take a husband. Perhaps she was an *epiklēros* heir, that is, a female child who is the inheritor of the property in the absence of a male heir.[20] This daughter would later marry Nicanor. In the will there is no mention of her name, Pythia, which is reported to us by the Neoplatonists. Sextus Empiricus (*Against the Professors* 1.258), many centuries later, claimed to know that she married three husbands.[21] **"Aristotle's daughter Pythia was married to three men, the first of whom was Nicanor of Stagira (a relative of Aristotle), the second was Procleus (a descendant of the Spartan King Demaratus) who fathered two children with her, Procleus and Demaratus,[22] who both studied philosophy with Theophrastus, and the third was the doctor Metrodorus (a student of Chrysippus of Cnidus and follower of Erasistratus) to whom was born a boy called Aristotle"** (*testimonium* 11b).[23]

Aristotle also had a son, Nicomachus, who is famous because the ethical treatise entitled *Nicomachean Ethics* is addressed to him. It is not actually known whether he was the son of Pythia or Herpyllis, Aristotle's second female companion, or whether he was legitimate or illegitimate, or whether he was Aristotle's sole heir. The question is probably not worth the ink spilled on it, often large quantities, from the end of the nineteenth century until our times (see Gottschalk 1972, pp. 323–325, with bibliography and *status quaestionis*). It is unlikely that Nicomachus was the editor[24] of the ethical treatise known under the title *Nicomachean Ethics*, since he must have died rather young. In fact, he seems to be already dead at the time of the drafting of Theophrastus's will, in which his father's student Theophrastus, who was the guardian of Nicomachus for a certain period,[25] directed that a statue of him be made, saying **"it is also my wish that a statue of Nicomachus be completed, of equal size"** (Diogenes Laertius 5.52).

Now let's enter the sphere of pure gossip. Great awkwardness, on the part of both ancient authors as well as scholars of the nineteenth and early twentieth centuries, was occasioned by the figure of Herpyllis, a woman who "was good" to Aristotle, and for whom he wished to ensure a quiet existence. His will reads as follows: **"the executors and Nicanor shall take care also of Herpyllis, in memory of me, because she was good to me, including, if she desires to take a husband, seeing to it that she be given one not unworthy of us."** Otherwise, if she chose not to get married, Aristotle ordered that she be lodged in one of his houses, in Stagira or in the section of the house at Chalcis reserved for guests, and that these houses should be supplied with all the furnishings necessary, in the judgment of Herpyllis herself. Moreover, he set aside for her one silver talent, one servant, and two slaves (Diogenes Laertius 5.13–14). Concerning the status of Herpyllis, the sources are in disagreement; in the Greek version of Aristotle's will, Herpyllis is treated as a free woman and not a slave (Mulvany 1926), but in the Arabic version of the will, on the other hand, she is treated as a servant; **"judging from what I saw of her earnestness in rendering service to me and her zeal for all that was becoming for me, she has deserved well of me"** (Usaibia, *Aristotle's Will* 1e, tr. Düring 1957). It appears evident, in any case, that Herpyllis was a woman very close to Aristotle for a long period of time.

All of the ancients (Hermippus, Timaeus, Diogenes Laertius, the *Suda*, and Hesychius) speak of her as Aristotle's lover (*hetaira*), while the Neoplatonists preserve a total silence about her. Aristocles of Messene, who wanted to protect Aristotle's reputation in his *On Philosophy*,[26] said that the philosopher in the end married her. **"After the death of Pythia, the daughter of Hermias, he married Herpyllis of Stagira, of whom his son Nicomachus was born."** Among modern scholars as well, some have found it inconvenient that a great thinker such as Aristotle had a companion out of wedlock, and they say that in the end the philosopher married her, or else affirm that Herpyllis was only Aristotle's "housekeeper."[27] But the provisions of the will hardly seem like the ones that are to be made for a simple housekeeper, and, on the other hand, the fact that Aristotle wanted to be entombed close to Pythia, and the general tenor of the bequest, would lead us to think that Herpyllis enjoyed a status slightly inferior to that of his first wife.

Not mentioned in the will, because he was already dead, was Aristotle's nephew Callisthenes, an important member of the family who had followed Alexander the Great on the expedition into Asia, with the well-known and tragic (for himself) consequences. We shall return to him below, in section 7.

Even if not all the information listed above is equally reliable, the family connections of the *genos* of Aristotle appear to me to be wide ranging and complex, more international than was the case for a typical Athenian family, generally proud of its local ancestry, and close to the networks of families of the archaic aristocracy. This is a family that was close to various "ruling classes" of its time, with ties to the courts of the Macedonian kings and the *diadochi*, to the tyrant of Atarneus, to the small towns of the Chalcidian peninsula and, later, perhaps, also to the royal family of Sparta. As we shall see below, the links of discipleship and family relationship tend to intermingle; Aristotle's most important pupil, Theophrastus, acted as the executor of his teacher's will, and his pupil, Demetrius of Phalerum, became a friend of Aristotle's stepbrother and adopted son Nicanor, while two of Aristotle's grandsons, Demaratus and "young" Aristotle, were welcomed during the lifetime of Theophrastus into the community of Peripatetic philosophers (Diogenes Laertius 5.53).

4. A PROVINCIAL PUPIL

In this section, we shall focus primarily on the external events that marked the early phase of Aristotle's life in Athens, referring the reader to other more important works for the question of his philosophical relationship with Plato and the development of his philosophy. The information that we possess concerning this period of Aristotle's life in Athens is concerned exclusively with his activity as a philosopher and a pupil of the Academy. "**Aristotle** [. . .] **became a pupil of Plato at the time of Nausigenes.** [. . .] **It is therefore not true, as these slanderers claim, that Aristotle became a follower of Plato at the age of forty, at the time of Eudoxus** [. . .] **according to the research of Philochorus**" (*Vita Marciana* 10–12). "**He encountered Plato and spent twenty years with him** [367–347], **having joined at seventeen**" (Diogenes Laertius 5.9). "**In the archonship of Polyzelus** [367/6], **after the death of his father, he came to Athens, being in his eighteenth year, and after he joined up with Plato, he spent a period of twenty years with him**" (Dionysius of Halicarnassus, *First Letter to Ammaeus* 5.2).

Aristotle conformed to a tradition, attested to as early as the period of the Sophists,[28] of choosing a famous master from whom to learn philosophy. We know nothing specific about his reason for coming to Athens. As I have already noted above (p. 11), the Arabic biographer Usaibia stated that Aristotle's guardian, Proxenus, entrusted the young man to Plato, because Proxenus and Plato were friends. Other authors make up other hypotheses.[29] One could hypothesize, for instance, that

Aristotle decided to study with a master of philosophy because he was interested in this discipline by reading some Platonic dialogue; in fact, one of the purposes of the dialogues was exactly this, to attract the best and the brightest to philosophy.[30]

What did Aristotle find when he arrived in Athens to study philosophy? According to H. von Arnim's reconstruction (1898, ch. 1), the earliest Sophists were itinerant teachers, not tied to any town or city (Isocrates, *Antidosis* 156), and their courses did not last a long time. In the course of time, however, full-fledged schools developed, with their own fixed group of students, who attended a course of lessons for a number of years in order to acquire *paideia*, some with a view to becoming philosophers, others simply to get a general education.[31] It is worth noting that in Diogenes Laertius the relationship between the masters of the lesser Socratic schools and their pupils is indicated by the term *diakouein* (2.111, 2.113, 2.126), which implies attending a course over time and not merely listening to a single public lecture; and the pupils of Stilpo were discussed in terms (2.113) that imply a remarkable familiarity and a long-term relationship, such as *apespasen, zēlōtas esche, prosēgageto,* and *apheileto.* Even the word *hetairoi,* which was sometimes used to describe the pupils of these philosophers, indicates the existence of a fixed group. And so Aristotle's decision entailed, at the very least, a commitment to stay in Attica for a long period of time.

In Athens at that time there were various active schools, and even though there is (from a theoretical standpoint) a vast gulf separating Plato and other teachers, such as the masters of rhetoric like Alcidamas and Isocrates, from the point of view of the public, Plato and Isocrates practiced the same "profession." The Platonic Academy appeared from the outside to be just another of the numerous residences or schools (*diatribai*) differing from the others only in terms of the program of study.

Aristotle very likely became one of Plato's pupils immediately, and did not attend any other schools.[32] Ancient sources attest to a certain degree of jealousy among the various masters, who struggled to keep their pupils from being taken away by others. Aristotle probably entered the Academy in 367/366 BCE, during the archonship of Polyzelus (according to Apollodorus, followed by Moraux and Düring), or in 368/367, during the archonship of Nausigenes (according to Philo-chorus, followed by Gigon, Berti, and Chroust), at the age of seven-teen or eighteen,[33] and stayed in the school for approximately twenty years, until 347. In 367/366, Plato was not in Athens, because after the death of Dionysius he had left for Syracuse, where he would stay for three years. Somehow a legend arose that during this three-year period Plato left Eudoxus in charge of the school, but there appears to be no evidence to support this.[34] The most recent editor of the fragments of Eudoxus even doubts that Eudoxus was ever a member of the Academy, and thinks rather that Eudoxus had a school of his own in rivalry with Plato's Academy.[35]

Aristotle remained at the Platonic Academy for roughly twenty years, from 367/366 to 347 BCE. Right from the beginning, or else at some point during his stay, he decided not to limit himself to receiving a general philosophical education, but to devote, in accordance with a specifically Platonic doctrine, the rest of his life to philosophical discus-sions and to a way of life dedicated to the cultivation of the intellectual virtues (*Republic* VII 536d–540c). Therefore, unlike the students of the Sophists and the orators, Aristotle's purpose in attending Plato's school was not to learn a technique that would put him in a position to pursue a profession and earn his living, but rather to realize a choice of a way of life. Often, as we shall see below (section 10, p. 70), modern critics iden-tify this decision as a professional choice, similar to the one to set out on a career as a professor in a modern university, but the comparison is not without its dangers.

In Athens, Aristotle lived as a *metic*, that is, an alien resident, subject like all his fellow metics to various obligations and prohibitions:[36] he had to pay a tax to the state, while citizens were exempt from taxes; he had to procure a *prostates*, an Athenian citizen who was his legal sponsor; he had to register as resident in an Attic *demos* (we do not know which one); he had to serve, in case of need, as a soldier in the army, or in the navy; he could not take any part in the political life of the city, nor could he hold a magistracy, nor could he own any real estate in Attica; and this last point, as we shall see, is linked to certain problems in the founding of the Peripatetic school. The condition of the metic was in no way despicable or servile, and at the beginning of Plato's *Republic*, the honest metic Cephalus is treated with great respect. As for Aristotle, Whitehead has maintained that, while there is no evidence that he enjoyed any special status over other metics (as Chroust, Grayeff, and others have supposed), his writings show no trace of any particular frustrations on this account.[37] And, on the other hand, we should also keep in mind the fact that Aristotle's scientific works are almost silent about his personal affairs.

Concerning the issue of the relationship between Aristotle and Plato, there are two distinct traditions: some sources maintain that relations between master and student were always cordial, while other sources claim that there was a falling out. This is in a way related to the issue of how to evaluate the philosophical distance between the positions of the two men; those who believe that there were no fundamental doctrinal disagreements usually maintain that their relations were cordial, as occurred in the Neoplatonist biographies. For example, the Neoplatonic biography of Aristotle affirms that "**Aristotle did not build the Lyceum in opposition to Plato while he was living** [. . .] **for he remained faithful to Plato until his death**" (*Vita Latina* 9 and 25, and *Vita Marciana* 9; see Düring 1957, pp. 256–258 and 357).

The reports that establish respect between Plato and Aristotle emphasize the fact that the master supposedly admired a very peculiar, and very anti-Socratic, way of doing philosophy on his student's part. Aristotle is said to have frequently walked out on the discussions in the school to be by himself reading books,[38] and Plato found nothing to laugh at in that, though he tried courteously to involve the solitary young man in the school discussions. Every so often it is suggested, most recently by Düring (1966, p. 13), that the young Aristotle who is a character in Plato's *Parmenides* might be a portrayal of the historic Aristotle.

On the other hand, those who admit that there were differences of thinking between Plato and Aristotle often think about there being a personal conflict as well. In antiquity it was thought that Aristoxenus, a student of Aristotle, had accused Aristotle of opening a school of his own before Plato's death. To the later ancient scholar Aristocles of Messene, this was an unbelievable report. "**Who could believe the things said by the musicologist Aristoxenus in his *Life of Plato*? During his** [Plato's] **wanderings and his absence, he** [Aristoxenus] **says that certain people, who were foreigners, rose up against him and established a Peripatos in opposition to his. Now some people think he said these things about Aristotle, though Aristoxenus refers to him consistently with reverence**" (excerpted in Eusebius 15.2.3 = *testimonium* 58d). "**So Aristotle did not build the Lyceum in opposition to Plato, for which Aristoxenus was the first to denounce him, followed by Aristides, if he remained faithful to Plato until his death**" (*Vita Marciana* 9 and *Vita Latina* 9; see also Aelius Aristides, *Oration* 46 (249.10) = *testimonium* 61a). In Diogenes Laertius (5.2), we find this famous anecdote about Aristotle: "**He left Plato while he was living; so they say he remarked that 'Aristotle kicked us out, just like colts kick out the mother who gave them birth.'**" On these texts, see below, chapter 4, section 2 and n. 20.

It is not known how much truth there is in all this; most of these reports were invented much later by later scholars, Hellenistic or Neoplatonic, who were probably influenced by the shifting relations between the Academy and the Aristotelian Peripatos over the course of the history of the two schools (Düring 1957, pp. 315–336; Gigon 1958, pp. 160+; Gigon 1962, pp. 44+). Fortunately, we have the word of Aristotle himself on this matter. From the text of Aristotle's works, the clear conclusion to reach is that there were doctrinal differences between Aristotle and Plato, which however did not result in personal conflict. In fact we can read, in *Nicomachean Ethics* I.4 (1096a11–13), that Aristotle finds it an obstacle to his examination of the notion of a Universal Good that "**the men who introduced the Ideas are friends of mine,**"[39] clearly a reference to Plato. A very cordial relationship between Aristotle and Plato is also suggested by the so-called *Elegy to Eudemus* (on this, see section 1.1C of chapter 4), which includes a celebration of Plato's personality and philosophy; Aristotle speaks of his friendship for "**a man whom the bad are forbidden even to praise | who proved it clearly, alone or the first of mortals | by his own way of living and his methods of reasoning | that man's goodness and happiness come together | but now no one is able to accept this ever**" (verses 3–7, fr. 673 Rose 1886 = fr. 2 Ross). It is well known that in certain parts of the *Metaphysics*, when Aristotle speaks of the proponents of the theory of ideas, he uses the first-person plural. This is a sign of at least a long-standing familiarity with the Academy, and a sense of community among Aristotle and the others (see Berti 1977, p. 20), though it is not really a sign of adherence to the doctrine in question; this was affirmed by Jaeger (1923, pp. 227–230) but denied by Cherniss (1935, pp. 488–494).

Compared with the no-holds-barred manner of polemic that was typical in antiquity, various instances of which have been mentioned in the preceding pages (Aristotle's enemies said that he was a lover of pleasure, that he was a glutton, that he had devoured his father's estate, and then chosen a military life, where he turned out unsuccessful as well, and then got involved in selling drugs, that he was a Johnny-come-lately Sophist with an insatiable appetite, greedy, devoted to serving his mouth), Aristotle's method of debate, like that of Isocrates, appears very moderate to us, since he refrains from any use of vulgarity. This is especially true of his polemics with his colleagues in the Academy, in his engagement with whom he goes only so far as a certain ironical observation, or else a certain venomous aside. For instance, he made two sarcastic comments at the expense of Speusippus in his *Metaphysics*: "**But nature does not seem to be episodic, to judge from appearances, like a bad tragedy!**" (XIV (N).3, 1090b19–20), and "**All the units become something that is good, and there is such a great abundance of goods!**" (XIV (N).4, 1091b25–26). Again, earlier in the same discussion, he lashed out briefly against Xenocrates, saying that "**it is evident from these considerations as well that the worst alternative is the third** [sc. the one of Xenocrates], **that the number of the forms is the same as the mathematical number, for this requires two errors to be combined into one opinion**" (XIII.8 (M), 1083b1–3). But there are also expressions of personal esteem, all theoretical disagreements aside, such as his evident respect for Eudoxus. "**His arguments were convincing because of his virtuous character rather than by themselves, for he was thought to be exceptionally self-controlled**" (*Nicomachean Ethics* X.2, 1172b15–16). This of course does not amount to great praise on the theoretical level.

A relationship of this sort, based on personal esteem, is understandable if we consider the relationships, made up of a sense of spiritual community (*koinonia*) together with a commitment to independent research, that can be concluded to have existed among the members of the Academy, as well as among those of the Peripatos, in the early phase of the history of these schools. In the Academy, there was radical criticism of both the doctrine of Ideas and Plato's doctrine of principles: Speusippus rejected the Ideas, while Xenocrates accepted the existence of ideal numbers; Aristotle harshly criticized the cosmology of the *Timaeus*, while Philip of Opus, on the contrary, developed its astronomical science in particular. Later, in the Peripatos, Theophrastus criticized many of Aristotle's theological beliefs in his own *Metaphysics*, as well as the Aristotelian idea of "place" (fr. 146 FHSG), the use of such expressions as "per se" (*to kath' auto*) and "the thing itself" (*to he auto*) (fr. 116 FHSG), and the Aristotelian theory of the active intellect (fr. 307a FHSG). We know from Cicero (*Letters to Atticus* 2.16.3) that Dicaearchus rejected the superiority of the intellectual life of study (*bios theōretikos*) over the political life (apparently in his *Tripolitikos*; see *Letters to Atticus*, 13.32.2), and in so doing rejected not only a view held by Theophrastus but also the very theoretical foundation that supported the existence of the Peripatetic school. But none of that resulted in any personal attacks.

In all probability, this relationship between masters and students was based on free discussion and a fundamental agreement in choosing the problems to be discussed, rather than the solutions to be espoused. This became impossible later, in the more dogmatic Hellenistic and Neoplatonic schools, where many of the stories mentioned above, about the conflicts between Aristotle and Plato, were invented. And even nowadays, theoretical differences between scholars can lead to harsh debates, fierce battles, stinging witticisms, every available way to express a reciprocal irritation, in some cases very explicitly; and at times it seems difficult for us to recover the admirable equilibrium of these early Greek masters.

Despite not wishing to talk about the issue of the development of Aristotle's philosophical thinking, it seems within the limits of this study to make some reference to the activities of study and research that Aristotle undertook in the Academy. This is an extremely important topic about which, unfortunately, we have very scanty information. We do not really know how work was actually organized inside Plato's school, and the hypotheses put forward have been many and varied (see the overviews by Isnardi Parente 1974 and 1986). Limiting ourselves strictly to what directly relates to Aristotle, it is in his works that we find some indications, and these indications show us Aristotle committed to amassing data in many differing fields of research: astronomy, collections of proverbs, and studies of dialectic and of rhetoric.

In a passage from his work *On the Heavens*, Aristotle states that he had personally observed (*eōrakamen*) the moon in a half-full phase pass in front of Mars, and Mars, hidden by the moon, then emerge from behind it (II.12, 292a3–6); "**In certain cases this has actually been clearly visible; in fact, we have observed the moon, when it was at the half, overtaking the star of Ares** [sc. the planet Mars], **which was covered up by its black** [shadow], **but came out visible and bright**." Modern astronomical data permit a calculation of the date and time of this observation, within a small range of possibilities. It probably took place between 20:12 and 21:30 on the evening of 4 May 357 BCE, when Aristotle was twenty-seven years old and had been a member of the Academy for ten years (see Natali 1978). It might also have taken place late in the evening of 20 March 361, according to the most recent study of the question (Savoie 2003; the remaining possible date of this observation in Aristotle's lifetime is much later, on 16 March 325, but if this was the occultation in question, Aristotle's work *On the Heavens* must be among the last works he wrote.) We must assume that this was not a casual observation but rather formed part of an activity of scientific research, in which the examination of celestial motion played an important role.[40]

Although Plato in *Republic* VII dismissed the importance of astronomical observation (529c–530b), there are records of astronomical observations by other students of Plato, besides Aristotle, such as Philip of Opus. "**This is also how the observations found in Philip about atmospheric conditions were established, as well as the discoveries of the heavenly motions on the basis of astronomy**" (Proclus, *Commentary on* Timaeus I, 103.3–6). Eudoxus of Cnidus wrote two books of astronomical observations: one, the *Phainomena*, containing astronomical observations that he made in Citium, and the other, the *Enoptron*, containing observations Eudoxus made farther south, in Athens or Cnidus, according to Lasserre (1966, p. 181).

Apparently, then, the research activity that Aristotle pursued at the Academy focused, from the beginning, on the subjects of astronomy and natural science.[41] For that matter, many authors agree that, in addition to dialectical discussions, members of the Academy carried on scientific activity involving the observation of natural phenomena, and that this was accompanied by the analysis of concepts in a strictly logico-philosophical way. This is confirmed by considerable evidence, of which the most striking is a renowned fragment by the comic author Epicrates[42] caricaturing the students of Plato, who were intent on dividing up the natures of things (i.e., the natural kinds) and were perplexed by the question of where to place a gourd within their conceptual divisions (*diaereseis*).[43] In this setting, empirical observation hardly seems separate from metaphysical analysis and dialectical discussion; rather, it seems to be part of that process, serving the role of providing the facts and the experiences that the metaphysician must "save" or, rather, which he must justify.

One report, found in Athenaeus (2, 60d–e), indicates to us another field of research that Aristotle pursued in the Academy; **"Cephisodorus, a student of Isocrates,[44] in his *Against Aristotle* (a work in four books) criticizes the philosopher for making proverb collections of no value"** (*testimonium* 63d). This research into proverbs is also a facet of the attention given by Aristotle to common opinion and to the *phainomena*, those impressions and beliefs that seem evidently true to various people. A theoretical study must take ample account of these facts, as Aristotle tells us in his *Metaphysics* (Book II (a).1, 993a30–b5); **"the theoretical study of the truth is in a way difficult and in a way easy. An indication of this is the fact that nobody is able to reach the truth satisfactorily, nor completely misses it; but each one says something true about nature, and while individually they contribute nothing, or not much, to the truth, from the conjunction of all we get a considerable amount. 'Who could fail to hit the doors?' as the proverb goes."**

Popular sayings and proverbs are frequently used by Aristotle in his works (for a list of passages, see Bonitz 1870, *s.v. paroimiai*). He gathered them not out of ethnological interest but as a collection of information to be used in the physical sciences as well, for instance, astronomy.

The collections of popular sayings are used in the cosmological research of Aristotle, in various surviving texts; for instance, in his *On the Heavens* I.3 (270b13+), Aristotle seeks confirmation of his theories in common beliefs and proverbs, stating that men have always, back to the earliest antiquity, called the material of which the sky is composed "ether"; and in *Meteorology* I.3 (b16–30), the same thing is repeated (on these passages, see Natali 1977). Aristotle, from his earliest days of activity as a scholar, shows a special interest in widely held beliefs, more than Plato ever accorded to them. This activity of learned research, of collecting the most widely varying facts, such as this collecting of the proverbs, the popular maxims, and the sayings of the ancients, for instance, will remain one of Aristotle's distinctive traits (see Moraux 1951, pp. 128–129 and 334, and also below, section 2 of chapter 3, pp. 104–107).

Many authors, including Zeller (1897, 1:17n3), say that one of Aristotle's first activities in the Academy was to offer a "course" in rhetoric. It seems difficult to believe, however, that there would ever have been interest within the Academy for any teaching of rhetoric that would be technical and practical, like that found in the school of Isocrates (von Arnim 1898, p. 19). There is no other student of Plato, as well, of whom we have reports of "courses" properly so called; and modern authors who write about this topic sometimes project the structure of a modern university onto the organization of Plato's school.[45] One could rather consider it to have been a study concerning the nature of conviction, more theoretical than technical, like the one contained in Book I of the *Rhetoric*. The rivalry between the school of Isocrates and that of Plato, documented by many sources, as well as by the above cited text written by Cephisodorus, may have led the members of the Academy to examine more deeply the nature of persuasion and to take notice of certain fundamental claims of Isocrates; but I cannot imagine a rivalry between Aristotle and Isocrates in the narrowly technical area of the training of orators.

On the other hand, however, there are some ancient authors, such as Philodemus of Gadara, Cicero, Quintilian, Strabo (14.1.48), and Syrianus, who speak of certain "courses" of rhetoric offered by Aristotle (*testimonia* 32a–e and 33). They tell the story that Aristotle, at a certain point in his "career" as a teacher of philosophy, and therefore not right at the very beginning of that career, changed his theoretical opposition to rhetoric, and began to teach this *technē*. Philodemus goes on the attack against Aristotle on this matter, near the end of Book VIII of his treatise on rhetoric, a book written on a roll of papyrus broken into two scorched part-rolls found in Herculaneum (*P.Herc.*832 and *P.Herc.*1015), yielding mostly legible tops and bottoms of columns, but not their middle portions. (We refer to the edition of the text in the reconstruction and edition of Blank 2007, by the reconstructed column numbers as well as papyrus line numbers.) Near the beginning of this extended polemic (col. 192: *P.Herc.*832, 36.1–6), he mentions "**what they proclaim ab**[out] **Aristotle, that he used to train** [students] **in the afternoons, commenting, 'It's a shame to be silent and let Isocrates speak.'**" After a little more than a column, Philodemus sarcastically imagines one scenario where it might make sense to teach rhetoric: if someone "**lacks the necessities of life but might have to a certain degree a facility for rhetoric because of certain causes**[46] **that go ba**[ck to his yo]**uth, perhaps in a way he might for a short time make a good living by teaching it to some of those who solicit him as a teacher, until he can return to his proper subject of philosophy, as he would with reading and writing and gymnastics and any subject which as a child he picked up because of his parents' upbringing**" (col. 194: *P.Herc.*1015, 49.1–19).

Next follow several paragraphs of criticism directed against the profession of teaching rhetoric, and then Philodemus returns to personal attack, saying, "**nor was Aristotle very philosophical when he did what we hear told about him along with his rebuke. Why was it more shameful to be silent and let Isocrates speak?**" (col. 196: *P.Herc.*832, 40.1–8). To this rhetorical question comes a rhetorical reply: "**if deeds are advantageous, so is speaking, even if he didn't exist; but if neither are, nor is giving speeches, even if there were thousands of him, so that Aristotle's knocking him down whenever possible wouldn't seem to be actually motivated by resentment**" (col. 197: *P.Herc.*1015, 52.10–19). In the middle of this column some lines of text are missing, but when it resumes, the subject has not changed, and Philodemus is still attacking: "... **but not by reference to the natural goals; if he was using these, how could he fail to consider it a shame to speak** from the rostrum things that make him resemble those orators who slave for wages, more than those philosophers who equal the gods? And why, along with his exhortation of the young towards the worse, did he also hazard terrible revenge and hostility on the part of the students of Isocrates, as well as the other sophists?" (cols. 197–198: *P.Herc.* 832, 41.5–14 + *P.Herc.* 1015, 53.1–6). Two columns later, Philodemus finally reaches the end of his polemic against Aristotle on rhetoric, before moving on to attacking his interest in political thought. Apparently, Aristotle opposed "the rhetoric which seemed similar to that of Isocrates, which he mocked in a variety of ways, but not political rhetoric, which he considered to be different from that other kind. If, then, he offered training for this kind, not the didactic kind, it was ridiculous for him to say that it was a shame to allow Isocrates to speak, since he was not going to speak in the same way as him. I'm not even mentioning the fact that of those who studied rhe[tor]ic with him, not one has gone down as a shin[ing example] of either of them" (cols. 199–200: *P.Herc.* 832, 43.1–14 + *P.Herc.* 1015, 55.1–3).[47]

Cicero also refers to Aristotle's rivalry with Isocrates and his witty quip at his expense (*De Oratore* 3.141). "Aristotle himself, when he saw Isocrates flourishing with fine students because he [Isocrates] turned his discussions from lawsuits and political cases into empty elegance of speech, altered almost the whole form of his own teaching, and quoted a verse from *Philoctetes* with a slight alteration; he said, 'It's a shame to be silent and let barbarians speak' (but he [Aristotle] altered this to 'let Isocrates speak'); and after that he decorated and illustrated all his erudition, and combined knowledge of facts with practice in oratory" (*testimonium* 32a). In other works, Cicero refers to this episode in the following terms (*Tusculan Disputations* 1.7; see also *De Oratore* 14.46): "Aristotle, a man of the greatest genius, knowledge, and resources, when motivated by the renown of Isocrates the orator, began to teach young men to speak and to join intelligence with eloquence" (*testimonia* 32b–c).[48]

Not all of this information is 100 percent reliable. Philodemus of Gadara often makes use of very old Epicurean documents in his polemics, but here he mixed together various events that had occurred in different periods; in fact, he talks about the research into constitutions allegedly jointly conducted by Aristotle and his student Theophrastus (col. 198: *P.Herc.* 1015, 53.7–19).[49] **"Of course, he was greatly admired for his ability, but disparaged for his subject, and that's why he got caught like a thief collecting the laws, together with his student, as well as such a quantity of political constitutions, and legal judgements about the localities and the right times, and everything, as much of such . . ."**

So it is difficult to say whether the information that Philodemus gives us actually has anything to do with Aristotle's first stay in Athens in the Academy.[50] As for Cicero, it often seems that his chief purpose is to produce an argument that is rhetorically pleasing, more than to provide us with historically precise information. Employing a rhetorical device that derives distantly from the Aristotelian theory of the right mean, Cicero at times depicts characters from the cultural history of antiquity and has them evolve from opposed positions to a kind of right mean. (For a more detailed analysis of Cicero's method of constructing anecdotes, see Natali 1985.)

What is common to many of these sources is the idea that, at a certain point, Aristotle supposedly changed some aspect of his educational practice, and declared, "It's a shame to be silent and allow X to speak," and decided to begin teaching rhetoric.[51] It seems clear to me that these sources do not confirm the modern notion that Aristotle taught his first "course" of instruction in rhetoric in the Academy, because they maintain unanimously that Aristotle changed his educational methods and began to teach rhetoric only at a certain point in his development.[52] They know nothing about any content of the instruction, and they connect his interest in rhetoric with his interest in political life; Philodemus naturally criticizes all of this, while Cicero predictably approves of it wholeheartedly. We know from various sources that Aristotle wrote a work, perhaps in the form of a dialogue, entitled *Gryllus*, to mark the death of Xenophon's son at the battle of Mantinea (362 BCE), but we have no reliable indications about the content of this work.[53] The attempts so often undertaken to flesh out this ghost work, attributing to it parts or concepts of the first two books of the *Rhetoric*, can only remain hypotheses.

We do, however, have a document that dates from the period when Aristotle was offering instruction in the Academy. In the last chapter of *Sophistical Refutations*, which is generally thought to be a youthful work, Aristotle summarizes the purposes of the treatise and underscores the importance of his work, in which, for the first time, the syllogism is examined. "**Now then, we decided to discover some ability to make arguments** (*dunamin tina sullogistikēn*) **about what is proposed on the basis of what we started out with as being the most well reputed opinions; for this is the function of dialectic as such, of the skill of putting to the proof**" (183a37–b1). "**Now then, it is evident that what we decided to do has reached a satisfactory end, and we must keep in mind what has been settled about this subject** (*pragmateia*)" (183b15–17). "**Now on the subject of rhetoric much had already been said, and a long time ago; but about making arguments** (*sullogizesthai*), **on the contrary, we had absolutely nothing earlier to tell you about, except what we have labored for a long time in searching to study** (*tribēi zētountes*). **And if it seems to those of you who are viewing us that, out of such things as existed in the beginning, the investigation is now satisfactory, more than the other subjects that are based on adding to what has been transmitted** (*ex paradoseōs ēuxēmenas*), **then what remains, for all of you who have listened to our work, is to be forgiving of what has been omitted, and to be very grateful for what has been discovered**" (184a8–b8).

In contrast with rhetoric, a subject upon which numerous textbooks already existed for a long time, dialectic found a systematic form for the first time in the work of Aristotle. He stated that he had labored for a long time over these subjects (*tribēi zētountes polun chronon eponoumen*) and that he hoped for the indulgence and gratitude of his audience. What can we draw from this passage? First of all, that Aristotle in the Academy offered lectures, dedicated to the illustration of the various dialectical forms, by way of reading such *logoi* as the *Topics* and *Sophistical Refutations*; moreover, that he spent a great deal of time on the study of dialectic during this period; in the third place, that he apparently always paid special attention to the comparison between rhetoric and dialectic, a comparison that is present in this text, as well as in the beginning of the *Rhetoric* and in the lone fragment of the lost dialogue

Sophist.[54] All the same, here too there is no mention of a "course on rhetoric," and it would seem that the central focus of Aristotle's attention during these years had been dialectic, whereas rhetoric was pressed into service primarily as a point of comparison; on this, see Berti 1977, pp. 175+.

5. A SUDDEN INTERRUPTION

In the year 348 BCE, Philip of Macedon conquered Olynthus, and in 347 the anti-Macedonian party of Demosthenes took power in Athens. In that same year, Plato died, and Speusippus became the head of the Academy after him.[55] **"Now then, Spe[usippus] succeeded him as head of the school. Philochorus** [says that when Speu]**sippus** [dedicated] **the Graces in the *mousei*[*on*] he was then** [in] con[trol] **of it, and on them is i**[nsc]**ribed: Speusipp**[us] **dedicated these Goddesses of Grace to the s**[acred] **Muses, offering gifts for the sake of lea**[rn]**ing."**[56] And in this same year Aristotle left Athens, perhaps together with Xenocrates. **"When Plato died in the first year** [of the 108th Olympiad], **at the time of Theophilus** [348/347 BCE], **he** [Aristotle] **set out to stay with Hermias and remained three years** [347–345] (Diogenes Laertius 5.9). **"When Plato died in the archonship of Theophilus** [348/347], **he** [Aristotle] **set out to stay with Hermias, the tyrant of Atarneus, and spent a period of three years with him"** (Dionysius of Halicarnassus, *First Letter to Ammaeus* 5.2).

In the most recent studies, there has been much discussion whether Aristotle's departure from Athens was caused by events within the school or by external political events. Those who believe that the death of Plato was the decisive cause of his departure, as does Jaeger (1923, pp. 135–144),[57] think that Aristotle was driven away by doctrinal disagreements with Speusippus, and was signaling in this way his distance from Platonism. Others who think, along with Zeller (1897, 1:19), that the reasons were not reasons of "theoretical" rivalry, but what we would define today as "academic politics," tend to suppose that neither Aristotle nor Xenocrates would have accepted the naming of Speusippus as the head of the school. A judgment of this sort presupposes in the Academy a job of "scholarch," with specific administrative functions and a special moral authority over the other constituents of the community. That is acceptable for dogmatic schools, such as the Epicureans (see below, section 3 of chapter 2), in which it was important that the scholarch be a faithful follower of the master's thought, but such an idea seems far less appropriate for the more liberal schools of Plato and Aristotle.

Those who, on the other hand, believe that Aristotle had already, at the time of Plato's death, taken an independent philosophical position think that there is no reason to accept that Plato's death would have triggered a philosophical crisis in Aristotle, and they therefore judge it possible that the departure of Aristotle from Athens is due to external reasons, to a worsening of the political climate.[58] This entails accepting that Aristotle already in this period represented an openly pro-Macedonian position, such as would make him invidious to the Athenians in a moment of crisis such as that which followed the conquest of Olynthus. The words of Demochares quoted above (section 2 of chapter 1) would support this hypothesis, but it would seem that these words were spoken forty years after the event and in a different historical moment. It is not possible to establish anything certain on this point, because neither of these two hypotheses has yet found any unimpeachable arguments in the texts.

6. AT THE COURTS OF PRINCES AND KINGS

6.1. ATARNEUS

The period from 347 to 335 BCE is the most obscure time in Aristotle's life. After he went away from Athens, his tracks appear more uncertain, and the reports on his movements appear more doubtful than before. It is reasonably certain, all the same, that he spent three years at the court of Hermias, the tyrant of Atarneus. "**When Plato died in the first year** [of the 108th Olympiad], **at the time of Theophilus** [348/347 BCE], **he set out to stay with Hermias and remained three years** [347–345]; **and he went to Mytilene at the time when Euboulus was archon, in the fourth year of the 108th Olympiad** [345]. **And at the time of Pythodotus he went to stay with Philip, in the second year of the 109th Olympiad** [343], **Alexander being already fifteen years old** [thirteen, according to Düring 1957, pp. 34 and 254]" (Diogenes Laertius 5.9–10). "**When Plato died in the archonship of Theophilus** [348/347], **he set out to stay with Hermias, the tyrant of Atarneus, and spent a period of three years with him before departing for**

Mytilene in the archonship of Euboulus [345/344]. **He left there to stay with Philip in the archonship of Pythodotus** [343/342], **and spent a period of eight years with him as tutor to Alexander**" (Dionysius of Halicarnassus, *First Letter to Ammaeus* 5.2–3).

Perhaps the acquaintance between Aristotle and Hermias, discussed by Didymus Chalcenterus in the passage quoted below, was due to the fact that Proxenus was from Atarneus; some scholars have hypothesized that in 347, after Aristotle left Athens, he simply decided to go back to one of the cities where he had personal ties.[59] If the statement of Strabo quoted in note 61 is to be taken seriously, Aristotle was accompanied by his fellow Academic philosopher Xenocrates, a native of Chalcedon on the Bosphorus, a city not far from Assos; but Strabo is the only source of this report.[60] Afterward, Aristotle spent two years in Mytilene, and then for another three years served as the tutor of Alexander the Great. We do not really know what he was doing during the other four years.

Hermias of Atarneus is nowadays known primarily because he was a friend of Aristotle, but he was a very well-known and much-discussed character in antiquity.[61] Without mentioning his name, Demosthenes reports (*Fourth Philippic* 32) that "**the man who is the agent and accomplice of all of Philip's machinations against the King** [of Persia] **has been seized, and the King will hear of all these deeds, not from our accusations** [. . .] **but from the man himself who organized them and carried them out**." Nineteenth-century philologists speculated that the person linked to Philip of Macedon, to whom Demosthenes refers anonymously, was in fact Hermias of Atarneus. This hypothesis has been confirmed by the discovery of a somewhat damaged papyrus fragment from a work commenting on the *Philippics* of Demosthenes by Didymus Chalcenterus (an Alexandrian scholar of the first century BCE), who, in connection with that passage, explains the reference in Demosthenes at some considerable length.[62]

The purpose of the scholar's comments is to provide a sketch of the controversies concerning the figure of Hermias. "**Since** [a great dif]-**ference is to be heard among those who trans**[mit stories about Hermias for the sake of] **the receptive ears** [of those who nowadays] **busy themselves with such things, I think I should speak about this** [at greater length]. **For some recol**[lect the man] **as the best, others, by** contrast, as the worst" (col. 4, lines 59–65, as edited and supplemented by P. Harding 2006). Didymus then quotes Theopompus, who, in the forty-sixth book of his *Philippics*, reports Hermias as being a eunuch and a Bithynian, who seized Assos and later conquered Atarneus and the surrounding territory. According to Theopompus, he was the cruelest and wickedest tyrant of all, he used drugs against his enemies, and he treated many of the Ionians abusively. In the end, Theopompus concludes, he was punished for his misdeeds, by being seized and dragged before the king of Persia, at whose hands he endured considerable physical abuse before being crucified (4.66–5.21).

This same Theopompus, however, in a *Letter to Philip* (a passage also cited by Didymus, at 5.24–28 and 5.52–63, rather damaged lines), says that Hermias had acquired a certain fame among the Greeks. In this *Letter*, apparently written during the lifetime of Hermias, he is described as being "**refined, and a lov**[er of beauty] (*philokalos*). **And, despite being** [a barba]**rian, he does philosophy with the P**[lato]**nists, and, although he was born a slave, he competes in international festivals with expensive teams. And despite possessing rocky crags and tin**[y land] **he got** . . . [*twenty-three lines are too damaged to be intelligible*] . . . **Plato** [. . .] **and into the surrounding country he led his army** [. . .] **and Erastus and Aristotle** [. . .] **for which reason indeed they all** [. . .] **afterwards,** [when others] **had** [come] **he gave them so**[me land] **as a gift.** [. . .] **And he changed the tyranny** . . . **to a milder system of rule. For this reason he also ruled over a**[ll the neigh]**bo**[ri]**ng country as far as Assos, when** [. . .] **to the above-mentioned philosophers** [. . .] **the city of Assos. Of th**[em] **he was most** [recep]**tive to Aristotle, and** [his disposition to]-**wards him was very familiar.**"[63]

Among Hermias's supporters there was also Callisthenes, who recalls his death in heroic tones. In the account of Didymus (5.66–6.18), according to Callisthenes, "**not only was he this so**[rt of man when he was far from] **dangers, but even** [when he found himself] **close to them he continued to remain the same, and he gave the great**[est proof of his virtue then,] **in the man**[ner of his death.] **For the bar-barians observed** [his] **courage** [with astonishment.] **Indeed the King, when** [question]**ing him and hearing** [nothing] **different from the same stories, was impressed by his courage and the steadiness of his**

demeanour, and it occurred to him to let him off completely, thinking that if they became friends, he would be one of the most useful. But when Bagoas and Mentor objected, out of resentment and
the fear that if released he might be foremost instead of them, he
changed his mind again; but when [he] passed sentence, he granted
him an exemption from the mutilations that take place there, [on
account of] his virtue. Now the existence of such moderation [on
the part of] enemies is totally incredible and [greatly contrary to] the
cus[tom] of the barbarians. [. . .] Phil[ip . . .] about to [. . .] for him to
[send a mes]sage to his [friends and his com]panions that he had done
nothing un[worth]y of philosophy [or dis]honorable.'"

This mention of Hermias's death leads us directly to recall the poem
written by Aristotle, described by Didymus as a hymn (*paean*), cited next
in his text (6.22–36).[64]

O Virtue, won by much toil of the mortal race,
You are the prettiest prey in the hunt of life;
For your beautiful form, O Virgin,
To die, is in Greece a fine fate to strive for,
As well as enduring fierce trials unending.
Such fruits as this you cast into hearts,
As good as immortal, and better than gold,
Better than parents, and languid-eyed sleep.
For your sake, even the godlike
Hercules and the sons of Leda
Held up under many labours
When [hunting for] your power;
Longing for you, Achilles and
Ajax went to the house of Hades;
For the sake of your lovely form, the scion
of Atarneus forsook the rays of the sun.
Wherefore the glory of his deeds,
And he, shall be exalted by the Muses,
The daughters of Memory, they who
Exalt the majesty of godlike Hospitality,
And the privilege of lasting Friendship.

Didymus then recalls (6.39–43) that Aristotle erected a monument to Hermias at Delphi; the monument still existed in Didymus's time, and on it was the following inscription:

Here lies, breaching the law sacred to Blessed Ones,
A man killed by the king of bow-bearing Persians,
Not besting him plainly in dread combat with spears,
But using the trust of a most treacherous man.

But it doesn't end there; there were further polemics to reckon with. Didymus then cites (6.46–49) from a book about Theocritus of Chios written by a certain Bryon, who states that Theocritus composed the following hostile epigram, apparently in response to the above epigram by Aristotle:[65]

To Hermias the eunuch, and slave of Eubulus as well,
This empty tomb was raised by Aristotle's empty mind.
Impressed by the belly's lawless nature, he chose to dwell
In the outlet of Borboros' stream, not in the Academe.

Lastly, Didymus concludes (6.50–59), there are even differing accounts of where Hermias was captured and how he died. Hermippus, in the second book of his *Aristotle,* says that Hermias died in prison, but others say that he was tortured and crucified, as Didymus had mentioned earlier (5.19–21), relying on Theopompus. A third version was supplied by Callisthenes, who states, as we saw above, that Hermias suffered appalling treatment with conspicuous bravery, without admitting anything to the king about his plots with Philip, which earned him an exemption from mutilation.

The result of these conflicting reports and opinions, in which some glorify Hermias and others consider him a villain, is that the reports about him are completely confused and contradictory. What is certain is that Hermias was the tyrant or dictator, after Eubulus, of Atarneus, the birthplace of Proxenus, who was Aristotle's adoptive father or guardian. Besides Theopompus and Strabo (13.1.57), Diogenes Laertius and others say that Hermias was a eunuch, a former slave of Eubulus, the former tyrant of Assos (who had been a banker), and then was himself tyrant (see *testimonia* 21–24).[66] In 345/344, in 343, or in 341/340, according to the various reconstructions,[67] as Didymus and Strabo tell us, Hermias was captured and killed by Mentor, a mercenary in the service of the Persian king. His reign therefore did not last a long time, five or ten years at the most. It seems clear from Aristotle's *Hymn to Hermias* that Hermias was a Greek and not a barbarian, as Theopompus claimed in the passage quoted above; but it was customary among Greek authors, when engaged in a polemic, to call everyone barbarians (see Mulvany 1926).

Some sources that tend to praise Aristotle, such as the Neoplatonic biographies, prefer to pass over in virtual silence this relationship with so questionable a figure; among the biographers of this tradition, his stay at the court of Hermias is mentioned only in Usaibia, and the mention is brief (*Life of Aristotle* 5, tr. Düring 1957). The school of Aristotle by contrast, beginning with the master himself, always defended the memory of Hermias;[68] Aristotle celebrated his virtues in the *Hymn* and with the epigram, both cited above. The metric form of the poem was first studied by Festa (1923) and later Bowra (1938), who argued that the very form of the poem indicates that it was composed to be sung in chorus, and thinks that it was sung every day at Aristotle's table. This story, as Athenaeus clearly tells us (15, 696a), is tied to the question of the trial for impiety brought by the Athenians against Aristotle; see below, section 9 of chapter 1, pp. 61–62. Didymus Chalcenterus, as we have seen above, cites the treatise that Aristotle's nephew Callisthenes wrote about Hermias, in which a favorable approach is evident, making Hermias out to be virtually a martyr to philosophy. Later, in the first century BCE, the Peripatetic Apellicon wrote another treatise, defending the friendship between Aristotle and Hermias from defamation (see section 1 of chapter 4). And so the tradition favorable to Hermias continued throughout the history of the Peripatetic school, both to celebrate the tyrant and to defend Aristotle from the accusation of having ties to a man considered by many to be despicable.

In general, there are no significant traces of the events of Aristotle's private life in his works. Aristotle mentions Eubulus in *Politics* (II.7, 1267a31–37), without naming Hermias;[69] and in the *Economics*, a later work written by a member of the Aristotelian school, Hermias is cited (II.2, 1351a35), but there is no talk of his friendship with Aristotle. The friendship between Aristotle and Hermias, all the same, is proved with certainty by Aristotle's so-called *Hymn to Hermias*, mentioned above (and on this see section 1.1C of chapter 4). In this text, the references to the "majesty of godlike Hospitality" and to the "privilege of lasting Friendship" testify to the nature of the friendship between the philosopher and the tyrant. Some believe that Aristotle had a role as political adviser to Hermias, in accordance with the Platonic tradition; see Mulvany 1926, p. 164, and Weil 1960, p. 15).

We know that Aristotle married Pythia, a person who was certainly very close to Hermias, and who is mentioned in Aristotle's will (see above, section 3 of chapter 1, pp. 14–15). Gigon calculated that there are no fewer than six different versions of the relationship between Pythia and Hermias: daughter, granddaughter, concubine, niece, sister, and sister adopted as daughter.[70] In his *On Philosophy*, Aristocles preserves part of a letter said to be from Aristotle to Antipater, which seems to express a need on Aristotle's part to defend his marriage; he tells Antipater, "**I married her after the death of Hermias,**[71] **out of good will toward him, and in any case she was sensible and good**" (excerpted in Eusebius 15.2.14 = *testimonium* 581).

Hermias had relationships not only with Aristotle but also with the Academy at large. As we can conclude from the passage quoted above, and from numerous other sources, several students of Plato had already got there before Aristotle, notably Erastus and Coriscus of Scepsis (*testimonia* 10T5–7 Lasserre 1987). Coriscus of Scepsis was the father of the same Neleus of Scepsis who became a student of Aristotle in the Peripatos and inherited the library of Theophrastus, according to Strabo 13.1.54 (*testimonium* 10T3 Lasserre 1987) and Diogenes Laertius 5.52 (we shall discuss the fate of these libraries below, in section 3 of chapter 2). Therefore, there existed a definite relationship between the Platonic school and Hermias, but it is not easy to establish either its origin or its nature. Some ancient sources speak of a sojourn spent by Hermias in the Platonic Academy (Theopompus and Hermippus, cited above, and Strabo 13.1.57, cited in note 61), but the name Hermias appears in none of the lists of the students of Plato (for these lists, see Lasserre 1987, *testimonia* 1T1–9).

Moreover, from the Platonic *Sixth Letter*, purportedly sent by Plato[72] to Hermias, Erastus, and Coriscus, in order to exhort them to get along together, it appears that Plato had not yet met Hermias. "**It seems to me, without yet having met him, that Hermias has a natural ability of this sort** [sc. practical political ability], **and has acquired skill through experience**" (322e6–7). And the letter makes it out that the connection between the Academy and the tyrant depended on the fact that Erastus and Coriscus, students of Plato, had become friends of Hermias, in a relationship that was useful for both. "**You are living as neighbours one to another, and you have an obligation to help each other as much as possible. For Hermias, neither the great number of horses he has, or of other military armaments, nor even his gold, add overall to his power as much as his having lasting friends of sound character**" (322c–d). Erastus and Coriscus, on the other hand, need a statesman who can protect them, so that their studies would not get neglected (322e–323a). In the passage cited above,[73] Hermippus describes the relationships that Hermias maintained with Plato's students and, on the basis of this fragmentary information, some have supposed that Hermias actually entrusted the Platonists with a city they could rule, Assos. But from the text of the *Sixth Letter*, nothing would seem further from the interests of Erastus and Coriscus than to receive the gift of a city, even a small one like Assos, to rule over; in fact, they "**lack the wisdom to defend themselves against the wicked and the unjust, as well as a certain ability for aggression,**" and they are "**inexperienced** (*apeiroi*)" (322d–e). Nor is there any mention of any role as political advisers that the two of them supposedly played under Hermias, as certain modern critics believe (e.g., Gaiser 1985, p. 17).

It is true that in a treaty between Hermias and the city of Eretria, carved on a stone inscription that is still preserved (Dittenberger 1915, no. 229), there are several mentions of Hermias "**and his associates**" (*kai hoi hetairoi*). Jaeger (1923, pp. 112+) and others such as Gaiser (1985, p. 20) have thought that they could identify these *hetairoi* as Erastus and Coriscus; and Pavese (1961) actually thought that they were Aristotle and Xenocrates, and he believed that Aristotle had been part of the government. This is pure speculation,[74] and it is in no way likely that the *hetairoi* were the philosophers. The story is told, in the ps.-Aristotelian *Economics* (2.2, 1351a33–37), that Mentor of Rhodes, after taking Hermias prisoner and seizing his fortresses, left in place the "overseers" (*epimelētai*) that Hermias had posted there. When these overseers felt more secure and brought back into light the riches that they had concealed, Mentor arrested them and stripped them of everything. It is clear from this passage that those who were in charge of governing the fortresses, such as Assos, on behalf of Hermias, were no philosophers, who fled when the tyrant died, but simple soldiers, as is shown by their conduct. It is also noteworthy, in this text, that there is no moral judgment whatever and no expression of support for Hermias; that characteristic differentiates this text from all the other passages of Peripatetic origin about Hermias (see van Groningen 1933, p. 172). The judgment offered of Mentor in *Magna Moralia* (1.34, 1197b21–22), by contrast, is much harsher; Mentor is said to be clever (*deinos*) even though he is wicked (*phaulos*). According to the *Suda* (*s.v.* "Hermias" = *testimonium* 24), Hermias is said to have written a treatise on the immortality of the soul in one book, following Aristotle's doctrines, but no one believes this.

Aside from these reports, there is not much information about what Aristotle was doing in Assos. From Wilamowitz (1893, 1:334) and onward, it was thought that Aristotle had participated in the discussions of a school of philosophers (this is also stated by Jaeger, Bidez, Bignone, Gauthier, and various others).[75] According to Jaeger (1923, p. 149), this school was an offshoot of the Platonic Academy, set up to realize on a smaller scale the political attempt that failed at Syracuse. And, in fact, the sources that are hostile to Plato give a long list of students who tried to apply in their own cities the political doctrines of their master;[76] but that there was in Assos a relationship between philosophers and a tyrant, like the one theorized by Aristotle in which the government follows the advice of the philosophers, is not at all certain. If this modern hypothesis were to be confirmed, the short duration and tragic end of the tyranny of Hermias would certainly not provide much supporting evidence for the practicality of the Aristotelian formula, nor for the quality of the advice given by the philosophers to the tyrant.

While we cannot say anything precise about the political role of Aristotle and his colleagues, there is however fairly certain evidence of the existence of a community of philosophers at Assos;[77] Theopompus, in the passage quoted above, states that Hermias engaged in philosophy together with the Platonists, even though he was a barbarian and a slave; and Philodemus of Gadara, in his *Index of Academic Philosophers,* speaks of a *peripatos* where philosophers gathered.[78] "**They had been invited by Her[mias] in a very kindly way earlier, too, but then, because of the death of Plato, he urged them even a b[it mo]re. On their arrival, he** [gave] **them everything in common and allowed them to li[ve in] a city, the city of Assos,**[79] **where they re[sid]ed and did philosophy, meeting together in a single** [Peri]**patos, and Hermias provided them, it** [seems,] **with every**[thing nec]**essary.**"[80] Moreover, Aristotle often cites Coriscus, especially in *Metaphysics* and in *Eudemian Ethics,* as an example of an "individual substance," and this has led some to think that the passages in which his name appears were written when Aristotle, Erastus, and Coriscus were discussing topics of first philosophy together.

According to what little we can gather from these sparse reports, the community of Plato's students in Assos was not divided by any substantial disagreements, and Philodemus emphasizes that they all belonged to a single Peripatos (concerning the meaning of this term, see section 4 of chapter 3). This does not necessarily mean that in this period Aristotle had no distinct philosophical positions of his own. It indicates rather that the habit of study and discussion acquired in the Academy was carried on in Asia Minor as well, presumably on the basis of comparing different opinions on similar problems, problems that all Academics concurred in considering important and worthy of attention. We shall return to this point later.

Many have remarked that the data on the life of the animals collected in *Research on Animals* show that Aristotle conducted a large part of his biological studies over the course of the years from 347 to 335 in the Troad, at Assos and Atarneus, and then on Lesbos, and then in Macedonia, because many of the observations pertain to species common and in some cases indigenous to those regions (Thompson 1910 and Lee 1948). But this reasoning, which at first seemed unquestionable, has been opened up again for discussion more recently, and with good reason; in his *Research on Animals,* Aristotle worked primarily from written sources, including Homer, the poets, and Xenophon, and not from personal observation (Solmsen 1978; but see Byl 1980, pp. xxxviii–xl and 1–135). All the same, we cannot rule out that Aristotle dedicated part of his time in Assos and Mytilene to biological research. A theory that Theophrastus met Aristotle before the latter's stay on Mytilene, that he took part in the Peripatos at Assos, and that he wrote his work *On Fire* at Assos, has been hypothesized by Gaiser (1985, esp. pp. 28–36), but without any secure textual basis.[81]

Around 345/344 BCE, Aristotle left Hermias and moved over to Lesbos, perhaps to conduct research, in the view of Lee (1948, p. 64), or perhaps because of his newly born friendship with Theophrastus, in the view of Regenbogen (1940, col. 1357) and Berti (1977, p. 29). There he made the acquaintance of other people, and other students of Aristotle came from Lesbos, such as Phanias and Praxiphanes, as remarked by Bignone 1936 (2:43–44); Bignone also claims that Aristotle also founded a school in Mytilene (1936, 1:411+), but this is a doubtful business.[82]

6.2. MACEDONIA

According to the ancient chronologies, in the years 343–335 BCE Aristotle lived in Macedonia, first as the tutor of Alexander and later, when Alexander was appointed regent by his father Philip in 340, as a private citizen. The evidence about this period in Aristotle's life is fairly thin, as Zeller had long ago noted (1897, 1:21–22). The chief source for the event in Aristotle's life that took him to Macedonia is Plutarch, who writes in his *Life of Alexander* (7.2) that, since Philip **"didn't have much faith in teachers of music or the general curriculum to provide him with attentiveness and discipline [. . .] he sent for the most well esteemed and well versed of the philosophers, Aristotle, and paid him a suitably handsome tuition"** (*testimonium* 25a). The description of this event given by Plutarch is part of the tradition of fictionalized biographies that were extremely popular with the Hellenistic and Roman public; at that point in time, Aristotle was certainly not famous, and the further details given by Plutarch appear to be invented. He writes that Philip assigned to the teacher and pupil a temple of the Nymphs at Mieza in the district of Emazia, where in Plutarch's time one could see the marble seats and the shady lanes frequented by Aristotle and Alexander. Even today, anyone who goes to Mieza will find archaeological excavations with the sign "School of Aristotle," but the whole thing is not credible. According to Plutarch, Aristotle taught Alexander ethics, politics, medicine, and all his esoteric doctrines (including the treatise on first causes entitled *Metaphysics*); and he prepared for him a critical edition of the *Iliad*. Plutarch tells us that the relationship between the two cooled off little by little, even though Alexander remained passionate about philosophy; indeed he took with him into Asia Anaxarchus of Abdera, a follower of Democritus, and he gave fifty talents to Xenocrates (in order to irritate Aristotle, said many; see Diogenes Laertius 4.8).

Others who speak of the relationship between Aristotle and Alexander include Quintilian, Dio Chrysostom, Justin, and all the Neoplatonic biographies (*testimonia* 25a–h). The information given us by these sources is largely the product of fantasy, but the encounter between the two of them must have actually taken place,[83] even though several ancient sources that speak of Alexander make no mention of his relationship with Aristotle.[84] In fact, the Stoics, who consider Alexander a model of moral depravity, never mention Aristotle as having been responsible for his education (see Stroux 1933 and Chroust 1966, p. 128). All the same, there is sufficiently ancient evidence linking Aristotle and Alexander to allow us to accept the traditional report. In his *Memoranda*, Alexinus of Elis (a student of Eubulides and a contemporary of Zeno the Stoic) related a conversation that Alexander had with his father Philip, in which the son complained about the *logoi* of Aristotle. In his *On Philosophy* (fr. 2 Chiesara), Aristocles held that **"even the stories of the sophist Alexinus can be reasonably judged ridiculous; he depicts Alexander as a boy speaking with his father Philip and scorning the *logoi* of Aristotle and instead approving Nicagoras, known as Hermes"** (excerpted in Eusebius 15.2.4 = *testimonium* 58e); but what is ridiculous is the belief in a human Hermes, not the implication that Alexander knew the *logoi* of Aristotle.[85]

It is no easy matter to establish what these *logoi* were, whether lectures or treatises, or even the famous *logoi exōterikoi,* the popular published works of Aristotle. In fact, we know nothing certain about what Aristotle may have taught Alexander, but the question has aroused the

imagination of modern historians. Their opinions more or less reduce
to three: (A) Aristotle taught Alexander his entire system, including
metaphysics, ethics, and politics;[86] (B) Aristotle taught Alexander traditional Greek culture, including epic poets and tragedians (despite the
low esteem in which these authors were held in the Academy);[87] (C)
Aristotle taught Alexander dialectic. This latter report might be confirmed by the *Letter to Alexander* of Isocrates, in which he states that
Alexander rejects no part of philosophy, not even *eristic*, that is, soph-
istry (*tōn te philosophiōn . . . tēn peri tas eridas*), given that Isocrates generally uses this expression to refer to those who dedicate themselves to
investigations of a theoretical or dialectical nature (*Helen* 1; see Eucken
1983, pp. 9–10), including the members of the Academy (*Antidosis* 258).
From the point of view of Isocrates and his conception of philosophy,
the differences of theoretical position between the various philosophers, such as Antisthenes, Socrates, Plato, and Aristotle, might well
have appeared to be of very little relevance; he states in general that
the ruler should not get into discussions with his subjects, or be contradicted, but he should guide them by making use of the philosophical
logoi that are appropriate for making good choices, both in public affairs
and in private matters, that is, the *logoi* of Isocrates himself (*Letter to
Alexander* 3–4). If the letter is authentic, the report, however vague and
imprecise, would be so ancient as to be incontrovertible, but there are
doubts about its authenticity.[88]

No hypothesis is really entirely demonstrable, and we must come
to a halt in the face of conjectures. We have seen that Plutarch believed
that Aristotle had taught Alexander his entire philosophy; others thought
it was a good idea to invent Aristotelian texts specifically addressed to
the young prince. That is why we find, both in the traditional corpus of
writings by Aristotle and in other collections, works dedicated to Alexander such as the *Rhetoric for Alexander*, or the letter to Alexander on government, preserved in Arabic translation (see below, pp. 123–124). However, none of these writings is certainly authentic, and they testify only
to the effort made by ancient intellectuals to fill this lacuna, which was
in its own right a source of the greatest curiosity; what could the greatest philosopher of antiquity have taught the greatest conqueror in the
universe? To put it kindly, however, their perhaps adequate theoretical

abilities were of no assistance in this literary effort of theirs; nothing astonishing, nothing worthy of the occasion, and nothing appropriate to the great names of each of the personages is to be found in the pseudonymous Aristotelian writings for Alexander.

We also have a few fragments of a treatise *On Royalty*, in which some see traces of the instruction given by Aristotle to Alexander; and among these is the famous advice that "**it is not necessary for the king himself to do philosophy; rather it will hinder him, but** [. . . the king] **should be open to hearing and being persuaded by those genuine philosophers whom he encounters**" (Themistius, *Oration* 8, 107c–d). Despite the lack of information that faces us, many link this episode instead with the Academic doctrine on the necessity of giving a philosophical education to a king, rather than with any events in Aristotle's biography (Rose, Robin, Jaeger, Prächter, Bidez, and Randall; for a good overview of the question, see Berti 1977, pp. 29–30, and Laurenti 1987, pp. 867–909).

Another famous piece of advice that Aristotle is said to have offered to Alexander is to "**behave towards Greeks as their leader** (*hēgemonikōs*) **and towards foreigners as their master** (*despotikōs*), **taking care of the former as friends and kinsmen and dealing with the latter as animals or plants**" (Plutarch, *Alexander: Fortune or Virtue?* I.6, 329b; see also Strabo 1.4.9). This advice, however, tends in the opposite direction from the policy of racial assimilation encouraged by Alexander. Its attitude is certainly in keeping with the opinions concerning barbarians that we find in Aristotle's writings, but it might well be thought that it would have been difficult for Alexander to have felt the need to ask Aristotle for advice on how to govern; the relationship of the king with the philosophers would appear to have been set up rather differently, and the Callisthenes affair suggests that Alexander was not very docile, nor was he receptive to the advice of philosophers. But, on the other hand, Aristotle wrote a book called *Alexander*, subtitled *Concerning the Colonies* or *Concerning the Colonists* (*Alexandros ē hyper apoikōn* or *apoikiōn*); these titles are listed both in Diogenes Laertius (5.22) and in the list of Aristotle's writings found in the anonymous ancient *Life of Aristotle* (sc. the *Vita Menagiana*; see below, section 1.3 of chapter 4), so it is fairly certain that an Aristotelian text with such a title existed.[89] (However, it is not certain that the advice that Plutarch preserves is derived from this work, where it is placed in the editions of Ross 1955 and Laurenti 1987; other scholars have seen it as a fragment from a *Letter to Alexander*, on which see below, p. 122). We have no certain information on the circumstances in which Aristotle wrote this work on colonies, and we have only a vague report about its contents and no certain fragments (see Laurenti 1987, pp. 911–959). The same is true for the Arabic text published by Bielawski and Plezia under the title *Lettre d'Aristote à Alexandre sur la politique envers les cités*: this work is generally considered to be pure compilation, done by someone who was very familiar with Aristotle's treatises; for the discussion on this point, see below, pp. 123–124.

Some have tried to guess what Aristotle might have taught Alexander by examining Alexander's political decisions, at least his most respectable ones. Jaeger claims that Aristotle suggested to Alexander the idea of unifying Greece under Macedonian leadership (1923, pp. 156–160). But this is an uncertain matter. Wilamowitz had earlier noted that Aristotle in his *Politics* limits himself to the problems of the *polis* (1893, 1:336, 365–369), and that in this work the idea that Greece could become a politically unified entity is not there; rather, he states that the small *poleis* should continue to exist. It is, of course, true that in the *Politics* (VII.6, 1327b32–33), Aristotle mentions the unification of Greece against the barbarians, but what he was thinking about is rather a unification (perhaps federal) among the various cities (*mias tugkanon politeias*), and there is not a word about any role for the Macedonian kings in this context; this silence is important and makes an evident contrast with clearly pro-Macedonian positions, such as that of Isocrates. Even Isocrates openly advises the unification of Greece against the barbarians, under the leadership of Philip of Macedon; he says that only Philip can successfully unify Thebes, Argos, Sparta, and Athens, and can succeed in defeating the king of Persia (*Philip* 16, 41–45, 57, 68+, 80, 88, 139). It is worth the trouble to emphasize this difference of positions, because modern historians usually view the Peripatetic school as a sort of cultural "fifth column" of the Macedonian kingdom in Athens (for a recent example, see Will 1983, p. 54n39).

In the passage from Timaeus of Tauromenium quoted above (section 3 of chapter 1, p. 10), the historian, who was younger than Aristotle by a generation, at once connects and contrasts Aristotle with Alexander the Great's expedition into Asia. But, as was the case with Hermias, there is no reference whatever in the works of Aristotle that have survived to his relationship with Philip or Alexander, nor is Macedonia the object of any particular appreciation, support, or explicit praise; rather, in *Politics* VII.2 (1324b9–22), the Macedonians are listed among non-Greek peoples, along with Scythians, Persians, Thracians, Celts, Iberians, and Carthaginians,[90] and, just like Plato (*Gorgias* 470d+), Aristotle considers the Macedonian royal family as an example of barbaric customs in his *Politics* (on this point, see Wilamowitz 1893 (1:348), Ehrenberg 1938 (pp. 62–102), and Weil 1960, pp. 184–185, 195, 198–201, and 215–217). This contrasts, once again, with what Isocrates says in *Philip* (105+), where he attributes to the Macedonian royal house the glories of Hercules. Aristotle never mentions any events in the life of Alexander or his wars; for instance, when he speaks of Thebes, he does not mention the fact that Alexander razed it to the ground, nor does he ever mention the expedition into Asia and the destruction of the Persian Empire. An ancient tradition holds that Alexander sent Aristotle botanical samples and exotic animals for his biological studies from Asia, but there is no trace in the writings of Aristotle of any of this; the reports that we find in his *Research on Animals* (IX.1, 610a15+) on India and its fauna, such as elephants, are entirely a matter of fables and legends.[91]

The main events in Alexander's reign are instead mentioned by the subsequent Peripatetics. There may be a reference to the fall of the Persian Empire in the ps.-Aristotelian *Economics* (I.6, 1344b34), which speaks of Persian customs in the past tense, but it is chiefly Theophrastus who, in his *Research on Plants,* offers specific reports. He recalls the expedition of Alexander (1.4.1, 4.7.3), he mentions a specific place in the city of Babylon (2.6.7), he describes the amazement of Greek and Macedonian soldiers when they found themselves confronted with unknown plants and herbs (4.4.1–10), such that they tried to identify them by giving them the names of the plants of their own countries, and he mentions the name of the personal physician of Alexander (4.16.6).[92] The difference between his perspective and that of his master is considerable.

Here we can only mention a fragment of the text *On Fortune* by Demetrius of Phalerum, reported by two historians, Polybius (29.21.3–6) and Diodorus Siculus (31.10.1–2), in which the orator and politician comments on the fall of the Persian Empire and predicts the end of the Macedonian kingdom. **"If one takes into consideration not limitless time nor many generations, but merely these last fifty years up to now, you will recognize in them the toughness of Fortune. Fifty years ago, do you think either the Persians or the king of the Persians, or the Macedonians or the king of the Macedonians, if one of the gods had predicted the future to them, would ever have believed that by the present time, not even the name of the Persians would have remained at all, they who were masters of almost the whole world, and that the Macedonians would now be ruling over everything, they who formerly didn't even have a name? No, in a way the Fortune that breaches contracts in our lives, produces new things beyond our power to think about, and displays her power in ways beyond belief, is now too, I think, showing all humans, by sending the Macedonians to dwell in the prosperity of the Persians, that she is lending them these good things until she wishes to do something else with them."** The comment is strange coming from a politician who built his career on support from Macedon and who attained supreme power in Athens only as the "administrator" (*epimelētēs*) of Cassander (Diodorus Siculus 18.74.2; see above, section 3, p. 13).[93] Polybius quotes the prediction as a comment on the Roman conquest of Macedonia (29.21.2), and he affirms that Demetrius's intention had been **"to show humans that Fortune is changeable."** Modern historians who have studied this passage generally consider it to be a sinister prophecy of the fate of the Macedonian monarchy, or as an expression of pessimism, whether personal on the part of Demetrius or general on the part of all Greeks at the end of the fourth century BCE. This passage is generally linked to the fragments of Theophrastus on the power of fate (fr. 487–501 FHSG), but Theophrastus is referring to the lives of individuals, not entire peoples; in his *Consolation to Apollonius* (6, 104d), Plutarch tells Apollonius that **"all of us have suffered the same thing. 'Fortune is aimless,' says Theophrastus, 'and is terribly good at stealing away the things we work for and overturning apparent prosperity, since it has no prescribed time.'"**

Yet arguably the matter could be understood differently; according to my hypothesis, Demetrius does nothing more here than apply to the events of his own time certain distinctions practiced by the Peripatetic school. In Aristotle's view, that which depends on "luck" (tychē) falls into the sphere in which human actions are undertaken (*Physics* II.6, 197b2–8) and corresponds to that which happens "by accident" (*kata sumbebēkos*) (II.5, 197a5–6; II.5, 197a32–35; II.6, 197b23–24; II.6, 198a6–7). It is not possible to have a science about things that happen by accident, according to Aristotle. Not only does this limitation apply to small-scale everyday events, but it may also be characteristic of events of large significance (*Metaphysics* XI (K).8, 1065b1). But what could it mean to say that events such as the collapse of world empires happen as the result of *tychē*? In our view, that which distinguishes, in Peripatetic philosophy, between events such as the rise and fall of great hegemonies and the political organization of the *polis* is that events of the first sort are in a certain sense irrational, beyond scientific and political knowledge; the cities, on the other hand, are the ultimate end, the culmination of the genetic development of the forms of human community, the highest level that man can attain, in which his social nature finds its fullest realization (*Politics* I.2). No major novelties or later innovations in the form of the human community are predicted after the birth of the *polis* (*Politics* II.5, 1264a1–5). Therefore it is possible to have a theoretical understanding of the *polis*, an understanding expressed in Aristotle's *Politics*, while this is not true of the affairs of kingdoms. For that reason, Aristotle seems more interested in questions of constitutional and social history than in the *histoire événementielle* of his times.

We do not really know what connections there were between Aristotle and Alexander after Alexander assumed the throne (335/334 BCE) and stopped attending the philosopher's lectures. Plutarch tells us that relations between the two became increasingly chilly, and modern scholars think that this development is due especially to their disagreement over the way that Alexander treated the Persians after conquering their empire, as we have seen above. That there actually was a disagreement of this type between the Greeks and Alexander is the clear conclusion to be reached from the episode of Callisthenes (on this, see below, section 7 of chapter 1). But to maintain simultaneously, as has indeed happened, not only that, on the one hand, Aristotle gave advice to Alexander but also, on the other hand, that he was the head, at least spiritually, of a sort of "Greek nationalist party" among the circle of Alexander's friends, a party that attempted to oppose the policies of the king (see Wilamowitz 1893, 1:339), and, on a still other hand, that he was the head, at least spiritually, of a sort of "pro-Macedonian party" in the *polis* of Athens, as various modern historians have claimed from time to time—all this is not very credible. Aristotle's chief interests were, surely, the theoretical life, philosophical research, and philosophical reflection; and, after the Macedonian period, the affairs of the kingdom of Macedonia and the development of Aristotle's political thinking seem to have developed along their own lines, independent of one another.

In general, the contemporaries of Aristotle seem not to have been particularly impressed by the fact that Aristotle was the teacher of Alexander; the fact did not attract universal attention, and it was only in later periods that it was considered the most exciting episode of Aristotle's life. Chroust maintains that the shift in appreciation took place in the time of Andronicus of Rhodes, and in connection with his edition and publication of the works of Aristotle (1966, pp. 130–131); see below, section 1 of chapter 3.

Aside from the question of Alexander's education, ancient sources attest to other relationships between Aristotle and King Philip of Macedon. We have already seen above (section 2 of chapter 1) the accusation of Demochares, according to which Aristotle was present in the Macedonian camp in 348 BCE during the siege of Olynthus, and the story about the destruction and reconstruction of Stagira. Just as questionable are the reports according to which Aristotle wrote works for Philip (*Vita Marciana* 4 and *Vita Latina* 40). The work in question is listed in the catalogs under the title *Decrees of Cities* or *Greek Cities* or *On Localities* (see Diogenes Laertius 5.26, and frs. 612–614 Rose 1886 = frs. 405 and 407 Gigon 1987). It is supposed to have been written in order to help Philip eliminate the disagreements and territorial disputes among the Greek cities, in order to found a Pan-Hellenic league (Bergk 1887, p. 483; Nissen 1892; Wilamowitz 1893, 1:305; Pohlenz 1929; Tovar 1943), but others reject the entire story, or are rather skeptical (Heitz 1865, pp. 263–264 and Moraux 1951, pp. 122–123). Philodemus of Gadara was thought to have claimed that Aristotle dissuaded Philip from attacking Persia (*testimonium* 31); but this is not a trustworthy report, especially if we compare it with others, according to which Aristotle had an unwavering anti-Persian attitude and had urged Alexander to attack Persia, and in any case the textual basis of the report is not sound.[94]

Perhaps Aristotle remained in Macedonia for a few years after 334/335 BCE. This is affirmed by Hermippus in Diogenes Laertius 5.2 (in 5.4 the version is different), according to whom Aristotle had been an ambassador of Athens to Philip (see also Philodemus of Gadara in the *Index of Academic Philosophers*).[95] If we trust the discoveries of Lee (1948, p. 63), Aristotle undertook various biological research projects in Macedonia as well, and therefore spent a certain amount of time there. But, as we have seen above (p. 41), these claims are now questionable again. A fragment of a letter attributed to Aristotle in ps.-Demetrius, *Elocution* (29 and 154) contains this curious statement: **"I went from Athens to Stagira because of the Great King, and from Stagira to Athens because of the great winter."** It is not clear what this means (see Prächter 1926, pp. 350+, Düring 1957, p. 400, and Plezia 1961, p. 121), but to the Greeks the Great King was the king of Persia, not the one in Macedonia. We cannot therefore interpret this as a reference to a political mission undertaken by Aristotle on behalf of Philip of Macedon.[96] The passage was held to be an invention by Zeller (1897, 1:21n6).

At this point I should perhaps draw some conclusions from this discussion of relations between Aristotle and Macedonia. It seems that we are faced with two sets of discordant facts, which lead to differing conclusions. On the one hand, there is a whole series of historical data suggesting fairly close relationships on the part of Aristotle and his family with Macedonian notables; to begin with, the presence of Aristotle in Macedonia as Alexander's tutor is reliably documented, and Aristotle probably had a relationship with Philip, and it seems that Aristotle was, for a time, one of those numerous well-known and intelligent Greeks who, according to Isocrates (*Philip* 19), lived in Macedonia and had relationships with the king; again, Aristotle's nephew Callisthenes accompanied Alexander to Asia, though with unfortunate results; Aristotle was later accused by the Athenian democrats, as we have seen, of being a friend to Macedonia; finally, certain pupils of the school, such as Demetrius of Phalerum, were dependent on the power of the Macedonians. Even Hermias, who had a close relationship with Aristotle, is described by Demosthenes as an "**agent and accomplice of Philip.**" Even though it is possible to argue over each individual fact, the accumulation of elements is fairly impressive.[97]

On the other hand, there is the undeniable fact that, in Aristotle's treatises, even in *Politics*, the political power of Macedonia in Aristotle's time remains completely invisible, and the few references to Macedonia found in the work are either cold or almost hostile. Aristotle, in contrast with Theophrastus, refrains from even mentioning any specific events from Alexander's expeditions. This total silence is broken, of course, by the indirect reports on the works that Aristotle is said to have dedicated to the Macedonian monarchs, which we have discussed above; but this does not take away from the fact that in the treatises that survive, that is, in the most well-researched theoretical works, Aristotle maintains an attitude of complete detachment. It would be difficult to characterize the *Politics* or the *Constitution of Athens* as texts compiled in order to defend and sustain the political influence of Macedonia in Athens, like the *Philip* of Isocrates, for these were works connected with teaching in Aristotle's school, directed to pupils among whom must have been many Athenian citizens. This is a case, therefore, in which biographical information can have a negative influence on the study of a work; to interpret the *Politics* as Kelsen does (1937–1938), as an explicit defense of hereditary monarchy in general and an implicit defense of the Macedonian monarchy in particular, and to see the ethical ideal of the theoretical life as nothing more than a prop for monarchic government, is to close off the path to a correct interpretation of both the value and the meaning of these fundamental works in the history of thought.

7. THE ADVENTURE OF CALLISTHENES

Callisthenes of Olynthus,[98] Aristotle's nephew or cousin,[99] was famous throughout history for the episode in which he took part in Alexander's campaign against Persia, as well as for being put to death by Alexander himself, on the accusation of having conspired against the king. Because he died before Aristotle, he is not mentioned in his will; therefore, we do not exactly know the degree of family relation between the two, nor do we know anything about Damotimus, the father of Callisthenes. The figure of Callisthenes, however, confirms what was said before; among many of these philosophers and men of culture, there existed close ties of family and of friendship, to the point of making philosophy appear on some occasions as the specific pursuit of a certain family or clan (*genos*) and its closest friends.

According to the account in Plutarch's *Life of Alexander* (55.7–8), Callisthenes was raised by Aristotle, probably after Philip had destroyed the city of Olynthus (*testimonium* 28c), and may have lived with Aristotle at Assos or Mytilene.[100] Indeed, we have already seen that Callisthenes wrote a treatise on Hermias, in which he showed that he had some familiarity with the personality of the tyrant (see section 6.1 of chapter 1), and this familiarity places him in close contact with the affairs of Aristotle (Jacoby 1901, Jaeger 1923 (pp. 115–116), Wormell 1953, Chroust). Later, Callisthenes collaborated with Aristotle in editing a catalog of winners of the Pythian games (see section 8 of chapter 1).[101] It would seem that the pair collaborated fairly continually, at least until 334 or 331 BCE, when Callisthenes left with Alexander on the campaign against Persia. Callisthenes wrote a *History of Greece* in which he recounted the history of Greece from 386 to 356 BCE, a book about the Sacred War, and a work on the *Deeds of Alexander*.[102] It is not at all certain, however, that Aristotle entrusted his young relative with responsibilities for research projects in biology and geography, as some historians have supposed. It is not known to what degree the philosophy of Aristotle influenced the historiographical work of Callisthenes; some say greatly (Jacoby 1923, *ad loc.* and Jaeger 1923, pp. 318+), others say not much (Bosworth 1970). If we possessed entire works by Callisthenes, we would certainly know more. He supported Macedonian policy in his works and, according to ancient sources (Diogenes Laertius 5.4 and 10; *Suda, s.v.* "Callisthenes"), Aristotle gave him a recommendation as the historian of the expedition of Alexander.[103]

With the disgrace, imprisonment, and execution of Callisthenes, Aristotle's group of friends suddenly found itself in the floodlights of high-level politics of the time, as Gigon remarked (1958, p. 188). The facts are recounted in Plutarch (*Life of Alexander*, chs. 52–55) and Arrian (4.10–14), in substantially the same way; Callisthenes is presented by these authors as a figure with the character of a Cato and an enemy of flattery, with a somewhat arrogant personality and very conscious of his dignified position. Completely opposite to him was the Democritean philosopher Anaxarchus of Abdera,[104] also a member of Alexander's expedition, who was described as a man willing to engage in any form of flattery. Apart from a few secondary episodes, the major clash between Callisthenes and Alexander took place because of the king's demand that he be saluted with genuflection by the Greeks and the Macedonians, as his new Persian subjects did. Callisthenes refused, with a certain haughtiness, and both Plutarch and Arrian say that he had been right in substance but excessive in the manner of his refusal.[105] Rumors also circulated that he gave general support to the traditionalist tendency, namely to those groups of Greeks and Macedonians who opposed the evolution of the royal dominion of Alexander into a sort of oriental monarchy. Many modern historians have accepted this version (e.g., Schwartz 1901, col. 1889); others instead (e.g., Jacoby 1923, *ad loc.*), relying on certain statements of Plutarch and Arrian, believe that Callisthenes did not really oppose the Persian policy of Alexander, but that the difference between the two of them arose mainly because the king and the historian both had ugly personalities that were destined to clash with each other. However this may be, Callisthenes was involved in a conspiracy to assassinate Alexander, organized by the king's pages who were young aristocrats of Macedonian origin, was imprisoned, and died. There are various versions of his death: that he was hanged, that he was devoured by a lion (Diogenes Laertius 5.5), or that he died of disease and harsh treatment in prison (see Prandi 1985 for an examination of the various versions offered by ancient historians).

Aristotle mourned the loss of his relative and colleague (Diogenes Laertius 5.5 and 39), and Theophrastus commemorated him in a book entitled *Callisthenes* or *On Bereavement*, very little of which survives beyond the title (Diogenes Laertius 5.44), but in which Theophrastus spoke about the importance of fate in human affairs and its connection to the character of the individual (Cicero, *Tusculan Disputations* 3.21 and 5.25; ps.-Alexander of Aphrodisias, *De anima mantissa* 186.28–31). This reference to the problems that stem from the individual's character accords with the reports of historians on the harshness of Callisthenes's character that are found in Plutarch, Diogenes Laertius, and Arrian, in whose opinion the fate of Callisthenes was determined above all by his lack of *savoir faire.*

Some say that after this episode the Peripatetic school became fiercely hostile to Alexander.[106] The rumor is ancient, and in the tradition there remain traces of conflict and serious clashes between Aristotle and Alexander.[107] There are certain ancient writers (such as Plutarch, Arrian, Dio Cassius, and Pliny) who believed the story that Alexander had been poisoned by Antipater, acting in concert with Aristotle (*testimonia* 29a–d); but other historians who report the poisoning of Alexander (such as Curtius Rufus, Diodorus Siculus, ps.-Callisthenes, and Julius Valerius) do not report any participation on the part of Aristotle (see Plezia 1948). Dio Cassius tells the story (77.7) that the emperor Caracalla, for whom Alexander was the greatest hero in human history, believed so completely in the reports that Alexander had been assassinated with Aristotle's help that he expelled the philosophers "**called Aristotelians**" from Alexandria, had their books burned, and destroyed their *sussitia,* namely the rooms dedicated to their common meals and their meetings (*testimonium* 29d). It is unlikely that the story about the participation of Aristotle in the murder of Alexander is true.

The idea that there was hostility between the Peripatetic school and Alexander is also widespread in modern scholarship. It is difficult to see how this hypothesis could fit in with the idea, also generally accepted by historians, that the Peripatetics were the cultural "fifth column" of Macedonian politics in Athens; I have already expressed my reservations on this point.

8. ATHENS REVISITED

"**His arrival at Athens was in the second year of the 111th Olympiad** [335 BCE], **and he lectured in the Lyceum for thirteen years** [335–323]" (Diogenes Laertius 5.10). "**After the death of Philip in the archonship of Evaenetus** [335/334], **he returned to Athens, and taught in the Lyceum for a period of twelve years**" (Dionysius of Halicarnassus, *First Letter to Ammaeus* 5.3). The most important event of the second part of Aristotle's life was undoubtedly his decision to return to Athens and open an independent school there, separate from

Plato's. This was probably a decisive factor in the preservation of his work. In fact, we do not have the complete works of any philosopher of the time who worked outside of Athens, and, among those who worked in Athens, not one of the writings of the students of Plato has been preserved.

The fact should be emphasized that Aristotle decided to open a school of his own in Plato's own city, Athens (see Berti 1977, p. 31). This indicates a will to be independent, if not to be in opposition; evidently he did not wish to return to the group of Academics. The institution of an independent community, dedicated to the discussion of problems similar to those dealt with in the Academy, but distinct from those examined, for instance, in the school of Isocrates, can only indicate a will to establish his own independence of thought, though remaining within a partly shared tradition, and a desire to give birth to an autonomous community of discussion, in which the usual philosophical terms—"theory," "philosophy," "dialectic," "wisdom," and "conduct" (*praxis*)—would take on a new and original meaning, different from the use made by the master Plato and his older fellow students. For this reason, it seems to me that the claims of the Neoplatonic biographers cannot be accepted when they maintain that Xenocrates and Aristotle were the joint heirs to Speusippus and that, by common consent, they carried on the work of the school in two locations that differed only spatially, the Academy and the Lyceum (see Jaeger 1923, pp. 428–430, with Gigon 1962, p. 46).[108]

Wilamowitz (1893) has appositely noted that the period in which Aristotle returned to Athens was a period of restoration; cults were being reopened and ceremonies that had been abandoned got back their honored status, the fleet and the arsenal underwent restoration, and the city was generally trying to return to normal. On a strictly political level, however, after the fall of Thebes, Alexander's position as the head of the League of Corinth and the virtual leader of Greece was by then firmly established, and Athens had been obliged to accept the situation. The hypothesis that Aristotle had come to Athens with the express intention of getting involved in politics in support of Alexander, and as a spokesman for the Macedonian court, is a product of modern authors and is not attested by any ancient source.

Düring went further and stated that Aristotle's arrival in Athens went wholly unnoticed (Düring 1957, p. 460 and Düring 1966, p. 20), and that Aristotle remained a fairly obscure philosopher, unknown for the duration of his stay in Athens. The first part of this judgment seems to me reliable, as far as one can tell from the weakness of the indications and the lack of certain information, but about the second part there can be legitimate doubts. The very quantity of attacks and polemics on the part of his contemporaries, well documented by Düring (1966, p. 26), suggests that Aristotle and his followers were not in fact obscure characters but were fairly well known, at least in the circle of "philosophers" and educated people, even if the comic playwrights failed to make Aristotle the butt of their jokes, as they had done to Socrates, Plato, and other well-known philosophers. Aristotle therefore does not seem to have enjoyed the vast public notoriety that Socrates and Plato had among their more humble fellow citizens, but rather to have been a philosopher who was well known primarily among educated people.

For that matter, when compared with what can be read in the works of Isocrates and Plato, the works of Aristotle show a more relaxed attitude, less preoccupied with how philosophical studies were judged by the ordinary citizen (see Natali 1987). And popular attitudes were also changing; compared with the reactions at the time of the first efforts of the Sophists and of Socrates, it seems that, over time, the existence of independent philosophical schools had become an accepted fact of life for the ordinary Athenian, and the fact that some young people got educated in philosophy prompted less and less scandal. On the other hand, the school of Aristotle, in its founder's time, could not have been very involved in the city's political life, despite the arguments of Wilamowitz (1881, pp. 181–186). For what happened after the death of Aristotle, see below (chapter 3).

In the last wills and testaments of the Peripatetic scholarchs (Diogenes Laertius 5.51–57, 5.61–64, 5.69–74), and from Hellenistic authors such as Antigonus of Carystus (cited in Athenaeus 12, 547d–e, a passage discussed below at pp. 93–95), we find a description of a Peripatetic school with a rather complex organization; it seems to be endowed with a garden, some houses, lecture halls, spaces for group banquets, and so on. Was the school like this during Aristotle's time as well? Bernays claimed that Aristotle, as a metic, could not own real estate in Athens, and for that reason, he asserts (1881, p. 108), it would not be surprising[109] if Aristotle had not left his students an autonomously organized school endowed with its own buildings, because the buildings where his lessons took place were not his property. Bernays observed as well that Theophrastus was the first Peripatetic to receive the grant of a right to own real estate (*egktēsis*) in Athens, through the efforts of the Peripatetic Demetrius of Phalerum, who in those years (316–306 BCE) governed the city (Diogenes Laertius 5.39). Düring and Brink believe that this evidence suffices to rule out the existence of an institutionally organized Peripatetic school as early as Aristotle's time, and they think that the school of Aristotle consisted only of a group of friends, with a very free and informal structure, dedicated to the study of philosophy (see Düring 1957, pp. 260 and 460, with Brink 1940, cols. 905–907).

All the same, a great many others, including Ross, Kafka, Prächter, Gauthier, Jaeger, and Chroust (1972a), have stated that the fact that Aristotle did not own real estate in Athens does not by any means exclude the presence of an organized school, which the philosopher could have directed in rented premises (as Lyco would later do; see Athenaeus 12, 547 d–e, cited below at pp. 93–94). In the texts of Aristotle, there are sufficient indications to document the existence of a rather complex teaching activity, very different from the free discussion while strolling that is typical of the time of Protagoras and Socrates. Concerning the organization of the school, see below, chapter 3.

Was Aristotle busy with political business during his second stay in Athens? We shall explore in detail below (section 2 of chapter 4) the entirely political interpretation given by Chroust of this period of Aristotle's life, but for now the following should be kept in mind: some ancient sources speak generically, without giving us too many clarifications, of a benefaction (*euergetein*) on the part of the philosopher toward the city (*Vita Marciana* 15–22); and Diogenes Laertius claims that Aristotle served as an ambassador for Athens (5.2), as did Xenocrates (4.8–9), Menedemus (2.140), and Arcesilaus (4.39). It is not clear how we should evaluate these reports, but some among the most important scholars, such as Mulvany (1926) and Düring (1957, pp. 58, 110, 232–234), hold them to be entirely unreliable.

Linked to this problem is the problem of how to interpret the information in Ptolemy's *Life of Aristotle,* in the version of Usaibia (*Life of Aristotle* 18, tr. Düring 1957), according to which the Athenians awarded *proxenia* to Aristotle, by decree of the assembly, for the benefits that he had brought to the city, and had commissioned an inscription to this effect on a column. "**In the inscription on this column, they mentioned that Aristotle of Stagira, son of Nicomachus, had served the city well by doing good and by the great number of his own acts of assistance and beneficence, and by all his services to the people of Athens, especially by intervening with King Philip for the purpose of promoting their interests and securing that they were well treated; that the people of Athens therefore wanted it to be quite clear that they appreciated the good that had come out of this; that they bestowed distinction and praise upon him, and would keep him in faithful and honored remembrance.**" Usaibia then relates that a certain "Himeraios" was opposed to these tokens of respect, and that he demolished the column where the inscription appeared (see section 1.2 of chapter 4).[110] Antipater had Himeraios killed for this,[111] and later on the inscription was restored by a certain "Stephanos," who added to the inscription the story of the misdeeds of Himeraios. It would have been difficult for Usaibia to invent all this, including the Greek names. There is a real historical person named Himeraius,[112] though it is not known who this "Stephanos" might have been. In the nineteenth century, Baumstark, Steinschneider, and Drerup defended the authenticity of the decree, while today opinions diverge; fairly favorable to the authenticity of the decree are Gigon 1958 (pp. 138–141 and 164), Gigon 1962 (commentary to section 59), Chroust 1967a, Chroust 1973 (pp. 139–141), and Chroust 1973a. The latter hypothesizes, not very reliably, that Aristotle defended the interests of Athens to Philip after the defeat of Chaeronea in 338 BCE; opposed to this is Düring 1957, pp. 239–241.

There is no detailed information about the activities undertaken by Aristotle at Athens, apart from teaching and discussing philosophical problems. What we have instead is information about a research project in history, a "commission" so to speak, given to Aristotle and his associates by the *Amphictyons,* the magistrates governing the games in honor of Apollo at Delphi. Despite the damage to the document, an inscription at Delphi demonstrates the reliability of the information, recording this work in the following terms. **"The temple keepers have decreed: since Aristotle of Stagira son of Nicomachus and Callisthenes of Olynthus son of Damotimus** [drafted] **at the request of the Amphictions catalogues of those who ha**[ve wo]n **the** [Pythian games] **fro**[m the time of . . .][113] **and also those who had organized the games since the begi**[nning,] **Aristotle an**[d C]**al**[li]**sthenes are to be prais**[ed] **and** [cr]**owned; and t**[he tre]**asurers are to** [bui]**ld the cat**[alogue into the tem]**ple by tr**[anscribin]**g** . . ." (Dittenberger 1915, no. 275 = *testimonium* 43). A few fragments of this catalog survive (frs. 615–617 Rose 1886 = frs. 410–414 Gigon 1987). It must have been carved on stone and placed in the temple, because in the accounts of the treasurers of Delphi there remains the notation of a payment to the stone carver Dinomachus for this work. On the basis of the sum that was paid, some reckon that the inscription comprised twenty-one thousand letters.[114] This demonstrates that, during his stay in Athens, Aristotle had relationships with people and institutions outside the city as well. This research was performed in collaboration with Callisthenes and must therefore have been done before the latter left with Alexander (334 or 331 BCE), but, according to the most recent research (Lewis 1958), the stele was not actually erected until 327, the year in which the payment of the costs of inscription was recorded in the Delphic account books.

Many say that during Aristotle's stay in Athens he made friends with the Macedonian regent, Antipater. This seems confirmed by the fact that twice in his last will and testament Aristotle mentions Antipater as his principal executor (Diogenes Laertius 5.11 and 5.13), unless this means only that Aristotle wished, through this legal pretense, to place his last wishes under the protection of the Macedonian power.[115]

9. TRIAL AND FLIGHT

In 323 BCE Alexander died, and in Athens the anti-Macedonian party became stronger again. In the same year Aristotle moved to Chalcis in Euboea, where he died the following year (October 322, according to Düring 1966).[116] Modern historians suppose that there is a certain connection between the two events. **"Then he set off for Chalcis in the third year of the 114th Olympiad** [322 BCE] **and died of an illness,** at the age of about sixty-three, in the archonship of Philocles, the same year that Demosthenes passed away in Calauria" (Diogenes Laertius 5.10). "In the thirteenth year, after the death of Alexander in the archon-year of Cephisodorus [323 / 322], he set off for Chalcis, where he died of an illness at the age of sixty-three. Now then, these are the facts transmitted to us by those who wrote about the life of the man" (Dionysius of Halicarnassus, *First Letter to Ammaeus* 5.3–6.1).

Almost all ancient authors report that Aristotle left Athens to avoid being condemned to death for impiety.[117] Indeed, a trial was commenced against him on those charges, more than seventy-five years after the death of Socrates—in other words, following a long period of relative tranquillity in which it seemed that the ancient distrust of philosophers had somewhat diminished, and that the practice of accusing philosophers of impiety had fallen out of fashion (see Derenne 1930, Marasco 1976, Dover 1976, and Humphreys 1978, p. 213). In contrast with the cases of Protagoras, Socrates, Theodorus the Atheist,[118] and similar cases, however, it would appear that the trial was not prompted by, or at least did not take as its pretext, the ideas professed by the philosopher, but rather by his public behavior, not directly linked to his ideas.[119] This must have depended on the changing times and also on the nature of Aristotle's philosophical research, which, on the one hand, was conducted on a level that was too abstract and complex to unsettle an ordinary citizen and, on the other hand, for theoretical and systematic reasons, was very careful to avoid excessively paradoxical and absurd positions like those of the Sophists.

Both ancients and moderns have thought that the accusation of impiety was an excuse to strike out at Aristotle for political motives, but they have identified these motives differently (see Gigon 1958, p. 178). The ancients thought it was the relationship between Aristotle and Hermias, whereas the moderns think it was the relationship between Aristotle and Alexander. The ancients, including Hermippus (cited below),[120] Diogenes Laertius (5.5), Mubashir (20, tr. Düring), and Usaibia (7, tr. Düring), basically think that the accusation against Aristotle was for his having treated Hermias as a deity, by praising him with the epigram and the *Hymn to Hermias* that was sung in his honor, as to a god.

Relying on Hermippus, a character in *The Learned Banqueters* of Athenaeus denies that this poem was a hymn (*paian*). "**But surely the song written by the extremely learned Aristotle for Hermias of Atarneus is not a hymn, as Demophilus who filed the indictment against the philosopher for impiety** [the text is corrupt at this point] **provided by Eurymedon, on the grounds that he impiously and shamefully sang a hymn, every day in the dining-rooms** [*sussitia*], **to Hermias. That there are no features at all of a hymn in the song, but that it a particular type of *skolion* in its very form, I will make clear to you from the text itself**" (15, 696a–b). The words of the song follow (696b–d), and then the character draws his conclusion (696e): "**now then, I don't see how anyone could discern anything in these** [verses] **that is specific to a hymn, since the writer clearly admits that Hermias is dead when he says, 'For the sake of your lovely form, the scion | of Atarneus forsook the rays of the sun;' and it does not even have a hymnal chorus.**" Various examples of hymns follow, each with its own refrain, followed by a quote from the *Defense against the Charge of Impiety*, an apocryphal work attributed to Aristotle (696e–697b). Boyancé believes in the truth of the accusations mentioned in this account (1937, pp. 299–310), that Aristotle ordered the singing every day, at mealtimes in his school, of a hymn in which Hermias was deified. However, this seems unlikely according to Gigon 1958 (p. 178) and Gigon 1962 (p. 75), since, if it had been true, Aristotle would have continued to celebrate the memory of Hermias every day for a full fifteen years, many of which were passed in Athens, before the Athenians found anything ridiculous in this practice.

The moderns, instead, hypothesize that the hostility against Aristotle erupted because the philosopher was considered a proponent of the Macedonian power. Diogenes Laertius claims (5.5) that the accusers of Aristotle were Demophilus and the *hierophant* Eurymedon,[121] as was also reported in the biography of Aristotle by Hermippus (cited above). Some have ventured that, because a *hierophant* is the highest priest of the Eleusinian mysteries, Aristotle must have attacked these mysteries.[122]

We do not necessarily need to think of a nocturnal flight; it seems that Aristotle left Athens with all his slaves and household possessions, but naturally this does not exclude the possibility that he was threatened with a trial. He headed to Chalcis, where he lived for a year and perhaps opened a school. Diogenes Laertius cites (10.1) a late Peripatetic scholar named Heraclides Lembus who tells us that Epicurus **"came to Athens at the age of eighteen at the time when Xenocrates was teaching in the Academy and Aristotle was teaching** (*diatribousi*) **in Chalcis"** (fr. 9 *FHG*; the passage does not appear among the *testimonia* in Düring 1957). Strabo also mentions the residence or school (*diatribē*) of Aristotle in Chalcis (10.1.11). According to Aulus Gellius (*Attic Nights,* 13.5), when Aristotle was dying, he named Theophrastus as his successor as head of the school, choosing him over Eudemus of Rhodes. Not all scholars accept these reports.[123]

Some traces of these events remain in the collection of letters attributed to Aristotle. In his *Miscellaneous Research* (14.1), Aelian notes that Aristotle is said to have been deprived of the honors decreed for him by the Amphictyons of Delphi (mentioned just above),[124] and that Aristotle himself supposedly wrote to Antipater as follows. **"About those things which were decreed for me at Delphi and of which I am now deprived, my present attitude is that neither am I greatly concerned about them nor are they of no concern to me at all"** (*testimonium* 67c). Some link this report to the accusations of impiety (Düring 1957, p. 401; Plezia 1961, p. 112; Dittenberger 1915, *commentary* to no. 275, citing similar cases), and there are traces of a violent anti-Macedonian reaction in Delphi in the years 324/323 BCE (Goulet 1989–2012, 1:423). In the Neoplatonic *Lives*, in Diogenes Laertius, and in various ancient authors,[125] there is mention of a complaint allegedly expressed to Antipater on Aristotle's part about his treatment at Athens, saying that **"it is hard to live in Athens; pear ripens upon pear, and fig upon fig."** The comment is obscure, but seems to be a protest against the Athenian denouncers or voluntary public informers known as "sycophants," a word evidently but obscurely derived from *sukon*, meaning "fig." A jest that Aristotle supposedly wrote to Antipater as he was about to leave Athens, as reported by various sources (the Neoplatonic *Lives* and other ancient authors),[126] is very interesting. He supposedly wrote, **"I will not let the Athenians sin a second time against philosophy,"** linking his case to that of Socrates and, at the same time, clearly taking the opposite decision from the one made by Socrates. The episode is a good reflection of the difference between the intellectual personalities of Socrates and Aristotle; this is a perfect case of the Italian proverb *se non è vero, è ben trovato* (if it isn't true, it's well made up).

Aristotle died in Chalcis in 322 BCE. Generally the ancients relate that he died of a stomach ailment, but there is no lack of more fictionalized versions.[127]

10. FROM TRADITIONAL CUSTOMS, A NEW MODEL

Ultimately, we know relatively little about the life of Aristotle, at least in comparison with the information we have about many philosophers closer to us in time; but when compared with the reports we have about other ancient philosophers and poets, such as Homer, Anaxagoras, Democritus, Theophrastus, and Strato, we have a reasonable amount of information, and these facts allow us to attempt an overall reconstruction, in broad outlines, of the figure he represents. In my view, with Aristotle a new kind of intellectual reaches its perfect development, different from the intellectuals of the preceding ages, and particularly important as a model for many centuries to come. In this intellectual figure, remarkably innovative aspects are mixed together with aspects that are entirely traditional. In this section I would like to try to describe these novel elements, and so let me begin by outlining what Aristotle was *not*.

Aristotle was not a charismatic personality like Empedocles, who dressed in purple and wore a golden crown (Diogenes Laertius 8.73), or like the Cynics Menedemus and Menippus, who went around dressed as sorcerers, with black capes, hats with the signs of the zodiac, and magic wands in hand, characters midway between priest, prophet, and sideshow charlatan.[128] Nor was he a paid teacher, like the Sophists or the masters of rhetoric such as Isocrates,[129] and for that reason he lacked certain characteristics of the Sophists, such as the need to advertise himself and a certain tendency to salesmanship, typical of all those who, in order to earn a living, need to seek students by showing off their own fame and talent.[130] As I shall explain in greater detail below, in Aristotle's case, his interests seemed to center around research rather than the teaching and the political training of his students.

The problem of whether or not he received fees for the lessons given to others is a very important issue in the definition of what kind of intellectual Aristotle was. All ancient sources insist on this point, even though not all the modern critics have devoted sufficient thought to the matter. It is well known that the impropriety of accepting payment for lessons constituted one of the cardinal points in the polemics of Socrates and some Socratics against professional Sophists, and that Socrates did not get paid for his teaching, though he did not reject occasional offers of help from his wealthier friends. The students of Socrates also respected, some more, some less, their master's position; a partial exception was Aeschines of Sphettus, who earned a living by composing speeches for the law courts after returning to Athens from Syracuse, though he did not dare to become a Sophist (Diogenes Laertius 2.62). Aristippus of Cyrene was the exception; he did get paid for his lectures and lived the life of an itinerant teacher typical of the Sophists, making long journeys in both Greece and Sicily. Perhaps it was to him that Xenophon was alluding when he said (*Memoirs of Socrates* 1.2.60), "**Some of them** [the companions of Socrates], **after getting from him a few bits for nothing, sold them to others for a lot.**"[131]

Like Socrates, Plato and his students, including Aristotle, refused to be paid for their lectures, or rather for the philosophical teaching imparted to their audience; but this decision did not have the same significance in the case of Socrates as in the cases of Plato and Aristotle. When Socrates decided not to accept the role of a salaried teacher, he did so at the price of a life spent in miserable conditions, and the same also happened to the Cynics; see von Arnim (1898, pp. 37+), who claims that Diogenes, Menedemus, Crates, and Metrocles became adepts of a gospel of poverty, that they taught philosophy not as a profession but to comply with "God's will," and that with this choice and by acting in certain manners, they embodied the purest type of Socratic personality. The decision of Socrates and the Cynics was a paradoxical decision, by the ethical standards common in the fourth century BCE, a decision that defied all the value criteria of ordinary Athenians; they always held it to be certainly true that a poor man, a bad administrator of his own family fortune, who was not concerned with maintaining or increasing his own wealth, would be considered to be a complete nobody.[132]

The attitude of Socrates and many of those who closely followed his example, in the face of such widespread opinion, was at the same time didactic and polemical. They based their activity as thinkers and teachers primarily if not exclusively on direct discussion, on personal contact with their students, on persuasion, and on empathy, trying to produce in their own students a conversion of sorts and an alienation from the lifestyle of ordinary citizens. The philosophical activity of Socrates gave rise to a particular type of human relationship. In Aristotle's view of the intellectual life, by contrast, there was no tendency at all to missionary proselytizing, to conceiving one's life choice as a "witnessing" involving not only narrowly intellectual work but also the entire personality of the subject.[133]

The fact is, for people such as Plato and Aristotle, the refusal to be paid for philosophical teaching, and hence to draw from philosophy the means of earning a living, assumed a very particular significance, contrasting with that of Socrates; and though in some respects Aristotle was living a life similar to the life lived by Socrates, he distanced himself decisively from the Socratic model of a "life dedicated to philosophy." Plato and Aristotle were rich men, in fact, from good families, who lived from their own resources.[134] They did not look to "philosophy" as a way of earning a living, nor did they choose to live in poverty in order to dedicate themselves to converting their neighbor; rather they chose the life of philosophy because they saw it as one of the possible responses, indeed, the best possible response, to the problem that faced all free adult Greek males who were sufficiently rich that they were not constrained to work, of how to occupy their *scholē*.

The *scholē* of the Greeks was not "free time" in the modern sense, in which one rests after the effort of working, by bowling or strolling or being with friends, so that one can then return to one's own job in society. It refers to that part of the day that is free from necessary commitments, the part in which we express our own individual character and articulate the meaning we wish to give to our own lives; it is not the time left over from the really important things but the most important part of our lives, the part in which we pose the question of what sort of person we are. For Plato and Aristotle, dedicating themselves to philosophy was also a choice of *bios*, of a way of spending one's life, and of best actualizing one's human capacities; it was, in a word, the choice of a way of being happy. For this reason, one could say that with Plato and Aristotle there was a progressive distancing from the original Socratic model. Of course, in many respects the influence of Socrates remained strong in both of them, especially where the role of dialogue and dialectic was concerned, because the Platonic dialogue somehow institutionalized Socratic discussion, and the Aristotelian treatises maintain a dialectical structure and were based on examining the opinions of experts. But it is precisely in this process of the "institutionalization" of dialectic that we see signs of development in the intellectual figure of the philosopher.

On the basis of these new premises, even the way of conducting a dialogue with one's interlocutors has changed. Aristotle's position is much "colder" and more rational than that of Socrates, and it is generally disliked by those who look to philosophical reflection to satisfy their emotional needs. The Aristotelian model of life and reflection gives the first place to the intellect, to investigation, and to intellectual discussion in which to develop convictions derived from the comparison of theses and theoretical positions. It gives the first place to purely rational argumentation, not emotional appeals or moral imperatives;[135] a secondary role is decisively assigned to personal interaction. Philosophical investigation is conducted, generally speaking, among a restricted group of colleagues, and the theoretical debate can even be set up with a thesis written in a book, without being face to face with the living person (see below, section 1 of chapter 3).

Plato's position strikes us as fairly close to that of Aristotle, apart from Plato's evaluation of the written word, because in both of them dialectic and discussion are more prevalent than giving witness to ethical values; but the student Aristotle lacked many of the main aspects of the cultural personality of his teacher Plato. Aristotle was a citizen of a tiny *polis*, he lived as an outsider all his life in a wide array of very different places, and this did not permit him to cultivate a true interest in the political life of a specific *polis* or to plan a direct political intervention, as did happen to a certain degree in the Academy (see most recently the overview by Isnardi Parente 1988, and below, section 2 of chapter 2). Any interest in politics appears to be present in Aristotle only in an

indirect form, as a scientific reflection on the *polis*. This situation, however, also rendered him immune to that vein of bitter polemic against
Athenian political life that continually flows through the works of Plato.
And yet it is true that, in the dialogue *On Justice* (fr. 1 Ross), mention
is made of an interlocutor who **"mourns the city of the Athenians"**
(ps.-Demetrius, *Elocution* 28), but the topic of that discussion, to judge
from the few surviving fragments, appears to be the search for what
rhetorical form is best suited to express commiseration, and not what
judgment to offer concerning the political life of the city of Athens,
according to Laurenti (1987, pp. 182–186).[136]

Returning to the life choices made by philosophers, the decision to
devote one's own life to philosophy was often presented in ancient texts
as the fruit of personal deliberation, sometimes almost as a conversion
(see Nock 1933, pp. 129+, and Gigon 1946), and certainly in many cases
that is what took place. But the biographical facts add certain rather complex and archaic nuances that allow us to understand the situation better.
In some cases, the decision to devote one's own life to philosophy appears
to have been a question of *genos*, a family affair, in an environment where
such decisions constitute distinctive features of an aristocratic family or
group of families.[137] We must remind ourselves on this point of certain
characteristics of an aristocratic frame of mind that are quite different
from our modern ones; hobbies and ways of spending their *scholē* are in
ancient culture definitely to some extent matters of individual choice,
but of individuals immersed in a very strong and clearly constraining
family context, in which the influence of custom and family traditions
is extremely lively. At times one has the impression that in the ancient
aristocratic families all the men, the sons following the fathers, devoted
themselves to the same diversions and the same activities. Thus in Pindar
we see that the family of Alcimedon of Aegina devoted itself to wrestling, the sons following the fathers (*Olympian* VIII), and the family of
Xenophon of Corinth had a tradition across the whole clan (*genos*) of vic-
tories in the various athletic games (*Olympian* XIII). In Athens, the wife of
Strepsiades, in the *Clouds* of Aristophanes (60–77), comes from a noble
family that is traditionally passionate about horses.

Even the dedication of oneself to literary and philosophical culture,
to the tutelage of the "sophists" and to one's own theoretical reflection,

can become, in this aristocratic context, the distinguishing characteristic of a noble house. The dialogues of Plato show fairly clearly by their choice of characters that Plato also meant to celebrate his own family as one of the most learned, and one of the closest to Socrates,[138] and one of those readiest to absorb his teaching, as he himself says in his *Charmides* (154d–155a). Socrates is narrating the account of his discussion with Critias, who was Plato's uncle and older cousin to Charmides, another uncle of Plato. **"By Heracles!" I said, "how irresistible you say the man [Charmides] is, if he has only one more thing little something in addition."—"What?" said Critias.—"If his soul," I replied, "has a good nature (*eu pephykos*). And it rather stands to reason, Critias, that he ought to be such a man, since he belongs to your household (*oikias*)." "Well yes," he said, "he is very much a gentleman (*kalos kai agathos*) in those ways too."—"In that case," I said, "why don't we undress that part of him and inspect it before the visible part? He is fully of an age now, I think, to be willing to have a conversation."— "Yes indeed, very much so," said Critias, "since he is actually a phi- losopher (*philosophos*), and also, as it seems to others as well as him- self, very much a poet."—"And that fine quality, my dear Critias," I said, "goes back a long way in your family, from your kinship (*syn- geneias*) with Solon."**

Of course, these ties were not binding, but we have seen that perhaps Aristotle attended the Academy because of the friendship that bound Proxenus to Plato; and then again, where Aristotle's descendants are concerned, philosophy became something of a family business, and between the master and his closest students bonds of affection and kin- ship were established. We can guess at similar relationships in other con- texts as well; Diogenes Laertius tells of an entire family, a father and two sons, who were influenced by Diogenes the Cynic to give themselves to philosophy (6.75–76), and another family of Cynics was that of Crates, his wife Hipparchia, and her brother Metrocles (6.96–98 and 5.94; see also frs. 5.H.19–26 [Crates], 5.I [Hipparchia], and 5.L [Metrocles] in Giannantoni 1990). On the other hand, as we shall see in greater detail below when we examine the last will and testament of Theophrastus, among the most natural candidates for membership in the philosophi- cal community established by the Aristotelians were family members and relatives of the master.[139] The same is true of Plato's school where Speusippus is concerned. Obviously, this is just a general trend; not all the relatives of the philosopher do philosophy with him, nor are the relatives and intimate friends of the philosopher the only ones to do philosophy with him, but for some members of the philosopher's circle this choice of way of life came about more easily and more naturally than for others—for instance, for a member of a family in which the traditional hobby is raising hunting dogs.

Plato and Aristotle did philosophy for their own pleasure, therefore, following their own particular traditions, and not in a professional or competitive context; their standards of success were therefore much different from our own. Aristotle declares this many times in his two treatises on *Ethics*, when he emphasizes the link between a life of theory and happiness, and when he praises the way of life chosen by Anaxagoras. The founding of a school, the gathering around oneself of a group of students and collaborators, and the dedicating of one's own life and all one's intellectual energy to making theoretical progress—all this should be seen, in the case of Plato and Aristotle, as a way of giving meaning to their own aristocratically affluent lives, and not as the choice of a social role, as a professional vocation, a *Beruf* in the Weberian sense.

It is often said, however, that Aristotle's life resembles that of a university lecturer, and occasionally we get to see the personal story of the greatest philosopher of antiquity expounded as if it had been the career of an older colleague of ours; we read that in the Academy Aristotle gave a "course" in rhetoric (presumably as a stipendiary assistant and not as a "full professor"), and that the *Gryllus* had been his doctoral thesis. We run a risk in making this comparison; even though it is not entirely mistaken, there are important differences that should not be overlooked. Certain distinctive characteristics of a professor or university lecturer would have been missing from the curriculum vitae of Aristotle: he did not work in an institutional context; he was not an employee of the state or even of a public or private research institute; and his activity was not marked by any need to advance himself or have a "career," as is so often implied in certain reconstructions of philologists and modern critics, who unwittingly project their own experiences and conceptual schemes onto the figure of the ancient scholar, as apparently similar to us as he is profoundly different.[140] Even the decision that Aristotle made, at a certain point, to return to Athens and open a school of his own was certainly not meant as a way to attain any "career advancement" that would be comparable to what an academic of the present day might aspire to after managing, with great effort, to move to a famous academic center.

This new cultural model was unquestionably prepared by the evolution of the Platonic Academy; but Aristotle is its most perfect and important product, on account of the great depth of his theoretical development, and on account of his awareness of developing the theory and putting into practice the model of a life in which happiness coincides with giving primacy to intellectual activity over all others, because only intellectual activity is perfectly human. In this sense, it seems to me that at times the importance of the Aristotelian lesson is nowadays rather underestimated, or that some of its most extreme and paradoxical aspects are excessively emphasized, to the detriment of the truly important ones.[141] The truly essential elements, it seems, were his development of this model and the fact that Aristotle opened up the road to a special way of understanding the idea of "doing philosophy" that was different from his predecessors. At the same time, he founded this model of intellectual life on a series of ethical and anthropological arguments and on a global conception of human nature, a conception that constitutes a coherent and complex theoretical system, which remained for a long time at the foundation of European intellectual consciousness.

CHAPTER TWO
INSTITUTIONAL ASPECTS OF
THE SCHOOL OF ARISTOTLE

1. THE THREE CONDITIONS OF THE THEORETICAL LIFE IN ARISTOTLE

In the *Nicomachean Ethics* Aristotle does not make it clear in an exact and explicit way whether the content of *theōria* involves a direct contemplation of the divine, a life of scientific research, or else a combination of both, in which knowledge of the divine is an aspect of a broader study of reality.[1] What he does, however, indicate with remarkable clarity are the external conditions needed to make such activity possible, and there is a substantial agreement between the *Eudemian Ethics* and the *Nicomachean Ethics* on the question of the amount and quantity of goods necessary for the *bios theōretikos*. At *Eudemian Ethics* VIII.3 (1249a21–b25), an effort is made to determine a criterion (*horos*) of selection for things that are **"naturally good but not praiseworthy,"** an expression Aristotle uses to designate external goods.[2] These goods are directed for an end (*telos*), and Aristotle criticizes the attitude that he defines as a "political disposition" (*hexis politikē*) with respect to these goods, that is, making them the goal of actions and virtues, behavior typical of the Spartans. According to Aristotle, the good life is not a means to acquire external goods; on the contrary, external goods are a means to a good life.

The list of these external goods is spelled out at *Eudemian Ethics* VIII.3: **"honor, wealth, physical prowess, good fortune, and power** (*timē kai ploutos kai sōmatos aretai kai eutychiai kai dynameis*)" (1248b28–29 and 1249b16–18), but obviously what Aristotle is seeking is a moderate amount of these goods, the right "mean" between extremes.[3] And to determine the right mean in Aristotle's philosophy, one must take into account the nature of the thing in question, proceeding, however, by a *via negativa*, that is, beginning with the opposite extremes and working back until one finds the right mean. In this way, we move from what is most known to us to what is most known in itself, because everybody knows how to recognize an excess which is too obvious, whereas the exact determination of the *meson* may itself cover a certain range (see *On Generation and Corruption* II.7, 334b26–30 and *Nicomachean Ethics* II.9), and it is not easy to find this range with precision. What is needed in fact is not to determine the right mean in absolute terms or in general, focusing abstractly on the thing in itself; rather, we must determine the right mean in concrete terms, and with reference to a specific situation, for this individual, the *meson pros hēmas*.[4]

A quantity of goods that actually hinders the attainment of the end for which they come to be chosen is bad, and for the philosophical life it is necessary to attain a moderate prosperity, commensurate with the end that is to be reached, and sufficient to assure freedom from need.[5] In this way the theory of the right mean of the external goods harmonizes with the theory of the mental and physical conditions of philosophical activity; as T. Tracy has shown, for *theōria*, which is the highest level of human activity, what is necessary is a state of moderation and calm in the psychological sense, a stable equilibrium of the functions and desires of the body and, above all, the right regulation of the fundamental emotions of pleasure and pain. Not only the higher functions of the psyche but also the vegetative and sensitive functions should operate at their highest states for there to be freedom to study scientifically, and a man should be free of emotions and desires that exceed the right mean. But because the internal equilibrium is not independent from that of the external environment (*periechon*), here we find that the two middles, external and internal, are both necessary and interdependent, given that psychological equilibrium and tranquillity also depend upon a proper organization of the external goods.[6]

On this topic the *Nicomachean Ethics* does not differ from what is said in the *Eudemian Ethics*. Here too Aristotle wants to demonstrate the superiority of the *bios theōretikos*, and he therefore focuses on how it affords a greater degree of self-sufficiency as compared with other types of happy lives. But to be self-sufficient, in the first place, one must first be free from need and possess a moderate fortune (*NE* X.7, 1177a28– 34 and X.8, 1178b33–35). In particular, it could be said that, compared with the political life, the theoretical life is more self-sufficient, given that a politician in order to live well must have access to wealth, respect, and power (*dynasteias*, X.7, 1177b13), while the efficacy of his actions is subject to the effects of the actions of others. There is no difference on this point between the two works; on the contrary, what was said before is repeated: the politician does not have sufficient tranquillity to think, and he searches to find the criterion or *horos* of the external goods of fortune, bound up with the sphere of what is noble (*to kalon*) (X.7, 1177b17). Because there is bound to be an ample margin of uncertainty in the successful outcome of his actions, the politician is naturally worried about contingent results, and his natural condition is that of *ascholia*, a complete lack of leisure that is not only external but also capable of disturbing the equilibrium of his internal functions (X.7, 1177b2–4, b17–18, 1178a9–22).

The right mean for the philosopher consists in not being very tied to external prosperity (*ektos chorēgia*, 1178a24–25) and not being worried about whether he is fully equipped with the goods of fortune. Nonetheless, this by no means amounts to a total rejection of them, as happened with the Cynics. The philosopher should, for his own tranquillity, avoid an excess of goods (1178b3–5), but he does require health, food, and whatever is indispensable for living (1178b33–35). Both in order to convince his interlocutors and in order to motivate them to accept these ideas, Aristotle then went on to demonstrate (1179a9–13), by appealing to Solon and his doctrine of moderation (*metriotēs*),[7] how this idea of his also fits in with traditional opinions. Indeed, for Aristotle the *metrion* constitutes the good in the category of quantity (*NE* I.6, 1096a25–26). Referring to independence from need and to free time (*scholē*) as values and as criteria for choosing the type of life to which to devote oneself, all that Aristotle is doing is linking the ideal of the theoretical life to well-known tendencies in Greek popular morality, transcending the Platonic oppositions between philosophy and common sense.[8]

The first condition necessary for *theōria*, possession of moderate goods and freedom from need, therefore constitutes the foundation of the second necessary condition, *scholē*, which is not so much a component of a happy life as one of its necessary conditions, declares Aristotle. These two things, components and necessary conditions of happiness, are different from each other, because in Aristotle's view the "component parts" possess certain characteristics from which the "necessary condi-tions" are excluded. "**These are not the same: having the things with-out which being healthy is impossible, and being healthy; and this is how it is in many cases, so that living a good life too is not the same as having the things without which this is not able to happen**" (*EE* I.2, 1214b14–17; see also *Politics* VII.8, 1328a21–26 and VII.9, 1329a34–39). The reason why the necessary conditions are not parts is based on the distinction between ends and means (*Politics* VII.8, 1328a28–33). The necessary conditions bear the same relationship to the parts of hap-piness as the tools of the mason do to the finished house; they are not part of it, but they are indispensable to its creation. And *scholē* is a condi-tion that becomes all the more indispensable the closer one comes to the peak of *eudaimonia*, the *bios theōretikos*. At the highest level of hap-piness, in its conception of the unmoved mover of the whole cosmos, Aristotle explicitly links *theōria* and *scholē*, making the most complete freedom from external conditions the foundation for the best life of the mind.[9] Such a level of independence from need is unattainable for humans, but even in the human world a partial liberation from needs and necessities is possible. Aristotle argues this with the example of the Egyptian priests, whom he refers to at the beginning of the *Metaphysics*. In Egypt, the conditions necessary for the development of pure theo-retical thought were the liberation of certain individuals, the priests, from the need to provide for their own survival, and their attaining a certain comfort.[10] According to Aristotle, *scholē* is a necessary condition for thought from another point of view as well; it distinguishes philo-sophical reflection from sophistical debate, in which the debaters do battle against their adversary in order to win and are driven by the need for self-assertion. What is needed in order to find truth, on the contrary, is tranquil reflection.[11]

The third condition of *theōria* serves in a way as a counterweight to the first two, both of which threaten to push the philosopher's life away from the right mean and toward an excess of solitude, toward the life of an outsider, like the life of Anaxagoras at Athens had been;[12] a philosopher needs friends. In *Eudemian Ethics* VIII.3 (1249b18), friends are listed among the external goods, which therefore can be taken to include ordinary friends, not interested in philosophy,[13] but in the

Nicomachean Ethics (X.7, 1177a34), Aristotle mentions "collaborators" (*synergous*); and so the one doubt is about whether Aristotle means to include, among the best conditions for doing philosophy, only the presence of collaborators in the dialectical discussions and the research enterprises of the Platonic approach to philosophy,[14] or also the presence of students at lectures and of less active listeners.[15] It should, however, be noted that this condition is not strictly necessary for reflection, in contrast with the first two conditions; a philosopher can be active even on his own, and the presence of friends only makes his condition better.

The relationship between self-sufficiency and friendship is also examined at *Eudemian Ethics* VII.12, and here Aristotle cautions against the theory that the happiest man, being self-sufficient, can have no need for friends; in fact, it is more pleasurable to share the activities that constitute the purpose of our lives with well-chosen friends, and to devote ourselves with them not only to the pleasures of the body but also to the study of the cultural arts (*theōria mousikēs*) and to intellectual discussion (*philosophia*) (1245a21–22). Pleasure is also increased by the act of collaborating (*synergein*), sharing the activities that constitute the highest good, namely studying together (*syntheōrein*) and rejoicing together (*syneuōcheisthai*, 1245b4–5). His only warning to keep in mind is that sharing goods and experiences at this level is reserved to rather restricted groups, because it would be hard to assemble a large number of men disposed to share such feelings (*synaisthēsis*), and one would not know what to do with them once they had been assembled (1245b23–25).

In order to clarify what Aristotle means by *synergoi*, we can look at the texts in which he speaks of his students and interlocutors. At *Nicomachean Ethics* IX.1 (1164b2–3), he is obviously talking about his students, who have a relationship with their master similar to that which binds them to the gods and to their parents, that is, a friendship of superiority (*philia kath'hyperochēn*, VIII.7, 1158b11–12), in which the two parties are unequal.[16] In contrast, at IX.12 1172a1–8, he speaks of the community of those who wish to share with their friends the activity they prefer, and who therefore gather together to pursue what is for them a real life choice, truly so called. Echoing a passage of Isocrates, Aristotle cites as examples of this the principal forms of Greek non-political social life (drinking at *symposia*, training in the gymnasiums, and hunting),[17] and he coins a new term to signify the theoretical life: *symphilosophein* (to do philosophy together), a word that we shall come across again below.

Unlike in the case of the students, in the community described in *Nicomachean Ethics* IX.12 there is friendship in the fullest sense of the term. Thus, the relationship described here seems to fit better than the relationship between master and student with the indications given by Aristotle in *Nicomachean Ethics* X.7. Among such friends in the full sense of the term, there is no relationship of pure justice (*dikaiosynē*), as there is in less complete relationships;[18] this too is an indication that will need to be taken up again below.

For now it can be said, on the basis of the three conditions established by Aristotle, that the life of the wise man is not conceived as a deprived life, far from the full development of human capacities; on the contrary, it is presented as the functioning at full stretch of an individual of the human species. It is not strange to us that Aristotle tried to recommend to others the sort of life that he and his friends chose for themselves, defending a conception of the good life that had developed in the Platonic Academy, if not earlier; and it has been widely and well noted that the end of the *Nicomachean Ethics* has a pronounced protreptic quality.[19] I believe that here Aristotle wished to speak about a comprehensive choice of life, not about a particular component of the happy life,[20] and that such a proposal would have had a certain, albeit limited, success among Athenians of a comfortable station.[21]

2. THE ORGANIZATION OF *THEŌRIA*: THE NATURE AND ORGANIZATION OF THE PHILOSOPHICAL SCHOOLS

The purpose of this inquiry of ours is not to assess the acceptability of Aristotle's proposal or the consistency there may be between this and the other doctrines of the philosopher, but to see whether all these values and practical suggestions for living gave birth to a particular organization for the philosophical life. We are interested in finding out whether, by making use of institutions already present in Athenian tradition, philosophy succeeded in creating for itself an autonomous zone to organize according to its own vision of man and his functioning (*ergon*).

A standard reconstruction of the Athenian philosophical schools was proposed some time ago, and it has dominated scholarship on the subject since the end of the nineteenth century. Although there are certain precedents, this reconstruction is in very large part due to Wilamowitz (1881), who proposed a bipartite vision, so to speak, of these institutions.[22] Basing himself on the presupposition that all ancient associations had a devotional character and that they were recognized as religious associations by Athenian law, which attributed to them the status of juristic persons, Wilamowitz distinguished both an external and an internal aspect of these assemblies of philosophers. From the external juridical point of view, they would have been religious associations (*thiasoi*) dedicated to the cult of the Muses. From the point of view of their internal organization, on the other hand, these schools (especially the Academy and the Lyceum) would have been precursors of the modern university; in them, scientific research would have been carried on by teams, scientific material would have been collected, museums of natural history would have been organized, and the work of research and teaching would have been undertaken by a division of labor among the various senior and junior "professors" who taught actual courses, with larger public lectures and smaller seminars, for which the professor would have needed to prepare notes, make use of lecture halls, and calibrate the difficulty of the subject matter according to the more or less advanced level of the audience. However, nobody has ever reached the point, as far as I know, of supposing that these schools held examinations and issued degrees, like modern universities.[23]

As early as 1901, T. Gomperz criticized this reconstruction, claiming that the elements described by Wilamowitz as typical of the *thiasoi*, such as the statues of the Muses and their worship, were also typical of other institutions such as gymnasia and schools for boys; these elements would therefore not be sufficient to identify the philosophical schools as religious associations. All the other scholars, however, accepted Wilamowitz's theses; for instance, in his 1909 study of the history of Greek institutions, Poland considered the results of the study of the philosophical schools by Wilamowitz to be definitive contributions. In more recent times, however, doubts have begun to surface again about the picture sketched above, and the reconstruction of Wilamowitz has been chipped and broken in various places. Some have claimed that the status of *thiasoi* was something more than a juridical fiction; Boyancé has said that the mystical and religious aspects of the philosophical schools should be taken seriously (1937, pp. 261+), and that the worship of the Muses was something for which the members of these schools had a profound feeling.[24] On another front, the comparison between the activities of ancient philosophical schools and those of modern universities was radically criticized by Cherniss (1945, pp. 72–73), and similar positions are obviously held by all medievalists who have worked on the origin of the modern university, who have always considered it to be a weird quirk in classical philologists to want to discern in the Athenian schools of Plato and Aristotle the model of the medieval *universitas studiorum*.[25]

Even more recently, Gottschalk, Lynch, and Wehrli have again taken up the criticisms that Gomperz directed against Wilamowitz. Gottschalk noted a series of historical inaccuracies and contradictions in Wilamowitz's writing and concluded that his book should no longer be considered an authoritative account. He claims that it is not admissible to affirm both that the ancient philosophical schools were *thiasoi*, institutions of common property, and that the scholarch was the sole owner of all the real estate.[26] Lynch devotes an entire chapter to his criticism of Wilamowitz, showing that the arguments of the German philologist are weak and in some cases contradictory; he argues in particular that no ancient source ever uses the term *thiasoi* to refer to the philosophical schools, not even in the last wills and testaments of the philosophers, and commonly used terms such as "free time" (*scholē*) or "course" (*diatribē*) were connected with the educational sphere, not the religious; that the philosophers were commonly held to be irreligious; and that Aristotle, when he speaks of the *thiasoi* and the *eranoi*, does not mention them as if he were a member.[27] The presence of sanctuaries of the Muses in the proximity or the interior of philosophical schools, according to Lynch (who here agrees with Gomperz), does not prove that the entire school was a confraternity dedicated to the worship of the Muses, because *mouseia* and statues of the gods were also found in elementary schools and in other communities.[28] He then repeats Gomperz's criticisms, and claims that the presupposition of Wilamowitz's view, that the philosophical schools were established as *thiasoi* in order to obtain the status of "juristic person," is unacceptable, because in ancient Greece this concept was not yet available.[29] Like Gomperz, Lynch also claimed that the trial of Sophocles of Sounion, who was condemned in 307/306 BCE for having proposed the establishment of state control over the meetings of the "Sophists," does not prove that these meetings had a devotional character. The discussion was then carried on in book reviews and in collections of studies. Wehrli (1976) supported Lynch with new arguments; in particular, he found that in the will of Theophrastus the philosophers were invited to manage jointly the real estate property left by the philosopher as the site of his school, and that the expression Theophrastus uses is "possessing it in common as if it were a temple" (*hōs an hieron koinēi kektēmenois*). This would indicate, according to Wehrli, that the property left by Theophrastus was not a genuine temple. This observation strikes me as convincing, and I shall add below a few other observations of this type.

On the other hand, more recently, some scholars have come to the defense of Wilamowitz's position, such as Isnardi Parente (1986), who gives a complete overview of the discussions and contributions later than 1970; despite noting that Lynch's thesis is almost entirely successful, she finds that Wilamowitz's position is still defensible, but she transposes to a later time their resorting to the legal expedient of passing off a community of philosophers as a *thiasos* of the Muses. In her view (Isnardi Parente 1981, pp. 141–150), this would have happened only when Xenocrates succeeded Speusippus, that is, when a non-Athenian became scholarch of the Athenian Academy, and she advances the hypothesis that the philosophers attempted in this way to give their schools a form of public recognition, a legal guarantee, and moreover that they would have been able to express their special type of spirituality, different from the common one.[30] It is difficult to say with any certainty how things went, and Wilamowitz's reconstruction remains largely hypothetical. As for the second point, I believe that the spirit of the Peripatetic school was different from the spirit of Plato's Academy.

Even if Lynch's criticisms of the thesis of Wilamowitz can be considered acceptable, what remains rather perplexing to me is the great determination shown by Lynch, when he tries to demonstrate that the philosophical schools were in the first place "educational institutions," in other words, if I understand him correctly, institutions that established themselves freely in the environment of the city with the purpose of educating the young. The city, in the reconstruction of Lynch, while not having a direct interest in the foundation of these schools, looked on them very kindly and granted them the use of public spaces in which to teach, such as gymnasia, in exchange for the prestige and fame that accrued from their activity. In this way, the Peripatetic school was established in mixed territory, partly public and partly private.[31] It is true that there is no lack of witnesses who talk about an activity of teaching on the part of the philosophical schools. The last will and testament of Aristotle (Diogenes Laertius 5.14) mentions a certain boy named Myrmex, for whom the philosopher directs that "**Nicanor shall be in charge of the boy Myrmex, so that he is brought** [back] **to his own people in a manner worthy of us, together with the assets that we received from him.**"

It seems clear that this Myrmex was a young man who had come to attend the school of Aristotle in Athens, or perhaps in Chalcis, just as in his time Aristotle himself had come to Athens to attend the school of Plato, and that Myrmex was then sent back to his family because of the death of the master, who likely did not foresee an uninterrupted continuation of the school's activities. In his *Life of Lyco* (5.65), Diogenes Laertius says that Lyco was extremely good at educating young boys; and in his *Life of Zeno* (7.10–11), Diogenes Laertius transcribes an honorific decree from the Athenians that Zeno the Stoic received for his qualities as an educator of young men. "**Whereas Zeno of Citium (son of Mnaseas) has been living for many years in the city as a philosopher** (*kata philosophian*)**, and has been in other respects a consistently good man who encouraged the young men who joined his group** (*sustasis*) **towards virtue and temperance, and urged them to do what is best, providing in his own life a model for all, a life consistent with the lectures he gave; the people has decreed (may fortune** favor) that **Zeno of Citium (son of Mnaseas) be praised, that he be crowned with a crown of gold according to law on account of his virtue and self-control, and also that a sepulchre in the** [cemetery of the] **Ceramicus be built for him at public expense.**" A suitable sum is to be expended on the memorial tablets "**such that everyone may see that the people of Athens honor the good, both the living and the dead.**" Therefore the philosophers dedicated themselves, among other things, to educating the young, just as all the Sophists since the time of Protagoras had done. On this point there is no doubt. But the problem lies in establishing whether educating the young was the principal activity of the philosophers, or whether the philosophical schools had been established in the first place to perform quite different functions, functions other than the education of the young or the worship of the Muses.

To me it seems that a reading of the ethical works of Aristotle can clarify this point, because the foundation of the Peripatetic school was not an event detached from the theoretical context in which it came into being; on the contrary, it was an attempt to apply practically the ideas of the master. In Aristotle's writings, certainly, there is no shortage of indications about how lectures should be given, on the relationship between teaching and research, and on the different types of people of whom the public is comprised, there are passages that provide a direct view of Aristotle's relationship with groups of students (for more on this subject, see section 3 of chapter 3), and so on. But these were principally, as far as we can tell, students who were already advanced on the path of the *bios theōretikos* and had decided to pursue the life of a philosopher, like Antimoerus of Mende, who, as Plato tells us with a smile, "**is the most famous of the students of Protagoras, and is learning the technique because he is going to be a sophist**" (*Protagoras* 315a). Even if there were any such young men in his school, Aristotle does not mention in his works any young men who came there primarily to receive a bit of "higher education." The nucleus of the philosopher's activity is not *didaskalia*, as Protagoras maintained it was for him, when he talked about traveling as a foreigner through the great cities of Greece, where he went around persuading "**the best of their young men to abandon their associations with other people, both familiars and strangers,** both old and young, and to associate with him, because they are going to be better by associating with him" (*Protagoras* 316c), but rather the pursuit of the *bios theōretikos.*[32]

Nor is the nucleus of the philosopher's activity the training of rulers in cities, as it seems to have been in Plato's school, at least according to certain interpretations. Its nucleus is *theōria,* the cultivation of the highest functioning of man. In his *Sophistical Refutations* 2, Aristotle clearly contrasts the activity of teaching, which proceeds by demonstrative syllogisms like those described in the *Prior Analytics,* with other more philosophical activities, such as dialectic and *peirastikē,* that is, the technique of examining the consequences of premises that appear acceptable to experts. According to the hypothesis of Lynch, the Aristotelian ideal of the *bios theōretikos,* of a life devoted to the activity of discussion and theoretical development, remained unrealized even in the place that at first glance might seem best suited for it, the school; and we are obliged to see this ideal not as a feasible program for living, even if only for a few, but as a purely utopian vision. Before we reach such a conclusion, however, it would be good to examine the problem a bit more closely.

3. THE ORGANIZATION OF *THEŌRIA*: PHILOSOPHICAL SCHOOLS AND PERMANENT INSTITUTIONS

If we turn to the historians who have studied the permanent institutions in this period of Greek history, apart from a range of disputed issues we will find a consensus on various facts and judgments that can be useful also to a historian of philosophy who wishes to reach an awareness of how philosophical ideas were experienced concretely, and how the scale of values professed by the philosophers was put into practice within the schools.[33]

It would appear that the custom of setting up what, to use a modern term, we would call "foundations" had become widespread in Greece as early as the sixth century BCE, if not earlier, in the sense of a perpetual bequest on the part of a private individual of a portion of his property, in real estate or else a sum of money. This bequest was meant to ensure the perennial pursuit (*eis aei*) of a specific goal, which is particularly important to the person making the bequest. In reality,

however, these "foundations" often lasted no more than a few generations.[34] Those who made the bequest usually prohibited it from being
alienated, and the revenues that accrued from the bequest were used
to attain the stated goal. The first foundations were of a devotional
character; for example, we know that a foundation was established at
Delos by Nicias, and as Plutarch tells us, Nicias "**consecrated a tract
of land he purchased for ten thousand drachmas, from which the
revenues were to be expended by the Delians on sacrificial feasting,
requesting from the gods many blessings for Nicias**" (*Life of Nicias*
3.7, 525b). And another foundation was erected by Xenophon at Scillus
near Olympia, as he himself tells us (*Anabasis* 5.3): "**Xenophon acquired
a plot of land to dedicate to the goddess** [Artemis]" (5.3.7). "**He built
an altar as well as a temple with the sacred money, and ever after
he would take a tenth share of the seasonal fruits of the land and
make a sacrifice to the goddess. And all the citizens** [of Scillus] **and
all the neighboring men and women took part in the festival**" (5.3.9).
"**Within the sacred space were meadows and hills covered with
trees, good enough for keeping pigs, goats, cattle, and horses, so
that the yoked animals that brought the people to the festival were
also sumptuously well fed. Surrounding the temple itself a grove
of cultivated trees produced such fruits as were edible. The temple
itself resembled a small version of the large one in Ephesus, and the
image of the goddess, despite being of cypress wood, seems to be
gold like the one in Ephesus. And a tablet stood beside the temple,
thus inscribed: 'This land is sacred to Artemis. He who holds it and
takes its produce must offer a tenth share every year in sacrifice. And
from the remainder he must outfit and keep up the temple. And if
anyone fails to do this, the goddess will look out for him'**" (5.3.11–
13).

Subsequently there were foundations for the most widely varied
purposes: to restore and maintain the walls of a city in good condition,
to provide food for the citizens, to take care of the worship of the gods,
to pay the costs of the office of gymnasiarch or of other public offices
(in this case the donor was named to the office in question for life, for
instance, "perpetual gymnasiarch," and anyone who actually performed
the job of the office in the course of time was considered simply a

substitute, *epimelētēs*),[35] to pay for the oil for young men who wanted to anoint themselves before wrestling,[36] and so on. Foundations were often established in order to commemorate the memory of the donor (*eis mnēmēn*), and to recall his desire to enjoy a good reputation (*philodoxia*).[37]

Of great importance were the educational foundations, in which the donor not only assumed the expenses of teaching the young people, of constructing and maintaining the *gymnasium*, and of paying the salaries of the teachers, but also dictated rules to be followed in the teaching. Often the founders were buried near the foundation and were venerated with a cult similar to that reserved for heroes.[38] Other foundations had a funerary function instead, and they sought to ensure the continuance of the funerary cult of the founder.[39] Often the members of the group that was entrusted to celebrate the funerary cult were the members of the donor's own family.

The Peripatetic school had its origin, in its institutional structure, in a donation of this type, which had characteristics that were very similar to those of the educational and funerary foundations just described; but, in contrast with what Lynch claims, the purpose of the bequest was not to ensure the education of the young. This can be attested by reading the wills of the philosophers preserved by Diogenes Laertius. It is common knowledge that there was nothing at all in Aristotle's last will and testament about a school, given that Aristotle as a metic could not own real estate in Athens to be left to his students (as Epicurus would later do), nor does it appear that he did so in Chalcis.

Theophrastus, on the other hand, was able to purchase a garden in Athens, with the support of Demetrius of Phalerum, and in the last will of this philosopher we can clearly see that he possessed real estate in Athens that he used to establish a foundation of just the kind described above. The subject of the bequest is a garden, which must have been the one just mentioned, a *peripatos*, and several houses. It is not perfectly clear just what this *peripatos* was; the name means "promenade" or "place in which to stroll," and it could be a colonnade, or else a tree-lined walkway.[40] In the same will and testament, provisions are made for the restoration of a sanctuary of the Muses: Theophrastus gives directions to restore the temple and the altar, and to place or return to their proper places some votive statues that were missing, including statues of Aristotle and Aristotle's son Nicomachus (the latter statue had yet to be sculpted)[41] and to fix in place several panels that had maps of the earth. This last provision would suggest there was some connection between the sanctuary and the teaching activity of a school, and it would justify the view of those who claim that maintaining the cult of the Muses was among the activities of the philosophical schools. I do not want to rule this out, or to deny that philosophers might have had a special care for the cult of the Muses. My point is different; I wish to firmly emphasize the fact that the principal purpose of the establishment of the philosophical schools was not the cult of the Muses but was something else, the implementation of the ideal of the theoretical life.

We should also point out that it is not certain that the sanctuary of the Muses formed part of the bequest; Theophrastus concludes the part of his last will and testament devoted to the restoration of the temple of the Muses (Diogenes Laertius 5.52) as if he was finishing part of what he needed to say, and then moving on to the next, commenting, "**so now, as for the things that concern the temple and the votive offerings, let them be done this way**." There follows in the will a bequest to Callinus of a small estate that Theophrastus owned in Stagira (see section 2 of chapter 1), and the bequest of Theophrastus's entire library to Neleus; and it is only at this point that he begins to deal with the garden, the houses, and the community of philosophers who were to make use of them.[42]

Let us examine the text (Diogenes Laertius, 5.51–53). Theophrastus directs that the funds at the disposal of his trustee Hipparchus are to be applied "**in the first place, to bring to completion the** [work on the] *Museion* **and the** [statues of the] **goddesses, and, even if something else stops it, to provide them with more beautiful ornamentation; then next, to place the image of Aristotle in the temple with the remaining votive offerings that were already in the temple; next, to build the small cloister next to the** *Museion* **no worse than before; and to set up the pictures** (*pinakas*) **on which there are the maps of the earth** (*gēs periodoi*) **in the lower cloister; and to outfit the altar as well, so that it may be perfect and elegant. It is also my wish that the statue of Nicomachus should be completed, of equal size; the cost of** the statue is in the hands of Praxiteles,[43] but the other costs should come from these funds, and it should be erected in whatever place seems best to those who administer the other written provisions of this will. So now, as for the things that concern the temple and the votive offerings, let them be done this way; but the small property at Stagira belonging to me I bequeath to Callinus, and all my books to Neleus, and I bequeath in perpetuity the garden and the *peripatos* and all the houses near the garden to those of my friends, hereinafter named, who wish to spend free time together and do philosophy together (*syscholazein kai symphilosophein*) in these places, since it is not possible for every person to be always resident, on condition that they not alienate the property nor privatize it in any way, holding it in common as if it were a temple (*hōs . . . hieron*),[44] and treat each other as friends and family, as is right and proper. Let the community consist of Hipparchus, Neleus, Strato, Callinus, Demotimus, Demaratus, Callisthenes, Melanthes, Pancreon, and Nicippus."

The foundation had property consisting of a garden, a promenade, and several houses. This property was left to a group of ten people, listed by name, as in the foundations for a funerary cult.[45] These were ten individuals bound to Theophrastus by special ties of friendship. In the will, the purpose of the bequest is clearly stated; the property is bequeathed "to those of my friends [. . .] who wish to spend free time together (*scholē*)[46] and do philosophy together." The term used by Theophrastus, *symphilosophein*, is important. As we have seen previously, this is a word invented by Aristotle in the *Nicomachean Ethics* to describe one of the ways of passing the free time of *scholē* with one's friends, when one enjoys freedom from the occupations required in order to live, in contrast with such traditional pursuits as hunting, going to the gymnasium, or indulging in group banquets (*Nicomachean Ethics* IX.12, 1172a1–8).[47]

The evident purpose of the foundation is to assure the philosophers the moderate prosperity and the freedom from need that we have seen constitutes one of the necessary conditions for dedicating oneself to philosophy in tranquillity; and, indeed, the entire complex was bequeathed only to those who are in a position to be able to live in the garden on an ongoing basis, since "it is not possible for every person to be always

resident," as Theophrastus himself tells us (5.53). This indication of the purpose is followed by a series of prohibitions, typical in these cases: never sell the land and the buildings, do not use them as private assets, but keep them for the purpose established by the donor, and use it in common, as if it were a temple. Like other donors, Theophrastus asks to be buried in the garden, with a funerary monument, which he himself provides the funds for erecting.[48] Then are prescribed relations of friendship among the members of the group, with a substantially equal relationship among them; the members of the community are enjoined to "**treat each other as friends and family, as is right and proper**" (5.53). The common possession of the garden and the houses was based on their mutual relationship of close friendship (*philia*) and kinship.

Those who have studied in juridical terms this type of ownership[49] have recognized that in the case of the philosophical schools we are in the presence of a sort of shared property based more on the goodwill of the members of the group than on any actual juridical norms, a relationship, that is, that depends primarily upon natural *philia*, as described by Aristotle in *Nicomachean Ethics* (VIII.9, 1159b25+ and VIII.11, 1161a25–30). It is a case analogous to the one of a group of brothers who, following the death of their father, decide not to split up the estate but to continue shared ownership; this is a type of shared property that was quite common throughout antiquity and which, according to Biscardi, is attested as persisting until the Byzantine era.

In this way an effort was made to put into practice the ideal of the *bios theōretikos*, and Theophrastus wanted to ensure its external conditions. The goal of the school was philosophy as a life choice, not the education of young people to undertake assignments assigned by the city, or to be successful in political life generally, as had happened in the time of the Sophists. All the same, this does not exclude either possibility: that the philosophers later taught the general public as well or that entry to the garden was reserved only to the ten members of the original group. In one source (Diogenes Laertius 5.37), it is said that Theophrastus had a huge number of listeners, more than two thousand, although that figure has been questioned by modern scholars.

The ten individuals to whom Theophrastus bequeathed the school must have had among themselves long-standing relationships of friendship and familiarity, relationships closer than those that exist nowadays between the professors of a single university department. Among them, six were also executors of the will of Theophrastus and therefore people with whom the philosopher was bound by ties of friendship and trust.[50] One of them, Neleus, was the son of Coriscus of Scepsis, who had accompanied Aristotle at the court of Hermias at Assos; so his friendship with Theophrastus probably dated from the moment that Theophrastus himself had become a student of Aristotle. To Neleus, Theophrastus left a special bequest, his own personal library, without by this act intending to establish any primacy of Neleus over the others,[51] given that Neleus was among those who wished to remain in the garden and devote themselves to philosophy. With this testamentary gift, Theophrastus had no intention of depriving the school of its library, which perhaps included the writings of Aristotle. This bequest, however, was the source of the legend, recounted by Strabo (13.1.54) and Plutarch (*Life of Sulla* 26), of the disappearance of Aristotle's works into a cellar during the time of Strato, a disappearance that deprived the Peripatetic school of the authentic views of the master, and which made all the more precious the republication of the Aristotelian treatises, first by Tyrannion, and later by Andronicus of Rhodes. We shall return to this point later (pp. 102–104).

Two others of the ten, Melantehs and Pancreon, were heirs to Theophrastus and therefore close relatives, possibly sons or grandsons, since Melanthes had also been the name of Theophrastus's father.[52] Perhaps the Demaratus mentioned in this list was Aristotle's grandson (see section 3 of chapter 1). Hipparchus, next, was the administrator of Theophrastus's assets in Athens. As the eleventh member, when he attained the proper age, Aristotle the younger, the son of Pythias and grandson of the philosopher, could be added to the list. Therefore, the original group of ten seems to have had this composition: six executors of the estate (among them a friend from his youth), two close relatives, the trustee of the estate, and one grandson of the founder of Peripatetic philosophy. The composition of the group seems anything but haphazard, and the life of philosophy almost seems like the business of a family clan, restricted to a small circle that mixed together relationships of kinship, of friendship, of business, and of culture.

There are also hints of ties of close friendship between Callisthenes and Theophrastus, between Theophrastus and Demetrius of Phalerum, and between Demetrius of Phalerum and Strato of Lampsacus, successor to Theophrastus as the head of the school, but listed in the last will and testament as an executor of the will. The same sort of ties can be found in later institutions; Taormina (1989, pp. 24–25) and Sorabji (1990, p. 8) describe the family relations between the ancient scholars who directed schools of philosophy in Athens and Alexandria, as follows: Iamblichus had as his students not only Sopater I but also that student's two sons, Sopater II and Himeraius, as well as the son of Himeraius, Iamblichus II, who in turn had as his student Plutarch of Athens; Hermias of Alexandria, for his part, married a relative of Syrianus, who was originally supposed to marry Proclus, and their son was Ammonius.

As was said above, there has been much discussion about whether this community was less a particular cult of the Muses (Wilamowitz) or whether it was more especially dedicated to the cult of the dead (Boyancé), either as a sort of hero cult or as a basic funerary cult.[53] There are also some who observe that the two things could go together, and that there are other examples of this in history (see the foundation of Epiketas, *Inscriptiones Graecae* XII/3, no. 330).[54] There are also some who believe, as we have seen above, that the school, in Aristotle's time, had the custom of commemorating Hermias of Atarneus with a daily ceremony.[55] This in no way diminishes the fact that the fundamental purpose for which these schools had been established was, above all, to enjoy free time (*scholē*) by spending it in "**relaxation and scholarship**," as Antigonus of Carystus puts it in a passage that we shall quote below (section 4, pp. 93–95).

4. SUBSEQUENT EVENTS

We know that Theophrastus was very successful with his teaching; according to Diogenes Laertius (5.37), two thousand pupils attended his lectures. That number is probably meant to indicate the overall number of all the students of Theophrastus, not the number of those who listened at the same time to one of his *logoi*. Despite this success,[56] his position was not invulnerable, and "**for a short time even he had to go into exile with all the rest of the philosophers, when Sophocles the** son of Amphiclides proposed a law that none of the philosophers is to be in charge of a school (scholē), **except by decree of the Council and the People; otherwise, death is to be the penalty. But right away they returned, the next year, when Philo prosecuted Sophocles for making an illegal proposal. Then the Athenians also repealed the law, fined Sophocles a penalty of five talents, and voted the recall of the philosophers, in order that Theophrastus also might return and be in the same circumstances**" (Diogenes Laertius, 5.38). Another parallel report, given by the *Onomasticon* of Julius Pollux (9.42), is that "**there is also an Attic law written against the philosophers, moved by Sophocles, the son of Amphiclides of Sounion, in which he made certain accusations against them and proposed that none of the sophists should be given permission to establish a school.**"

This event, which occurred in the years 307–306 BCE, is connected by all authors to the fall of the government of the Peripatetic Demetrius of Phalerum, who had done his best to favor the philosophical schools, helping both Xenocrates and Theophrastus (see section 3 of chapter 1). And indeed the decree of Sophocles of Sounion was directed against all the schools, as is shown by a polemical tirade written in those same years by the comic poet Alexis in his play *The Horseman*, roughly around the winter of 306, given that it presupposes that the decree of Sophocles of Sounion is in effect. A fragment of this tirade is reported by one of the characters in the work of Athenaeus (13, 610d–f). "**Then am I not right to hate all you philosophers, seeing that you hate literature? You are not the only ones whom King Lysimachus expelled from his kingdom by proclamation, as Carystius** [of Pergamum] **declares in his *Historical Notes*, but the Athenians did it as well. Alexis, at any rate, says this in *The Horseman*: 'So this is what the Academy is, this is Xenocrates? May the gods grant many blessings to Demetrius and the legislators, for they have hurled out of Attica into hell the men who transmit to our youth the power of *logoi*, as they call it.' A man named Sophocles also drove out of Attica all philosophers by a reso-lution** [in the Assembly]; **against him Philo, a student of Aristotle, wrote a speech, after Demochares, the cousin[57] of Demosthenes, had made a speech defending the resolution of Sophocles.**" This passage gives us a fairly precise account of the issue, which completes and confirms the information in Diogenes Laertius: on the one hand are the members of the democratic faction, such as the orator Demochares and this Sophocles, the son of Amphiclides of Sounion; on the other hand there are the Peripatetics, such as this Philo, who must have been a citizen, given that he was able to defend the school publicly, as noted by Wilamowitz (1881, pp. 263+). Theophrastus had apparently spoken before Demochares, who scored some points at his expense (Aelian, *Miscellaneous Research* 8.12).

Of the speech of Demochares in defense of the law of Sophocles of Sounion, we have a few fragments, the most important of which has already been quoted in section 2 of chapter 1, p. 6. The passages that survive show that the speech of Demochares was heavily based on political arguments. In his *On Philosophy*, Aristocles reports that Demochares **"said bad things not only about Aristotle, but also about the others"** (excerpted in Eusebius 15.2.6 = *testimonium* 58g); and from Athenaeus (5, 215c) we learn that he raised general doubts about the fitness of anyone educated in philosophy to act as a military leader, and that he cast aspersions on the prowess of Socrates,[58] saying that **"no one could make a spear point from a stick of savoury** [an aromatic herb], **just as no one could make a good general out of Socrates."**[59] He then went on to state that Aristotle betrayed his homeland, and that the students of Plato tried in every way imaginable to make themselves tyrants in their cities. With respect to other accusations against the philosophers, here the question of the impiety of philosophical doctrines, which led to the death of Socrates, seems not to have been mentioned any more, and the debate seems to have been conducted primarily on political arguments; only Alexis, in order to amuse the public, refers back to the old anti-Sophistic argument of **"the power of the *logoi*,"** with which philosophers supposedly turned the heads of young people, making them insubordinate and uncontrollable.[60] But the philosophers won the case, we do not know with what line of argument, and the school reopened.

At a certain point following the death of Theophrastus, the group to which the garden had been bequeathed elected Strato as its head, and, as such, Strato in his last will and testament bequeathed the school to Lyco. This change has been much discussed,[61] but it would seem to have been an exception to the rule; indeed, Strato seeks to excuse himself for the measures that he took, saying that the other members of the community were either too advanced in years or too busy (Diogenes Laertius, 5.62), and nevertheless he exhorts the other philosophers to collaborate with Lyco. Theophrastus too had excluded from the community those who were too busy to remain always in residence in the garden (5.53). Lyco, then, blended the model of Theophrastus with that of Strato, and he bequeathed the school to another group of ten students, charging them, however, to elect a scholarch from among their ranks (5.70). It is not really known what happened after that, but in the group of these ten students there was a young man who had lived for many years with Lyco and was considered by him as a son, who had the same name as him; this son called Lyco was also the trustee, along with a brother of his named Astyanax, of their father Lyco's estate (confusingly, there was a grandson of Lyco also called Lyco). Another member of the group Ariston of Ceos, who was, according to tradition, the successor of Lyco (the father) as scholarch of the Aristotelian Peripatos. But it is uncertain whether the school survived past the first century BCE.[62] In the wills of the successors of Theophrastus, there is no longer a repetition of the entire description of the bequest as done by Theophrastus; only Lyco exhorts his successors to keep the school open, to oversee the maintenance of its activity, and to foster its progress (Diogenes Laertius 5.70).

An admittedly polemical description of later developments in the school at the time of Lyco has been transmitted to us by Antigonus of Carystus. In a passage cited in Athenaeus 12 (547d–548b), Antigonus informs us that Lyco the Peripatetic, when "**he was head of the Peripatos, used to dine his friends with much expense and much pretense; apart from the entertainers brought in and the silverware and the textiles, the other arrangements and the elaborateness of the dinners and the hordes of serving staff and cooking staff were so excessive that many people were horrified and were repelled, despite wanting to join the school (**diatribē**), just as they would be cautious about joining a bad government regime that is full of public service and taxation obligations. For they had to be in charge of the regular running of the Peripatos (which was to ensure the decorous behav-**

iour of the debaters) for a period of thirty days; then, on the last day
of the month and the first of the next, having received from each of
the debaters nine *obols*, they had to include [in the dinner] not only
those who had contributed, but also the people Lyco invited, besides
those of the older men who attended administrative meetings at the
school (*scholē*), so that the money collected was not even enough to
pay for the perfume and the garlands; and they had to perform sacrifice as well as be administrator of the *Museions*.

"Now all this evidently has nothing to do with argument (*logos*)
and philosophy (*philosophia*), but is more appropriate to a life of
luxury and affluence. For even though some of those who were
unable to spend money on these things were excused from the duty
because their resources were limited and ordinary, still the custom
was entirely out of place. For surely it was not in order for those
who stream together and crowd in the same place to enjoy dinners
that last until morning, or to get drunk, that the followers of Plato
and Speusippus instituted these gatherings, but rather to display
themselves as revering the divine and associating with one another
in cultural pursuits, and, most of all, for the purpose of relaxation
and scholarship (*philologia*). Now all this became secondary in the
eyes of their successors to the fancy clothing and the extravagance
just described; nor do I make an exception of any of the others. And
Lyco was so pretentious that he took a twenty-couch room in the
most exclusive part of the city, in Conon's house, which suited him
for his parties. And Lyco was a good and skilful ball-player."

It is difficult to think that this description of the operation of the
Peripatetic school in the time of Lyco, given to us by Antigonus of
Carystus, is validly applicable also to the Peripatos of the time of Aristotle, or even the time of Theophrastus; in fact, the fundamental theme
of the passage is a denunciation of a "change" that is also a "decline."
Wilamowitz finds in this passage definitive proof of the religious character of the schools (1881, pp. 194–197); it names the office of a supervisor
of the good behavior of the students (*archēn . . . epi tēs eukosmias*),
who also looks after the rites honoring the Muses.[63] Wilamowitz believes
that in this passage with the term *presbuteroi*, a distinction is made
between the younger students and the more senior members of the

community, the ones named in the will of the previous scholarch who "participate in the succession." But the text of Antigonus could instead refer quite generally to those older students who attended administrative meetings at the school (*tous epimelōs synantōntas tōn presbuterōn eis tēn scholēn*).[64] The presence of the office of "**administrator of the Museions**" in this text is today the strongest argument in defense of Wilamowitz's thesis.

The fact remains that when Theophrastus established the foundation of the Peripatos in his last will, he did not include among the purposes of his bequest the worship of the Muses but only the pursuit of the theoretical life, and he defined the goods that constituted the common estate as something similar to a *hieron*, not something that was literally a temple. Antigonus of Carystus himself, at the end of the passage cited by Athenaeus, when he speaks of the purpose for which these schools were founded by "**the followers of Plato and Speusippus**," although he does mention a religious element, puts the emphasis on the intention to enjoy *scholē* as befits philosophers and wise men. This, in my view, remains the fundamental purpose of the institution of the Peripatetic school.

CHAPTER THREE
INTERNAL ORGANIZATION OF THE SCHOOL OF ARISTOTLE

1. THE COLLECTIONS OF BOOKS

There is no available external documentation concerning the organization and activity of the school in the time of Aristotle. Comic poets, who happily made fun of Plato, who was a citizen of Athens and member of a prominent family, paid no attention to Aristotle, who was an outsider, nor did the orators (with the exception of Demochares, as we have seen). We have no caricatured descriptions of the philosopher and his circle, as we do for Socrates and Plato. For this reason the Aristotelian treatises constitute almost the only source of information to help us understand how teaching and philosophical discussion were organized in the Peripatetic school at the time of Aristotle.

The scientific and philosophical research contained in the Aristotelian treatises is not of a kind that could be improvised while strolling under the porticoes of some random gymnasium, as was possible for the purely conceptual analysis of Socrates. The results that Aristotle reached are clearly the fruit of extensive investigations based on research (*historia*), of a complex systematic arrangement of the evidence (*phainomena*), and of an appropriate use of written sources. Let us begin with this third point.

From the time of his first stay in Athens, Aristotle stood out among the students of Plato because he preferred reading to public discussion. We referred in chapter 1 (p. 20) to the reports about Aristotle that contrast his habit of reading alone with the customs of the Academy, where discussion was general (and see n. 38 to p. 20). And in note 136 of chapter 1, we noted the irony with which Aristotle referred to those who "**have not read anything but the *Banquet* by Philoxenus, and not even all of it.**" It is not certain whether this anecdote, recounted in the Neoplatonic *Lives*, is historically reliable; some accept it, such as Düring (1957, p. 108) and Vegetti (1979, pp. 58–59), but others reject it, such as Gigon (1962, pp. 40–43). But there certainly remains in the collection of Hellenistic anecdotes a tradition whereby Aristotle was a passionate collector of books. Diogenes Laertius (4.5) tells us that **"Favorinus also says, in the second book of his *Memorabilia*, that Aristotle purchased the books of Speusippus for three talents"** (*testimonium* 42c). A very similar report reappears in Aulus Gellius (3.17), that **"it is also said of Aristotle that he bought a few books of the philosopher Speusippus, after the latter's death, for three Attic talents; this sum would be in our money seventy-two thousand sesterces"** (*testimonium* 42b).

And in Aristotle's own *Topics* we do find references to the use of written works. He says in this work that the *endoxa*, the reputable opinions that are starting points in dialectical demonstrations, can be taken either from oral tradition or from the written records of the sayings of wise men and experts. At I.14 (105b12–18), he lays out his plan for this process. **"It is also necessary to select from written sources, and to create lists for each kind under separate headings such as 'Life' or 'Good,' in other words everything good, beginning with what it is, and also to make a note of the opinions in each of them, for example, that Empedocles said there are four elements in bodies, for one might write down the comment of some reputable person."** We see here, for the first time (see Zadro 1974, p. 343), the principle upon which the doxographic collections would later be based, such as the *Opinions* (*Placita*) of Aëtius (see Diels 1879), which list the various opinions of the philosophers by topic, the formula of which is often traced back to the *Opinions of the Natural Philosophers* by Theophrastus. We often find the "philosophical" histories of Aristotle contrasted with these "doxographical" histories of Theophrastus; but the two approaches have the same origin, and simply represent two different levels of carrying out the same investigation. The practice of Aristotelian dialectic, which seeks to resolve *aporiai* by discussing and comparing famous opinions including those found in the books of previous philosophers, makes it useful and theoretically justified to organize collections of texts or summaries of the thought of different authors on this or that problem, in a way that permits dialectical analysis to be performed on this material. He says this in a well-known passage of his work *On the Heavens* (I.10,

279b4–12). "Having defined these terms, let's next say whether it is ungenerated or generated, indestructible or destructible, in the first place by going through what others have supposed, for the demonstrations of opposite theories are difficulties for the opposing ones. At the same time, as well, what we are going to say will be more readily believed by those who have previously heard the justifications for the disputed arguments, for the appearance of winning the judgment by default would apply less to us, since those who are going to judge the truth in a satisfactory way need to be arbitrators, not parties to the dispute."

In reference to the collections of proverbs that Aristotle assembled, we already touched on this point above (section 4 of chapter 1, pp. 25–26), noting that Aristotle believed that commonly held opinion is the repository of a kernel of truth, which gets recovered and clarified by philosophical investigation. In this context, the sayings of the learned and of the experts are especially worthy of attention, and should be collected. In the *Nicomachean Ethics,* in reference to the various opinions about what constitutes happiness (I.8, 1098b27–29), Aristotle writes that "some of these views have been stated by many men and in past ages, others by a few reputable men; and it is reasonable to think that neither of these views should be mistaken in all respects, but rather that they should get it right in some one respect, anyway, or even in most." For these theoretical reasons, the establishment of a small "philosophical" library would suit the conceptual schemes and methods of Aristotelian dialectic, even more than the Platonic Academy, and Aristotle is recorded by ancient sources as being one of those who were famous for having noteworthy collections of books.

One of the opinions that is most important and worth discussing, about what is good and what is bad, is the opinion of his teacher Plato. A great deal of Aristotelian thought has a direct relationship with Platonic thought, and not only with the "unwritten doctrines," of which Aristotle was one of the principal witnesses, but also with the dialogues that we possess. On the other hand, Aristotle almost never quotes Plato's dialogues directly, whereas he likes to quote various Presocratic writers in his treatises, so much that he is one of the main sources in which to find more or less literal fragments from these very ancient thinkers. For example, in his work *On Sense Perception* (2, 437b11+), Aristotle gives us a discussion of the theory that sight is fire, maintained by Empedocles and also accepted by Plato in the *Timaeus*. Whereas Plato's position is summarized in short phrases and rapidly refuted, Aristotle transcribes a long passage from Empedocles (fr. 84 Diels-Kranz). This way of proceeding is understandable only in a *logos* addressed to a public that has access to, or in any case has read, Plato's *Timaeus* but does not know the text of Empedocles directly; thus the master, quite correctly, gives his audience access to the text that is less available. The same thing occurs in chapters 5 and 7 of Aristotle's work on *Respiration* (472b6+ and 473b9+), and in other works.

There are also some curious passages, such as this one from *On Generation and Corruption* II.1 (329a13–16), in which Aristotle mentions the Platonic concept of the "Receptacle," with explicit reference to the *Timaeus*: "**what is written in the *Timaeus* is not at all defined, for he does not state clearly if the 'Receptacle' is separate from the elements, nor does he make any use of it by saying it is a substratum of what were said earlier to be elements**." The text continues with a summary of the principal positions of the *Timaeus* in order to show its inconsistency. What can we learn from this procedure? Cherniss was scandalized by this method of expression (1945, pp. 84–85); if Aristotle had been a student of Plato from the time of the writing of the *Timaeus* to the death of the master, how could he continue to have doubts of this sort? "Did he never happen to ask the master for an explanation? Or did he ask and receive no answer?" he wonders.

In my opinion, the solution is simpler; very probably in this case too Aristotle is addressing an audience with an enthusiasm for philosophy, an audience already directly familiar with the Platonic dialogue, so he did not slow down to cite the exact words, but he simply reported the gist of it and developed a number of criticisms of the text in question. If, as has been said, many Aristotelian theories were developed in critical response to positions taken by Plato and should be interpreted in light of Plato's dialogues, then it is likely that familiarity with those dialogues was one of the prerequisites for participation in the gatherings at Aristotle's school. Not an institutional prerequisite, of course, but a necessary condition for reaching the level of knowledge that is indispensable for taking part in the discussion. The different way that he refers to Plato's "unwritten doctrines" is also worth noting; Aristotle generally makes rather rapid and cursory reference to the dialogues, as if to well-known works, but dwells on his explanation of the unwritten doctrines, with which his audience was probably less familiar.

Those who have studied the development of Aristotle's school have noted that the theoretical influence of Plato's dialogues continued after Aristotle's death (see Wehrli 1959, 10:95–98) and that the Peripatetics such as Strato set forth their theories in the form of criticism of Plato's dialogues, not of Aristotle. The habit of reading and commenting upon the dialogues continued throughout the entire history of ancient Aristotelianism. Clearchus of Soli, for example, a direct student of Aristotle, but a passionate expert on topics in magic and mysteries, was engaged in commenting on the *Republic* and the *Timaeus*, which had been the Platonic works most often cited by Aristotle himself (Bonitz 1870, cols. 598a+). It is therefore reasonable to venture that part of the school's activity involved reading, commenting on, and critically discussing the writings of Plato.

The collection of *Problems* transmitted in the corpus of Aristotle's works has some interesting passages that are perhaps related to the school's activities. In several passages dedicated to questions about scholarship (*philologia*), Aristotle takes up two questions that can arise in a circle of friends dedicated to the theoretical life, conceived as reading of texts and discussion in common. The first question asks why it is that, "**for some people, when they begin to read, sleep overtakes them even if they don't want to, whereas for other people, who want to sleep, taking up the book makes them stay awake**" (XVIII.1, 916b1–3).[1] The answer is that it is due to the humors, melancholic or otherwise, of the individual in question. Another question asks "**why are contentious disputations** (*hoi eristikoi logoi*) **good for training** (*gymnastikoi*)?" (XVIII.2, 916b20). The answer is that, given that one either wins or loses, one is induced not to give up the dispute but to continue it or to start over and over, an excellent illustration of the so-called "agonistic mentality" of the Greeks, of their love for games in which it is clear who ends up superior to his adversaries. For the same reason, in these contentious disputations it is impossible to go on long goose chases (XVIII.8, 917b4–8).

We shall return briefly now to the stories of Aristotle's library, described in an exemplary manner and with great critical equilibrium by Moraux (1973, pp. 3–33). We have said that Aristotle was one of the first to collect books and establish a library, and we have seen above the importance given to reading and to written works in the context of the Aristotelian conception of dialectic. As Athenaeus tells us (1, 3a), he was renowned for his book collection, along with the poet Euripides (see Aristophanes, *Frogs* 943), and certain others such as a certain Larensis who **"owned so many ancient Greek books that he surpassed all who have been celebrated for their large libraries, including Polycrates of Samos, Pisistratus the tyrant of Athens [. . .] Euripides the poet,[2] Aristotle the philosopher** <and Theophrastus> **and Neleus who preserved the books of the two last named. From Neleus, he says, our King Ptolemy, surnamed Philadelphus, purchased them all and transferred those he had procured at Athens and at Rhodes to his beautiful capital, Alexandria"** (*testimonium* 42d). The passage in Athenaeus tells us that Aristotle's collection of books passed from him to Theophrastus, from Theophrastus to Neleus,[3] and from Neleus to the Library of Alexandria; this collection presumably contained not only the books that the philosopher had owned but also the philosophical treatises of Aristotle that we now possess. The interest of the Ptolemies in acquiring books is generally explained as arising from the close ties between the Peripatetic philosophers and the kings of Egypt; the ancient sources tell us that Demetrius of Phalerum collaborated on the organization of the great library,[4] and that Strato of Lampsacus took care of the education of Ptolemy Philadelphus (Diogenes Laertius 5.58).

We have some further information about which works comprised the collection of Aristotle's books or, rather, a collection of the philosopher's writings that is related to the book collection mentioned by Athenaeus (above). We find lists of works by Aristotle in Diogenes Laertius (5.22–28; see Düring 1957, pp. 29–56), in the *Vita Menagiana* attributed to Hesychius of Miletus (sixth century CE; see Düring 1957, pp. 82–89), and in the Arabic biography of Usaibia (Düring 1957, pp. 221–231). Of these catalogs, the last-named represents the state of the philosopher's writings prior to the edition done by Andronicus of Rhodes in the first century BCE, which basically arranged the philosopher's writings in the form in which they have come down to us. In contrast, the first two lists reflect an earlier state of affairs, and must have been edited at the end of the third century BCE, either in the Library of Alexandria (according to Düring and others), or else in the Peripatetic school itself.

This shows that in Athens, or in Alexandria, or possibly in both places, copies of the lessons and lectures that Aristotle had given in his school were preserved. Aside from this, we have other reports of the presence of the books of Aristotle in various places in the Greek world during the fourth century BCE. It seems that in Rhodes, Eudemus had a copy of the *Metaphysics* (fr. 3 Wehrli) and a copy of *Physics* (fr. 6 Wehrli). Most likely he also had a copy of the work that was later named after him, the *Eudemian Ethics*, and possibly the *Analytics* as well (see the discussion by Berti 1982, pp. 16+). In a work of unknown title (*P. Herc.* 1005, fr. 111), Philodemus quotes a letter by Epicurus in which he asks a friend to send to him Aristotle's "*Analytics* and *On Nature.*"

But with the passage of time Aristotle's works were read less and less; for example, there are solid reasons to doubt that the founders of the Stoic school had any direct knowledge of his words, though this issue has yet to be fully resolved.[5] When authors in Roman times tried to explain the drift of the Aristotelian Peripatos away from their master's interests, they thought it was due to the loss of the works of Aristotle. Thus was born a legend that attributed Aristotle's diminishing philosophical influence to chance events, not to any change in the theoretical interests of the philosophers of the Hellenistic age. This legend is cited by Strabo (13.1.54) and by Plutarch. Strabo, speaking of the city of Scepsis, notes that it was the birthplace of Erastus, and of Coriscus and his son Neleus, who was a student of both Aristotle and Theophrastus, and who "**inherited the library of Theophrastus, which included the library of Aristotle.**" Strabo says that "**Aristotle gave his library to Theophrastus, to whom he also left his school; and he** [Theophrastus] **is the first man, so far as is known, to have collected books, and to have taught the kings of Egypt how to arrange a library.**" In these few lines, Strabo relies on numerous unreliable reports: from the last will and testament of Aristotle it can be concluded that he did not leave Theophrastus either the school or the library; moreover, Theophrastus was not the first to collect books but was preceded by at least Euripides, as we saw above; furthermore, Theophrastus did not oversee the organization of the Library of Alexandria, which was assembled after his death, with the consultation of Demetrius of Phalerum.

Strabo then writes that Neleus **"took it** [the library] **to Scepsis and bequeathed it to his relations, ordinary people, who kept the books locked up without even being carefully stored. But when they heard how zealously the Attalid kings (to whom their city was subject) were collecting books to build up the library in Pergamum, they hid their books underground in a sort of trench. Much later, when they had been damaged by moisture and by insects, their descendants sold the books of Aristotle and Theophrastus to Apellicon of Teos for a large sum of money. And Apellicon was more of a bibliophile than a philosopher, and so, seeking to restore the parts that had been eaten away, he had new copies of the text made, supplementing the gaps not well, and published the books full of errors. The result of this was that the older Peripatetics after Theophrastus did not in fact have any books** [of their founders], **except for a few, mostly the exoteric** [published] **books, and were therefore not able to do philosophy in a systematic way, only to declaim** [rhetorical] **theses"** (Strabo 13.1.54). In his *Life of Sulla* (26), Plutarch tells us that in 84 BCE Sulla anchored in the Piraeus and took possession, among other things, of the library of Apellicon, which contained all the books of Aristotle and Theophrastus; then he brought these texts to Rome, and had them reordered by Tyrannion the grammarian; then Andronicus of Rhodes published and made a catalog of them. And Plutarch also repeats that the ancient Peripatetics were not well acquainted with the works of their masters, and he blames the heirs of Neleus of Scepsis, who had hidden the books.

The judgment rendered by Strabo and Plutarch against the Peripatos after Strato for not being familiar with Aristotle's ideas is historically accurate, and is shared by many modern historians. But the details of the whole story are quite perplexing, and there is no reason whatsoever to believe that Aristotle's writings simply vanished from the face of the earth until Cicero's time. However, for our purposes these questions are in the end secondary. What is important is the fact that the Peripatetic school appears always to have had a marked interest in the written word, both those of the master and those of others, and that a special attention to the fate of one's own library and one's own writings appears evident in the last wills and testaments of the Peripatetic scholarchs (see Gottschalk 1972, p. 319), as is shown by the lists of their works preserved in Diogenes Laertius as well as by a wide range of other indications.

2. METHODS OF GATHERING AND INTERPRETING INFORMATION

There has been intense critical discussion on the subject of Aristotle's methods of gathering and interpreting information, but it has focused for the most part on chronological questions, bound up with the problem of the "evolution" of Aristotle's thinking; scholars have wondered if Aristotle gathered the information that he used extensively in his works during his years of travel prior to returning to Athens, or whether the work of gathering the information took place entirely or largely during his later stay in Athens (see section 6 of chapter 1). To tell the truth, the question has always been posed with special reference to Aristotle's gathering of biological data, since for other kinds of data it has never been ruled out that Aristotle might have begun collecting when he was a student of Plato, and then continued thereafter for the rest of his life, also with the help of his students. This second question was of special interest because it was thought that his attention to so-called "empirical data" was tantamount to a separation from Platonism and the beginning of an "empiricist" phase in Aristotelian thought. Nowadays, nobody puts the question in these terms, and all agree that the study of diverse aspects of reality is not to be contrasted, neither in the Aristotelian Peripatos nor in the Academy, with their interest in research on first principles.

It seems fairly certain that collecting the most widely diverse data of experience was an activity already practiced in the Academy of Plato; and, as we saw above (section 4 of chapter 1, pp. 25–26), when he was still a student of Plato, Aristotle had assembled a collection of proverbs and popular sayings. Theophrastus himself tells us that, though Plato "**made the greater part of his study concern first philosophy, he also devoted himself to the evidence, and got involved in research**

on nature" (Simplicius, *Commentary on Aristotle's* Physics 26.9–15). This account seems to be in contrast with Plato's constant devaluation of the empirical observation of the stars, as compared with a study of the heavens of a purely mathematical and abstract sort, which Plato always preferred (*Republic* VII 529c, 530b, *Timaeus* 68b). But Plato also admitted the importance of investigating the presence of rationality in the world of becoming (*Timaeus* 29a–c), and from this point of view his position is not very far from the one expressed by Aristotle in *Parts of Animals* I.5 (see below, pp. 111–112).[6]

In the Academy, the idea of investigating rationality in the world of becoming was developed in a special manner. For example, we know that Speusippus wrote a treatise that goes under the title *Homoia,* or *Peri ta homoia pragmateia,* that is, *Resemblances,* or *Treatise on the Resemblances,* in which he collected material deriving from natural research and organized the specific data by the method of dichotomous division. It is thought that this treatise was meant to provide information that would be further examined in other, more theoretical, treatises (see Isnardi Parente 1980, pp. 214–215 and 377+, with Tarán 1981, pp. 65–68 and 256). This relationship between an "encyclopedic treatise" and a more "theoretical treatise" can also be found in the works of Aristotle—for instance, in the relationship between the *Research on Animals* and his other biological treatises. We shall take up this topic again shortly.

But what is meant by "data"? Is there really a concept of "empirical data" in Aristotle similar to our own? Or is it possible to distinguish various types of facts in his various works? In Aristotle's vocabulary there is no term that corresponds exactly to our scientific term "data," in the sense of factual information, especially information organized for the purposes of surveying, recording, classifying, and processing. The Aristotelian term that comes closest is *phainomenon,* which nonetheless has two meanings, according to Bonitz (1870): that of *res sensu manifesta* (a thing evident to the senses), and that of *animi cogitatio* (a thought in our mind), this latter meaning corresponding substantially to *endoxon,* reputable opinion. We see the first meaning in Aristotelian passages like the following: "**the end** (*to telos*) **of productive knowledge is the work** (*to ergon*), **whereas the end of knowledge in natural science is always, strictly speaking, the evidence of perception** (*to phainomenon . . . kata* *tēn aisthēsin)*" (*On the Heavens* III.7, 306a16–17). The second meaning can be seen in such passages as the following: a proposition is dialectical as opposed to deductive, if it assumes "**what is evident and reputable** (*tou phainomenou kai endoxou*), **as was said in the *Topics*"** (*Prior Analytics* I.1, 24b10–12). Similarly, in a passage where both meanings are in play, Aristotle criticizes the Atomists and accuses them of abolishing "**many reputable opinions and the evidence of perception** (*polla tōn endoxōn kai tōn phainomenōn kata tēn aisthēsin*)" (*On the Heavens* III.4, 303a22–23).

The ambiguity of the term *phainomenon* derives from the fact that, for Aristotle, the two meanings were not as far apart as they might appear to a modern reader,[7] influenced by Descartes, who established as the first rule of method in the Second Part of his *Discourse on the Method for Conducting One's Reason Well and for Seeking Truth in the Sciences* "never to accept as true any thing which I did not understand evidently to be such" (p. 18 Adam/Tannery). Aristotle considered as "data" both those which were observed and confirmed personally by the researcher and those which were attested by trustworthy persons. In his *On the Heavens* he writes, "**it seems not only that this argument testifies in favour of the evidence** (*ta phainomena*) **but also that what is evident** (*ta phainomena*) **testifies in favour of the argument. For every human has some notion concerning the gods, and everybody attributes the highest place to the divine**" (I.3, 270b4–7). In this passage, the first occurrence of the term *phainomena* is very close to our cognate term "phenomena," in the sense of "the evidence of experience," while the second clearly indicates common and widely held opinions, opinions that are evident to all people.

The collection of facts undertaken by members of the Peripatetic school reflects this fairly broad conception of what constitutes "data." In *Meteorology* (I.13, 350a14–18), Aristotle says that "**the greatest rivers appear to flow from the greatest mountains. This is clear to those who study the maps of the earth** (*tas tēs gēs periodous*); **for these are recorded according to their respective discoverers, in those cases where the authors were not eye witnesses.**" The expression that we find in this passage, *gēs periodos*, which can mean "description of the earth" as well as "map of the earth" (see Liddell-Scott, *s.v. periodos* III), reappears in *Politics* when Aristotle reports an observation about Upper

Libya made "**by some of those who have written descriptions of the earth** (*gēs periodoi*)" (II.3, 1262a18–19). The study of works of geography, as well as of history, is recommended for orators in his *Rhetoric* (I.4, 1360a33–37), because "**the descriptions of the earth** (*gēs periodoi*) **are useful aids to legislation (since from them we may learn the laws and customs of different ethnic groups), whereas what is useful for political deliberation are the researches of those who write about human conduct.**" The expression can be used to indicate travelogues, geographical descriptions, or even maps, as we shall see below. Likewise Theophrastus, who is considered much more of an actual "scientist" than Aristotle, opened one of his meteorological works with a reference to collecting information from others (*Weather Signs* 1).[8] "**We have recorded signs of rains, winds, storms, and good weather in what follows, as many as possible, providing some of them ourselves, and taking some from others who are not untrustworthy.**" Many critics have reproved Aristotle for using secondhand information, for instance Bourgey (1955, p. 11). But this denunciation is undeserved, if it is meant to suggest that Aristotle's methods were by the standards of the day sloppy and scientifically unsound; Aristotle's contemporaries simply had a different conception of what significant information ought to be gathered in order to give scientific explanations by means of causes and principles.

How were these data cataloged? In Aristotle's day, there was no such thing as an alphabetical order, or at least, it was never used; rather, the elements of a set were organized according to similarity in content. For instance, the so-called "philosophical lexicon" contained in *Metaphysics* V (Δ), which describes the ways in which a series of philosophical terms are used by experts, is not organized alphabetically, but by homogeneous groupings: first come the terms linked to the idea of cause (chapters 1–5), then those that express key concepts of what Aristotle calls "first philosophy" (chapters 6–8), then the ones linked to identity (chapters 9–11), and so on (see Reale 1968, p. 83). In the same way, the ps.-Aristotelian work *Definitions*, which contains a series of definitions of the philosophical terms most commonly used in the Academy, is organized by groups of subjects: definitions of ethics, politics, dialectic, and rhetoric (see Rossitto 1984, pp. 30–31).

The works that contain collections of facts often set out at their beginning the criteria by which the facts are arranged, so as to assist those who might need to find a specific piece of information. In the *Topics*, Aristotle organizes the subjects of the various arguments according to the division of the four predicables (accident, in Books II–III; genus, in Book IV; property, in Book V; definition, in Books VI–VII). These are organized into a series of subclasses, as described in the first book (I.10; see Zadro 1974, pp. 40+). In the *Research on Animals*, the material is organized according to criteria set out by Aristotle at the beginning of the work; his presentation of the various animal species divides the world of animate beings according to the ways they live, their actions, their character, and their constituent parts (I.1, 487a11). The division that Aristotle uses here shows the persistence of evident links with the Academic use of conceptual division or *diairesis*;[9] and the *Research on Plants* by Theophrastus is organized in a similar manner, according to a series of very similar differences: constituent parts, qualities, generation, and manner of living (1.1.1).[10] The presence of conceptual schemes of Platonic origin in Theophrastus has been emphasized by modern scholars, such as Steinmetz (1964, pp. 7+) and Regenbogen (1970, cols. 1470–1471).

On the other hand, rather than organizing facts by conceptual divisions, the second book of the ps.-Aristotelian *Economics* (dating from the end of the fourth century BCE), organizes in a roughly chronological way its presentation of stratagems whereby cities, princes, and military commanders have raised money when they needed some (see van Groningen 1933, p. 35). Indeed, its author says that he is collecting the results of a research enterprise (*historia*) into the actions of our predecessors (II.1, 1346a25–29).[11] It would be odd if the lists of the winners of the Pythian games, as well as the other similar works by Aristotle (discussed above; see section 8 of chapter 1), did not have the same ordering.

With respect to the traditional image of the Academy as a philosophical school dedicated to pure conceptual and abstract reflection, and of the Peripatos as a school engaged in empirical and scientific research in the modern sense,[12] one could say that the actual situation must have been far more nuanced, and the distinctions less clear. The *diairesis* appears to have persisted in the Aristotelian Peripatos, at least as a schema for organizing facts, albeit with modifications made to the rigid dichotomist schema of Plato (*Parts of Animals* I.2–3); it is assessed as a method of explanation (*Prior Analytics* I.31 and *Posterior Analytics* II.5) and criticized as such by both Aristotle (*Parts of Animals* I.3, 643a27+) and Theophrastus (*Research on Plants* 1.3–4; and see Wörle 1985, pp. 98+). At first sight, the differences between the Academy and the Peripatos in this period do not consist in directing their research efforts to studying different objects because they have different interests, but rather in different types of interpretation of the data being studied.

Aristotle's interpretation of the evidence to be accounted for, and his determination of their causes, was presented to his students in public lessons in which he read aloud his discourses, or *logoi*. The works of Aristotle that we possess, with some notable exceptions (such as *Research on Animals, Constitution of Athens,* the (mostly lost) published dialogues, and some other lost works of which we possess only a few fragments), are in fact a collection of *logoi* that he read aloud as a teacher. These lessons more or less resembled modern lectures, and the reading of these *logoi* constituted their publication, as Jaeger clearly showed (1912, pp. 131–148). Jaeger holds that in Aristotle's school lessons much the same things must have happened as in the lesson of Zeno, as related by the narrator at the beginning of Plato's *Parmenides* (127b–d). Zeno and Parmenides once came to the Great Panathenaic festival in Athens, and **"they stayed with Pythodorus outside the wall in the Ceramicus, and Socrates and many others with him went there because they wanted to hear the writings of Zeno; this was the first time they had brought them to Athens, Socrates being then very young. So Zeno himself read it out to us, and Parmenides was out of the house, and when the reading of the books was nearly finished, at that point Pythodorus came in from outside, and with him were Parmenides and Aristotle (the one who became one of the Thirty), and they heard only a little that remained of the text, though Pythodorus didn't, as he had heard Zeno before. Socrates listened, and then asked that the first thesis of the first book be read again. When this had been read, he said, 'Zeno, what do you mean?'"**

This lecture was held in a private home before an improvised audience. But similar lessons could also be held in public. Isocrates, for example (*Panathenaicus* 18–19), tells us of a public reading organized by a number of intellectuals in the Lyceum. **"Three or four of the herd of sophists, the ones who claim to know everything and suddenly show up everywhere, were sitting together in the Lyceum having a conversation about the poets, especially the poetry of Hesiod and Homer, saying nothing about them except to recite their verses and recall the most brilliant things said by certain others who were prior to them; and after the course** (diatribē) **they took met with the approval of the bystanders, the boldest one of them attempted to slander me, saying that I despise all such things and that I abolish all the philosophies** (philosophia) **and curricula** (paideia) **of the others, and say that everyone talks nonsense apart from those who are take part in my course** (diatribē)."

Schools must have operated in roughly the same way, as we see from another of Isocrates' orations (Panathenaicus 200), in which the orator allows us to catch a glimpse of work in his school. **"I corrected** (epēnōrthoun) **the written version of my speech up to what has been read so far, together with three or four young lads who are in the habit of taking courses with me** (syndiatribein). **When they went over it, it seemed good to us and to require only an ending, so it occurred to me to send for one of my associates who had served in politics under the oligarchy and had chosen to praise the Spartans, in order that, if we had overlooked something false in what was said, he might spot it and point it out to us."**

The "revision" that Isocrates mentions here was made aloud before an audience of students, and we may presume that the reading of Aristotle's logoi took place more or less in the same manner. Indeed, a similar situation is presupposed in a letter to Phanias of Eresus partly cited by Diogenes Laertius (5.37); Theophrastus, apparently in reference to the proof stage (peri tou deiktēriou) of publishing his works, commented **"in this letter: 'not that it's a festive party** (panēguris), **but it's not even an easy committee** (synedrion) **such as one would wish to have, and the readings produce corrections** (epanorthōseis), **and postponing and being careless about everything is no longer allowed by the current generation.' And in this letter he uses the term 'scholastic'** (scholastikos)." This incomplete sentence, a difficult text that has given rise to a variety of translations,[13] suggests to me that Theophrastus followed the same procedure described by Isocrates: the head of the school would gather together the most important students and read to them a text that that he had written so as to elicit suggestions for correcting and improving its exposition, before delivering it to a larger audience. Similar examples also appear in the Neoplatonic schools; in the commentary to the *Phaedrus* attributed to Hermias, Prächter observes that there is a narration of various academic discussions between Syrianus and his student Proclus (1909, p. 39).

This is all that is said in the ancient texts. The information is fragmentary and does not always directly concern the environment of the philosophical school; in fact, they describe, respectively, a public reading in a private home, a reading held in a gymnasium, the activities of a school of rhetoric, and the activities of a full-fledged philosophical school. Probably, however, many of the customs were more or less similar from school to school, and we can get at least a rough idea of how things happened in the schools on the basis of these data.

A typical characteristic of Aristotle's school, as we have said, is the idea that a good way of living the *bios theōretikos* is to devote oneself to collecting and explaining the most varied phenomena of the physical world. We cannot say that this is peculiar to the Peripatetics, because among the Platonists too there appears to have been something similar, as in the case of Speusippus, whom we mentioned above; but certainly in Aristotle we find an explicit, and rightly renowned, theorization of this position. In *Parts of Animals* I.5, 644b22+, Aristotle distinguishes, among all the perceptible substances, or "substances that exist by nature," those that are eternal such as the stars (for which sense perception provides few premises from which to begin research), from those that are corruptible, which we can get to know more, because they live among us (*dia to syntrophon*). According to Aristotle, knowledge of the principles of the stars and of the eternal sensible realities is more honorable and more pleasurable (*dia tēn timiotēra . . . hēdion*), even if more limited; corruptible substances, by contrast, give rise to an exceedingly great amount of knowledge (*epistēmēs hyperochē*, 645a2). In both cases, it is a matter of finding, in the world of sensible substances, a purpose that corresponds to the eternal and the "divine" (see 645a24–31). We do not find in these pages praise of pure empirical research, as Jaeger believed (1923, pp. 337–340),[14] but certainly Aristotle pays special attention to the pleasure that we can derive from the study of the physical world (644b34–35), and this characteristic distinguishes his thought from that of the other philosophers. Even creatures that are not pretty to look at, says Aristotle, are pleasurable to study, "**for even in those creatures that are unattractive to perceptual observation, their craftsmanlike nature provides tremendous pleasure to those who are able to recognize causes and are naturally good at philosophy**" (645a7–10). This point is important; scientific research into natural entities is not undertaken as an end in itself, or as an activity that is useful for the human community, but is proposed as the ultimate end, insofar as it is a way of actualizing the "life of philosophy," one of the possible practical realizations of the Aristotelian recipe for happiness, the life dedicated to intellectual activity.

Again this makes us come up against the difference between Aristotle's position and that of our own culture. Despite the fact that scientists today also take pleasure in engaging in the study of their own fields and dedicate all the time they can to research, they would hardly reply, if asked to justify their choice of this life, by reference solely to the joy and happiness that they derive from these activities, feeling that this is too subjective and trifling a reason, compared with the objective development of science and the progress of the human race. The reasons for which Aristotle praises the study of living creatures and sensible substances, therefore, demonstrate not a relative proximity to the modern conception of science, but how much historical distance there is between a Greek philosopher, even a "scientist" of the Aristotelian variety, and a modern researcher. The latter would judge the reasons of the former to be selfish and picayune, while the former would find the position of the latter to be a servile one, unworthy of free men. "**It is likely that the first to discover any skill at all beyond the common perceptions was admired by other humans, not only because there is something useful in the discoveries, but also for being wise and outstanding compared to others. But as more skills were discovered,** and some were directed to the necessities of life, others to pastimes (*diagōgē*),[15] the discoverers of such things were always taken to be wiser, because their knowledge did not aim at usefulness" (*Metaphysics* I(A).1, 981b13–20).

3. TEACHING SUPPORTS AND INSTRUMENTS OF RESEARCH

There are some who think that Aristotle, unable to own houses or land in Athens for legal reasons, limited his activity to giving lessons in public *gymnasia*, along with all the other so-called "sophists" (see Düring 1957, pp. 459+). But others object that this is impossible (e.g. Gigon 1958, p. 164, and Chroust 1972a, pp. 310–318). From Aristotle's works we conclude that his teaching activity required a few simple scientific instruments, and that they therefore must have been conducted in a different way from the free Socratic discussion described in the dialogues of Plato and Xenophon. The least dangerous way of reconstructing this "practical" aspect of Peripatetic research and teaching is to begin from the text of Aristotle's works, to search in them for some indication about how the work proceeded, the work of describing the manifold intricacies of reality of which the philosopher intended next to give a rational account (see also Dirlmeier 1962a).

Aristotle made use of tables and diagrams during his lectures. He recommends the use of diagrams in general in *Topics* (I.14 105b12–15), a passage that has already been partly quoted above (n. 38 to p. 20). "**It is also necessary to select from written sources, and to create lists for each kind under separate headings such as 'Life' or 'Good,' in other words everything good, beginning with what it is.**" Tables with the principal opinions of the philosophers on the themes of debate, therefore, must have been available to the members of the philosophical communities both Academic and Peripatetic.

In *Nicomachean Ethics* (II.7, 1107a32–33), a diagram displaying opposing vices and virtues is mentioned. The diagram has not survived, but we do have the one mentioned in the parallel passage of the *Eudemian Ethics* (II.3, 1220b36–1221a15). "**For the sake of example, let's take each of them and study them from the diagram:**

irritability	being not sensitive	good temper
rashness	cowardice	courage
shamelessness	shyness	modesty
lack of self-restraint	insensibility	self-control
resentment	unnamed	righteous indignation
gain	loss	the just
wastefulness	stinginess	liberality
pretentiousness	self-deprecation	truthfulness
smarminess	hostility	friendliness
servility	stubbornness	dignity
wimpishness	distress	endurance
vanity	meanness of spirit	greatness of spirit
extravagance	pettiness	magnificence
unscrupulousness	naïveté	intelligence

These passions and ones like them occur in the soul, and they are all so called either by being excessive or by being insufficient." And later in the *Eudemian Ethics* this table is recalled by Aristotle, when he reminds his audience that "**we distinguished also in the table rashness and cowardice as contraries**" (III.1, 1228a28–29).

Another table found at *De Interpretatione* 13 (22a22–31). "**Let's observe in the following diagram what we are talking about:**

able to be	not able to be
possible to be	not possible to be
not impossible to be	impossible to be
not necessary to be	necessary not to be

able not to be	not able not to be
possible not to be	not possible not to be
not impossible not to be	impossible not to be
not necessary not to be	necessary to be."

Such tables would have needed to be visible to everyone, and therefore written on or affixed to a wall. The lecture therefore required an institutional space and a special room, not just the strolling up and down that had been a feature of the teaching of Protagoras.

The use of drawings and diagrams is implicit in all the passages from Aristotle in which letters are used to indicate items; we shall mention just two for the sake of example. The first comes from Aristotle's analysis of justice in transactions in *Nicomachean Ethics* V.5, 1133a5–12. "**What makes the exchange a proportionate one is the conjunction in the diagonals, for example, a builder at A, a shoemaker at B, a house at C, and a shoe at D:**

The builder, then, must get from the shoemaker the latter's work, and must himself give him in return his own. If, then, at first there is proportionate equality, and then reciprocation happens, there will be what we said." The second comes from Aristotle's explanation of the apparent circularity of the rainbow (*Meteorology* III.4, 375b9–12). "**Let the outer rainbow be the** [line] **B, and the inner and primary one be the A; as for the colours, let the C be red, the D be green, and E be violet, and the yellow appears at the** [point] **F.**"

The lessons in biology presuppose that there were anatomical diagrams, which are cited several times in *Parts of Animals*. "**There must necessarily be something to receive it** [sc. food] **in turn from** [the stomach . . .] **These** [sc. blood vessels] **are to be observed in the *Anatomies* as well as in the *Natural Research*** [= *Research on Animals* III.3–4]" (*Parts of Animals* II.3, 650a28–32). "**The details of the dispositions of the different blood vessels are be observed in the *Anatomies* as well as in the *Animal Research*" (*Parts of Animals* III.6, 668b28–30). "**The way each of them is** [sc. the digestive organs of different molluscs] **must be observed in the *Researches on Animals*** [= *Research on Animals* IV.4] **and in the *Anatomies*, for some things are better clarified by argument, others by visually inspecting them**" (*Parts of Animals* IV.5, 679b37–680a3; and see III.14, 674b16–17 and IV.13, 696b15–16). "**The position the heart has relative to the gills is to be observed in the *Anatomies* in their visual aspect, and in detail in the *Researches*** [*on Animals*]" (*Respiration* 16, 478a34–b1; see also 478a26–28). Similar passages are also found in the *Generation of Animals*: "**these are to be observed in the images that are written out in the *Anatomies* and the *Researches*** [*on Animals*]" (GA II.7, 746a14–15; and see 719a10, 740a23, 753b18, 758a25). The last passage clearly shows that Aristotle made available to his students for ready consultation the work that we know as the *Historia Animalium*, or *Research on Animals*, and that this text was accompanied by anatomical diagrams, which were useful to consult (see Dirlmeier 1962a, pp. 20–22). In his *Research on Animals*, Aristotle mentions anatomical images, for example "**the things just stated are also to be observed in this drawing here**" (III.1, 510a29–30; and see also I.17, 497a32, III.1, 511a11–14, IV.1 525a7–9, IV.4, 529b18–19, IV.4, 530a30–31, VI.10, 565a2–13, VI.11, 566a13–15).

The treatise *Meteorology*, finally, makes frequent reference to geographical maps, models of the celestial globe, and star charts. "**The [zodiacal] circle as well as the stars in it may be observed in the diagram. As for the so-called 'scattered' stars, it is not possible to place them in the same way on the sphere** [= the model of the celestial globe] **because none of them has their apparent position permanently; but to those who look up at the sky they are clearly there**" (I.8, 346a31–35). "**There are two sections of the earth where habitation is possible: one is near the upper pole, the one near us, and the other is near the other one, the southern pole. And their shape is like that of a drum, for such is the shape of the earth if you draw lines from its center and make two cones, one based on the tropic circle and the other based on the polar circle** [literally: "the ever-visible circle"], **with their vertex at the center of the earth; and in the same way, at the lower pole, two other cones produce segments of the earth**" (II.5, 362a32–b5). "**This is why it is ridiculous how maps of the earth** (*tas periodous tēs gēs*) **are nowadays drawn; the inhabited earth is drawn as circular, which is impossible, according to the evidence** (*phainomena*) **as well as the argument**" (II.5, 362b12–15). "**Let us now explain their position** [sc. of the winds] . . . **One needs to observe the reasons for their position from the diagram** [= the wind rose]. **Now then, for it to be more distinct, the circle of the horizon has been drawn** (*gegraptai*); **this is why it is also round**" (II.6, 363a21–28). The phrase *tas periodous tēs gēs*, as we have seen above, has a twofold meaning: descriptions of voyages or travelogues, and the outlines or drawings that accompanied them. The passage at *Meteorology* II.5, 362b12 clearly refers to a celestial map. There were tablets with maps of the earth in the Lyceum at the time when Theophrastus wrote his will (see above, p. 86).

The use of all these visual aids (lists of noteworthy opinions, tables, diagrams, maps, wind roses, and anatomical illustrations) clearly indicates a teaching activity that was fairly institutionalized. Dicaearchus, one of Aristotle's students who was noted for having supported the superiority of the political life in opposition to the *bios theōretikos* supported by his master (see above, p. 23), is quoted by Plutarch (*Should Old Men Be Politicians?* 26, 796c–d) as criticizing the development of the philosophical schools, which had abandoned free Socratic philosophizing in favor of a more "scientific" approach that was less directed toward philosophical "proselytizing." "**Those who walk up and down under a portico are said to be 'doing a *peripatos*,' as Dicaearchus said, but not those who walk to the country or to see a friend. Doing politics is like doing philosophy; at any rate, Socrates did philosophy without setting up benches or seating himself on a throne, nor did he observe a fixed hour for lessons or for doing a *peripatos* with his companions; but even while fooling around with them, when that happened, while drinking with them, while on military campaign with some of them, while passing time with them in the agora, and, at the end, even while he was in chains and drinking the poison, Socrates was doing philosophy**" (*testimonium* 69a). It does not appear that this entire passage of Plutarch derives from Dicaearchus himself, and there are even some who believe that only the distinction of the meanings of the term *peripatos* derives from the student of Aristotle. But the polemic cited here corresponds very well to the image of his teaching that we can derive from the texts of Aristotle, and it is possible to see in this passage the protest of a rather traditionalist philosopher, steeped in conventional wisdom (see Wehrli 1944, 1:50–51), against the "scientific" development of the school, which had been made possible by Aristotle's definition of the theoretical life as the highest form of happiness.

4. TEACHING WHILE STROLLING

The school of Aristotle was called in ancient sources "Lyceum" or else "Peripatos." The first name suggests meetings held in the *palaestra* that the orator Lycurgus had caused to be built in the grove dedicated to the hero Lycos, the son of Pandion (Pausanias, *Description of Greece*, 1.19.3). Lycurgus "**created the *gymnasium* in the Lyceum, and planted** trees and built the *palaestra* . . . he created a list with all the acts of his administration and had it inscribed, for viewing by anyone who wished, on a pillar facing the *gymnasium* that had been established by him" ([Plutarch], *The Ten Orators* VII, 841c–d and 843f). In the Lyceum there was a dressing room and a covered gallery, according to Plato (*Euthydemus* 272e and 273a). Socrates often spent the entire day there (*Symposium* 223d). We have seen in the previous section (p. 110) that intellectuals liked to gather in the Lyceum. In fragment 1 (Müller) of the *Description of Greece* by Heraclides "Criticus" (third century BCE), mention is made of three *gymnasia*: the Academy, the Lyceum, and the Kunosarges, "all of them thickly planted with trees and grassy lawns. Festivals of every kind; recreation and pastimes for the soul from every kind of philosopher; many schools, frequent spectacles."

Aristotle's teaching, from what we have seen, was not such as to be capable of being conducted totally in an outdoor location, in an extemporaneous way. The site in which the teaching was carried out was very likely not the public gymnasium situated in the Lyceum; there are some (such as Gigon 1962, p. 64) who hypothesize that Aristotle and his students would meet in rooms located near the Lyceum, and that this was the origin of the name of the school.

The name *peripatos* means "promenade" or "place where one can stroll," after dinner for example (*Eudemian Ethics* I.2, 1214b23–24; see Bonitz 1870, *s.v. peripatos*). We have already seen that in the will of Theophrastus, the bequest that established the school included a garden, a *peripatos,* and several houses. It is not clear exactly what this *peripatos* was; it might have been a colonnade, or else a leafy walkway. The term later came to indicate the lessons of the "philosophical school," and it is used in this sense in the passage by Dicaearchus just quoted, in which the philosopher plays on the ambiguity of the term *peripatos* and contrasts the more usual meaning with the more technical one. Again, in the passage from Aristocles concerning the period that Aristotle spent in the Academy, cited above (pp. 20–21), the school of Plato was indicated with the term *peripatos*. Philodemus used the same term to describe the school run by Erastus, Coriscus, and Aristotle at Assos (see above, p. 41). In his will, Lyco uses *peripatos* to describe the buildings of the school, or the school itself (Diogenes Laertius 5.70).

It is unclear whether the students of Aristotle were called "Peripatetics" because the school had a *peripatos*, as stated in Plutarch's *Against Colotes* (14, 1115a) and Cicero's *De Oratore* (3.28 and 3.109), or else because the master loved to talk while walking, as attested by many ancient legends (Diogenes Laertius 5.2–3; see *testimonia* 68–71 in Düring 1957, pp. 404–411). The first hypothesis is preferred by modern scholars (such as Busse 1893 (pp. 835–842), Wilamowitz 1881 (p. 267), and Brink 1940, cols. 899–904, with an extensive history of the term). But the custom of teaching while strolling was an ancient one. In Plato's *Protagoras* (315b), Socrates describes the crowd of students of Protagoras who trailed after him, like the colleagues and assistants of the head physician of a modern hospital, finding it delightful to see, because "**it was beautiful how they took care never to get in the way in front of Protagoras; when he turned around they also turned with him, and those listening would split up in a rather nice formation on the two sides of him, and wheel around in a circle to get arranged behind him, very beautifully**." And Plato himself liked to stroll and talk, and the comedic writers of his time made fun of him for this, evidently not making any distinction between Plato and the Sophists. A character in the *Meropis* of Alexis associates strolling with Plato; "**you've come in the nick of time! I'm at my wits' end** (*aporoumenē*), **and walking up and down like Plato, and yet I've worked out no wise plan, I've only tired out my legs!**" (Diogenes Laertius 3.26). The same thing is said by the same author of Menedemus, who at times walked and at times taught lessons while standing still (2.130), and of Polemon, who was never seated when debating a problem (4.19). The question is not very important; the only things worth noting are that nothing of the sort is attested of the school of Isocrates, and that this habit seems to have been characteristic of philosophers.

CHAPTER 4
STUDIES OF ARISTOTLE'S BIOGRAPHY
FROM ZELLER TO THE PRESENT DAY

1. SOURCES OF ARISTOTLE'S BIOGRAPHY

For the contemporary reconstruction of the biography of Aristotle, we rely upon various kinds of surviving sources and *testimonia*, such as texts by Aristotle (in particular the fragments of the lost works and the texts of the surviving works, his last will and testament, his poetry, and his letters), official documents, ancient biographies of Aristotle, and *testimonia* from ancient authors. In this chapter we shall first have a look at what these sources are and what reliability each of them may have, according to the current opinions of scholars. A large part of this section derives from Düring (1957); I have updated the information provided by this magisterial work on the basis of later studies up to 1990, and I have revised its interpretations on a few marginal points. (For more recently published scholarship, see my author's postscript, below, p. 145.) I shall then, in section 2, look at the various phases of the history of studies on Aristotle's biography, and then I shall describe in broad outlines how the picture of the philosopher varies over different historical periods and in different cultural milieus during the past hundred years.

1.1. TEXTS OF ARISTOTLE

1.1A. Fragments of the Lost Works and Texts of the Surviving Works

From these texts it is not possible to gather much biographical material. Aristotle, it would appear, adhered to the Ionic scientific tradition of saying little about himself in his works, and we have nothing for him comparable to the *Seventh Letter* of Plato. It is therefore difficult to gather information about the external events of Aristotle's life from reading his works, except in a few obvious cases. For instance, it is safe to say that he had some kind of relationship with Themison of Cyprus, to whom he dedicated the *Protrepticus*,[1] and a passage of the *Nicomachean Ethics* (I.6, 1096a11–13) attests to his friendship with Plato, which is described by a vast tradition (although another very broad tradition attests the exact opposite, confusing doctrinal dispute with personal discord). Yet this information is not actually autobiographical in intent, just as the opinions expressed by Aristotle's contemporaries about him, generally very critical, are not actually serious works in the genre of biography. Beginning in the 1920s, as we will see, the philosophical works of Aristotle were analyzed to reconstruct the various phases of the "spiritual evolution" of the philosopher, and therefore also, indirectly, of his life.

1.1B. Aristotle's Last Will and Testament

Today there are no longer any doubts concerning the authenticity of Aristotle's will, on which see section 3 of chapter 3. It has been transmitted to us in two different versions, a Greek version in Diogenes Laertius 5.11–16 and an Arabic version reported in al-Nadim, al-Qifti, and Usaibia (on these authors, see below, section 1.3). These versions were published by the editors of the ancient biographies of Aristotle, and in Düring 1957 (pp. 238–241),[2] Plezia 1961 (pp. 67–70),[3] Chroust 1967, Chroust 1973 (pp. 183–120),[4] Plezia 1977 (pp. 35–42, together with the few related *testimonia*),[5] and Gigon 1987 (pp. 21a–b and 37b–38b).

1.1C. The Poems of Aristotle

The poems of Aristotle consist of five compositions, as follows.

Hymn to Hermias: cited in Diogenes Laertius 5.7, in Athenaeus 15 (696c–e), and in Didymus Chalcenterus, *On Demosthenes* 6.19–36.[6] There are modern editions in various texts, within the editions of Diogenes Laertius, Athenaeus, and Didymus, as well as in Rose 1886 (fr. 675), Ross 1955 (fr. 4), Plezia 1977 (pp. 4–5),[7] and Gigon 1987 (p. 20a).

Epigram for Hermias: cited in Diogenes Laertius 5.8, in Didymus Chalcenterus 6.39–43, and in the *Palatine Anthology* 7.107. There are modern editions in various texts, within the editions of Diogenes Laertius, Didymus, and the *Palatine Anthology*, as well as in Rose 1886 (fr. 674), Ross 1955 (fr. 3), Plezia 1977 (p. 5), and Gigon 1987 (p. 20b).

Elegy to Eudemus: partly cited in Olympiodorus, *Commentary on Plato's Gorgias* 41.9 (Norvin). There is a modern edition on pp. 115+ of the *Anthologia lyrica graeca*,[8] as well as in Rose 1886 (fr. 673), Ross 1955 (fr. 2), and Plezia 1977 (pp. 5–6).

In the catalog of the writings of Aristotle in Diogenes Laertius 5.27 (title 146 and 147), the opening words of two poems are preserved and are available in Rose 1886 (frs. 671 and 672), Plezia 1977 (p. 6), and Gigon 1987 (p. 24b). The poems were a hymn in hexameters to an unnamed god, and an elegy to Artemis.

1.1D. The Letters of Aristotle

Aristotle's letters comprise fragments 651–670 in Rose 1886, and they have recently been republished in Plezia 1961 and Plezia 1977, pp. 7–33, with the related *testimonia*. Their usefulness for the reconstruction of the biography of Aristotle naturally depends on a judgment about their authenticity, a very intricate problem. Zeller recommended that they be used in a limited way and with a certain carefulness (1897, 1:53–54), while Wilamowitz maintained that in all likelihood these are authentic letters, published to defend Aristotle from the calumnies of his enemies (1881, 151n15 and 1893, 1:339n39). On the other hand, while admitting that there might have been authentic letters of Aristotle, and that the Peripatetics might well have published an edition of them, Susemihl doubts that the letters we possess can be used to reconstruct the biography of Aristotle (1891–1892, 2:579–581); but he is open to accepting the authenticity of fr. 658 Rose (Plutarch, *Alexander: Fortune or Virtue?* I.6, 329b = fr. 6a Plezia 1977 = fr. 7 Plezia 1961), which includes the famous advice given to Alexander, to "**behave towards Greeks as their leader and towards foreigners as their master, taking care of the former as friends and kinsmen and dealing with the latter as animals or plants.**" (Other scholars, however, believe that this evidence is derived from Aristotle's work on colonies, entitled *Alexander*; see above, pp. 45–46.) In the twentieth century, Brink (1940, col. 913) returns to Wilamowitz's view, Plezia (1951, pp. 77–85) supports the authenticity of all the letters and produced editions of them in 1961 and 1973, and Moraux (1951, pp. 133–143) is more or less in favor of their authenticity. A limited utilization of the letters of Aristotle was also accepted by Jaeger (1923, pp. 5 and 259n2) and Düring (1968, cols. 163–165); the latter offers an excellent overview of the situation, and holds to be authentic at least the letters to Antipater, while the others are held to be inauthentic (see also Düring 1957, pp. 235, 286, 392, and 433–434).

On the topic of the letters to Alexander the Great, however, Pearson (1954) rightly noted that establishing the authenticity of a letter of which we have only a few fragments is practically impossible. Gigon (in 1958 (pp. 177 and 186), 1961 (pp. 18–20), 1962 (p. 14), and 1987, pp. 3b and 215a–b) strongly questions the authenticity of these letters (see also Berti 1977, p. 14). Gigon considers the surviving complete letters to Alexander to be certainly fabricated (almost everyone agrees on this point), and the others, those that we know through fragmentary quotation, to be highly questionable. Indeed, in Gigon's 1987 collection of fragments and *testimonia* published in the new edition of the works of Aristotle of the Academy of Science in Berlin,[9] there is no section devoted to the letters of Aristotle. Of all this material, Gigon publishes only a few fragments, which may not derive from the letters, and the fragments of letters included in the ancient biographies of Aristotle (frs. 8, 9, 11, 107, and 108, and *testimonia* 3, 5, 10, 16, and 23). As far as the fragments of other letters are concerned, Gigon believes that any and every citation of them should be confirmed with some passage in the reliably authentic works. Gigon's criterion is surely ideal, but it is difficult to implement because, as Wilamowitz reminds us (1881, p. 151), unlike the letters of Plato and Epicurus, which are doctrinal in character, Aristotle's letters, if they are authentic, form part of the philosopher's private correspondence. Doubts are also voiced concerning the authenticity of the letters by Chroust (1973, p. xxv); see also below, section 1.4.

A letter from Aristotle to Alexander the Great on his policy toward the Greeks and Persians had been published by Lippert (1891), and judged authentic by Nissen (1892) but spurious by many others. The letter has now been republished by Bielawski and Plezia (1970, pp. 161–166), who defend its authenticity (see further Plezia 1961, pp. 50–63 and 131–151). If it were possible to authenticate the letter, it would constitute a major contribution to our knowledge of the relationship between Aristotle and Alexander the Great. But the opinion of the Polish scholars mentioned has failed to take hold. Also on this question, Stern (1968) supplemented the Lippert edition with passages drawn from the new Arabic manuscripts, but without producing a definitive edition, and also without reaching definite conclusions; he did not exclude the authenticity of the letter. Arguments in favor of its authenticity can also be found in Sordi (1984) and Prandi (1984), on the basis of a comparison between this text and the fragment of advice transmitted by Plutarch (see above, p. 45), presumably in a *Letter to Alexander*, or else in a work entitled *Alexander*. But many doubts remain when the text of the letter is compared with the doctrines set forth in the *Politics*. Despite many textual similarities to passages of the *Politics* and *Nicomachean Ethics*, this text has a basic approach entirely different from that of the Aristotelian treatises. The central problem is no longer the *polis*, but a projected global state in which the city is being overcome and engulfed by a politically superior entity; but this view is entirely absent from the Aristotelian works that we know, as is argued by Thillet (1972, pp. 541–542). Opposed to the authenticity of this letter is also Wes (1972) and especially von Fritz (1972), who reconstructs the main points of the history of the matter; he considers the work a pure pastiche, made by someone who was familiar with the treatises of Aristotle and made particular use of the now lost works *On Royalty* and *On Colonies*. A recent full discussion of the problem is available in Laurenti (1987, pp. 942–948), who seems to be in substantial agreement with von Fritz. No one has ever suspected that the letters from Alexander the Great to Aristotle were authentic; on these letters, see Pearson 1954, Merkelbach 1954, and Boer 1973.

1.2. OFFICIAL DOCUMENTS

Three official documents survive.

1. The most important document is the inscription mentioning Aristotle and Callisthenes that was found at Delphi in 1898 and published in Homolle 1898 (see above, p. 60). The text, which has been repeatedly emended, can be found in Dittenberger 1915³ (no. 275), Düring 1957 (p. 339 = *testimonium* 43, with a discussion of the associated bibliography), and *FGrHist* 124T23. For the issue about its dating, see above, p. 60.

2. An inscription at Ephesus, published in Heberdey 1902, describes the privileges of *proxenia* conceded to "**Nicanor son of Aristotle of Stagira**." See Düring 1957 (p. 270 = *testimonium* 13 b), and above, in section 3 of chapter 1.

3. An honorary decree that the city of Athens is said to have conferred upon Aristotle, and inscribed on a column, is referred to in Usaibia's

Arabic translation of Ptolemy's *Life of Aristotle* (see section 1.3 below). Usaibia also states that a certain Himeraios knocked down the column upon which the inscription had been engraved. Antipater had him killed for this act, and later the inscription was restored by a certain Stephanos, who added to the inscription the story of the misdeeds of Himeraios (see section 8 of chapter 1, p. 59). It is unlikely that Usaibia could have invented all this, including the Greek names. Concerning this text, Drerup (1898) showed, by means of a comparison with similar decrees preserved in the form of inscriptions, that underlying the Arabic text must have been a very ancient Greek source, capable of reproducing exactly the distinctive forms of speech of genuine Athenian decrees. Düring thinks of it as a Hellenistic counterfeit (1957, pp. 232–236), given that, in his opinion, the other information that we have about the life that Aristotle led at Athens makes it unlikely that the Athenians would ever consider honoring Aristotle with a decree of this sort; but even from this point of view, the information seems to come from a good source, because it speaks explicitly about the fact that in Athens there were currents of opinion that were hostile to Aristotle. Gigon believes that it all must derive from the *Life of Aristotle* by Hermippus (1987, p. 7a).

1.3. ANCIENT BIOGRAPHIES OF ARISTOTLE

On Greek biography in general, see the classic works by Leo (1901) and Misch (1907), and the more recent studies by Dihle (1956), Momigliano (1971), and Gigon (1965). Specifically for Aristotle, the most important contributions are those by Wilamowitz (1881), Wehrli (1959),[10] and Huxley (1964); concerning the biographical tradition on Aristotle in the general context of Greek biography, see also Düring (1957, pp. 459–476), Gauthier (1970, his introduction to the second edition), and Momigliano (1971, pp. 69–105 and 113–130). It was only in a certain rather advanced phase of its development that Greek biography took the lives of philosophers as a subject. But it is difficult to find in that treatment any interest in history in the modern sense of the term, or any intention to place the philosopher in the context of his time and culture. As Steiner (1988) lamented (see above, p. 1), in these biographies what prevails is an interest in anecdotes, a quest for erudite curiosities, a reconstruction of his personality, and the reactions of the man; and when materials are lacking, they are ready to invent them. For instance, the Peripatetic Clearchus (who had Pythagorean tendencies) in his *On Sleep* tells of a conversation between his master Aristotle and a Hellenized Jew, who, by telling him stories of miracles, brings him around to a less rationalistic position (fr. 6 Wehrli). The story was judged authentic by Jaeger (1938a), who viewed it as documentation of the fact that Aristotle had a full-fledged school at Assos, already organized, but this view has not prevailed.

At a certain point within the Aristotelian school, a full-fledged biography of Aristotle was compiled. There has been much discussion as to whether Ariston of Ceos, according to tradition the scholarch after Lyco, actually compiled a *Life of Aristotle*; as we have seen, the proposition is doubtful (see Lynch 1972). Wehrli maintains that he did (1952, 6:65), and he collects a number of fragments (frs. 28–32) of his *Lives of the Philosophers*, all taken from Diogenes Laertius, and claims that the fact that the biographies of the Peripatetic scholarchs end with Lyco, the predecessor of Ariston, shows that Diogenes Laertius based his work largely on the work of Ariston in his composition of the section of the *Lives of the Philosophers* dedicated to the Peripatetics.[11] No one doubts that the "Peripatetic" Hermippus, an Alexandrian grammarian who lived in the second century BCE, practically a contemporary of Ariston, compiled a biography of Aristotle,[12] very likely of a predominantly laudatory character.[13] There are doubts about whether this writing has any scholarly qualities,[14] though it must have been impressive in its great display of erudition and its "research" into marvelous stories and curious anecdotes, so typical of its time. In general, it is said that this text must have been written for the purpose of providing "erudite entertainment," whatever it is that this obscure expression might mean; perhaps it would be better to speak of a "fictionalized biography." These characteristics will reflect on all the successors of Hermippus, in particularly Diogenes Laertius.[15] See Plezia 1951a, Düring 1957 (pp. 57–61, 263, 269, 278–279, 313, 346, 352, 406, and 464–467), and Chroust 1964. There is a collection of fragments of Hermippus in Supplementband 1 (1974) of F. Wehrli's *Die Schule des Aristoteles*, which was in 1999 superseded by the thorough edition of J. Bollansée.

1. The *Life of Aristotle* by Diogenes Laertius (5.1–35) is published in the general editions of Diogenes Laertius, among which we should mention Cobet 1850, Long 1964, and most recently Marcovich 1999, but it should be examined especially in light of the particular editions of the *Life*, of which the Buhle 1791 and Bywater 1879 editions have only historical value, while the most authoritative editions are in Düring 1957 (pp. 29–56), and Gigon 1987 (*testimonium* 1); see also Schwartz 1905, Moraux 1949, Moraux 1951, Moraux 1951a, Moraux 1955, Gigon 1958, Gigante 1962 (introduction), and Chroust 1965a. An overall examination of the scholarship and the problems created by this text is found in Moraux 1986, where we find his concise judgment on the worth of this biography: "in Diogenes Laertius the best is right next to the worst," in which "the best" is constituted by the chronology of the life of Aristotle (taken from Apollodorus) and by many ancient and authentic documents (such as Aristotle's will) and by the ancient lists of his works, and "the worst" consists of the fanciful details of which the work is full. An important characteristic of this biography is the effort it makes to be impartial; anecdotes that tend to show Aristotle in a good light and negative anecdotes are both reported with the same credence. The problem lies in the fact that they are in large part quite unreliable.

2. A brief *Life of Aristotle*, with a long list of his works, published for the first time in 1663 by Gilles Ménage, and therefore called the *Vita Menagiana* or *Anonymus Menagii*, but later attributed to Hesychius of Miletus (sixth century CE; see Schultz 1913), was then published in Buhle 1791, Westermann 1845, and von Flach 1882. Part of it is in the *Suda* (3929 Adler); there are editions also in Rose 1886 (pp. 9–18), Düring 1957 (pp. 82–89), and Gigon 1987 (*testimonium* 2). According to Düring this is a brief biography whose sources are as yet unknown, while Chroust (1973) claims that it derives from Hermippus and the Neoplatonists, concerning whom see below. There is also a brief life falsely ascribed to Hesychius, concerning which see Düring 1957, pp. 92–93.

3. The other biographies of Aristotle depend entirely or in part on the biography written by a certain Ptolemy, whom the Arabs called al-Garib (viz., "the unknown," or "the stranger"); this was long believed lost in every language, until allegedly found again by Professor Mushin Mahdi, who claims that the "Treatise of Ptolemy containing his testi-

mony about Aristotle, a catalogue of his writings, and part of his biography, dedicated to Gallo," contained in an Istanbul codex Aya Sofya 4833 (folios 10a–18a), is the original treatise of Ptolemy (see Düring 1971, Plezia 1975, and Plezia 1985). On the other hand, Düring states that the text of this codex is identical to the text of the biography of Usaibia, concerning which see below. This text was edited and translated into German by Hein (1985, pp. 388–446), who also studied its relations with other Arabic and Greek evidence; see my author's postscript, p. 146.

In the nineteenth century and at the beginning of the twentieth century, this Ptolemy was identified with Ptolemaios Chennos (a grammarian of the first century CE) by many scholars: Christ, Schmid, and Stählin (1912–1924, 1:723n4), Chatzis 1914, and many others, from Littig 1890–1895 to Plezia 1985. Others have claimed that the author was a Neoplatonist, who was cited also by Iamblichus and Proclus; see Rose 1854, Busse 1893, Moraux 1951 (pp. 292–294), Düring 1957 (pp. 209–211), Gauthier 1959 (p. 8), Dihle 1957, and Gigon 1965 (p. 10), while Moraux is not certain of this last indication (1973, 60n6). Plezia 1985 holds that he was a professor of Aristotelian philosophy from the fourth century CE, because his work is similar to writings by the grammarian Donatus.

On the reconstruction of this biography, see Düring 1957 (pp. 472–474), Chroust 1964, and Plezia 1985. This is an extremely laudatory biography, which leads us to think that the identification of the author as a Neoplatonist is the most reliable, given the tendency among Neoplatonists to reconcile the philosophies of Plato and Aristotle, and to celebrate in the most exalted language both the master and the student. In the account of Aristotle's life, reports that might have clouded his fame are passed over in silence; for instance, the story of his ties to Hermias of Atarneus, who had a bad reputation in ancient times, was eliminated. Then reports were added that increased Aristotle's fame; for instance, a legend was created about a voyage into Asia that Aristotle and Alexander made together. The general image of Aristotelian philosophy offered in this biography is the laudatory one typical of Neoplatonic commentators: Aristotle is the "divine Aristotle," his meeting with Plato was due to an oracle at Delphi, he was honored by Philip and Alexander, he had a great influence on Macedonian politics, he was a great benefactor both of individuals and of cities, he was accorded honors worthy of a hero after his death, and whoever visited his tomb came away purified in spirit. Despite this, the biography of this Ptolemy is a useful text, as it is based on good sources, such as Philochorus (on whom see below). It was written for the purpose of being used as an introduction to a reading of the works of Aristotle, perhaps in the school of Ammonius and his successors; see Busse 1893, Düring 1957 (pp. 107–119, 137–139, 158–163, 444–456, and 469–472), and Düring 1968 (cols. 170–172).

We have various versions of this biography, more or less complete, in four different classical languages. The *Vita Aristotelis Marciana*, preserved in a single Greek manuscript in the Biblioteca Marciana in Venice, was published in Robbe 1861, and then in von Flach 1882, Rose 1886 (pp. 426–436), Düring 1957 (pp. 96–106), Gigon 1962, and Gigon 1987 (pp. 28b–31a). The *Vita Lascaris*, according to Düring (1957, pp. 122 and 140–141), is only an excerpt of the *Vita Marciana*. Others, such as Tovar (1943) and Alfonsi (1949), think that it is the source of the latter. The so-called *Vita Vulgata*, which is also falsely attributed to Ammonius, was published in Rose 1886 (pp. 437–441), Düring 1957 (pp. 131–136), and Gigon 1987 (pp. 34a–36a). On this text, see also Busse 1893, p. 253n3.

There is a Latin version of this biography, called the *Vita Latina*, published in Rose 1886 (pp. 442–450), Düring 1957 (pp. 151–158), and Gigon 1987 (pp. 31b–34a).

There are two summaries of the Syriac translations of Ptolemy's *Life of Aristotle*, Syriac translations from which the Arabic versions were later done; these summaries, referred to as *Vita Syriaca* I and *Vita Syriaca* II, were published by Baumstark (1898). English translations are offered in Düring 1957, pp. 185–188.

The Arab tradition of Ptolemy is, along with the Greek tradition, the most important one. These are translations taken from a source that is independent of the Greek and Latin versions mentioned above, and which adds unique material, such as the reports on the Athenian honorific decree for Aristotle, and certain details on Aristotle's last will and testament; see Düring 1957, pp. 183–246. This tradition comprises different Arabic translations, done from the Syriac translations, by four authors, as follows: (1) Ibn al-Nadim, *Kitab al-Fihrist,* edited by Flügel-Rödiger (1871–1872, 1:246–252) and Müller (1873, with notes and translation);

other translations are in Baumstark 1898 and in Düring 1957, pp. 193–195. (2) Al-Mubashir, *Kitab mukhtar al-hikam wa-mahasin al-kilam*, edited by Lippert (1894, pp. 4–19); translations are available in Baumstark 1898 and in Düring 1957, pp. 197–201. (3) Al-Qifti Gamaladdin, *Tabaqat al-hukama*, edited by Lippert (1894); a paraphrase and partial translation are available in Düring 1957, pp. 208 and 211–212. (4) Ibn-abi-Usaibia, ʿUyun al-anba fi tabaqat al-stibba, edited by Müller (1884, 1:54–69); the translation in Düring 1957, pp. 213–231, was reprinted in Gigon 1987, pp. 36a–38b.

1.4. THE *TESTIMONIA* OF ANCIENT AUTHORS

The *testimonia* of ancient authors concerning the life of Aristotle were collected by Stahr as early as 1830–1832; and they were again collected, partially reedited, and extensively commented on, in the fundamental study of Düring 1957.[16] In this work we find a careful evaluation of the reliability of every single piece of information. Some further elements were added in Plezia 1961a. According to the studies of Foucart, Wormell, Düring, Gigon, Moraux, Gauthier, and Chroust, the opinions and the gossipy comments of Aristotle's contemporaries are the headwaters of two major biographical currents, one favorable and one critical, which influenced the entire later ancient biographical tradition. Even in the case of very ancient reports, then, it is necessary to weigh their reliability carefully.

Polemics among philosophers of different schools were a fairly common thing in ancient Greece, and, in the presence of a public opinion that was often indifferent or even hostile, the level of criticism was at times embarrassingly low; see Luzac 1809, Düring 1957 (p. 384), Sedley 1976, and Natali 1983. Aristotle himself was often a bit harsh with those who did not think like him; see section 4 of chapter 1. But his attacks never reached the personal sphere, which was in fact usually respected (e.g., Plato, Eudoxus); but the attacks described by Aristocles of Messene, our chief source for these early polemics,[17] had mainly to do with Aristotle's personality and way of life, and the level of these accusations justifies the disdain with which Aristocles of Messene regards these **"orators, whose names and books are both more dead than their bodies."**[18]

The first to launch polemics against Aristotle must have been the student of Isocrates, Cephisodorus, who reacted to the attacks against the rhetorical teachings of his master. These criticisms, according to modern reconstructions, were made by Aristotle during his first "course of lessons," delivered in the Academy and dedicated to rhetoric; but this is by no means certain (see section 4 of chapter 1). Apparently Cephisodorus wrote a treatise in four books entitled *Against Aristotle*, which is also important for the reconstruction of the evolution of the thinking of the young Aristotle. The passages are *testimonia* 58h, 59h, 63a–e in Düring 1957;[19] on Cephisodorus in general, see Gerth 1921.

Despite their theoretical disagreements, there are no documented polemics of Speusippus and Xenocrates against Aristotle. As we have seen in section 4 of chapter 1, Aristocles of Messene says that Aristoxenus, despite having nothing but praise for Aristotle in his *Life of Plato*, claimed in that work that some students rebelled and founded a Peripatos against Plato during his absence, and that unnamed others believed that this report refers to Aristotle;[20] and in fact in the *Elements of Harmony* 31.10–15, Aristoxenus speaks of Aristotle with great respect (see Bélis 1986, p. 45). A polemical dig against Aristotle can perhaps be seen as well in the criticism of Dicaearchus mentioned above (section 3 of chapter 3, p. 117), against the *bios theōretikos* and the life of study practiced in organized philosophical schools.

There is no shortage of accusations against Aristotle on the part of representatives of the other schools, such as the Megarian philosopher Eubulides of Miletus; concerning him, see Döring 1972 (pp. 102–104) and Giannantoni 1990 (1:591–592, 4:61–71, and 4:83). Eubulides wrote a book on the relations between Aristotle and Hermias of Atarneus and about relations between Aristotle and Philip of Macedon;[21] these passages are *testimonia* 58f, 59b, 62a–b in Düring 1957.[22]

Aside from these contemporaries, in the generation that immediately followed, we should mention the eristic Alexinus of Elis, who lived between the fourth and the third centuries BCE and carried on a long polemic against Zeno the Stoic; see Döring 1972 (pp. 21–27 and 115–123) with Giannantoni 1990 (1:401–408). Alexinus provides the earliest text to refer to a relationship between Aristotle and Alexander the Great (see section 6.1 of chapter 1), and he depicts Alexander as being full

of scorn for Aristotle's *logoi*; the passage in question is *testimonium* 58e
Düring 1957 (see section 6.1 of chapter 1). Moreover, the Pythagorean
Lyco of Tarentum (fourth century BCE) was the author of a very stupid
story about the number of saucepans owned by Aristotle, as reported
with disbelief by Aristocles in his *On Philosophy*. "**Surpassing in foolishness all** [the other accusations], **are what Lyco said, the one who calls
himself a 'Pythagorean': he actually claimed that Aristotle made
sacrifice to his dead wife, the same sort of sacrifice that the Athenians make to Demeter, that he used to wash himself in hot oil and
then sell this oil, and that, when he fled to Chalcis, the customs officials found on his ship seventy-five bronze saucepans**"[23] (excerpted in
Eusebius 15.2.8 = *testimonium* 58i).

The polemics of Epicurus and the Epicureans are on the same level,
and, for our purposes, the most important among the Epicureans was
Philodemus of Gadara. Concerning Aristotle and the Epicureans, there
are useful studies, aside from Sudhaus 1893, in Bignone 1936 and Sedley
1976. The texts are collected in Düring 1957: *testimonia* 58b and 59a–e
for Epicurus, and *testimonium* 31 for Philodemus.[24] From these texts we
can also derive some reports on Aristotle's teaching activity in the Academy. But for the most part we find only insults: wastrel, glutton, seller
of drugs (see section 3 of chapter 1).

As far as we can tell, some historians from Chios, such as Theopompus and Theocritus, conducted polemics against Aristotle, whom they
never forgave for his friendship with Hermias of Atarneus, because he
had intervened in the internal affairs of Chios. The Theopompus texts
are in Jacoby 1923 (*FGrHist* 115F250 and 115F291), and the Theocritus
texts are in Müller 1841 (2:86a–87b), and in the editions of Didymus;
they are also collected in Düring 1957 (*testimonia* 15c [Theopompus] and
15h, 58k, and 65b [Theocritus]). Other polemics against Aristotle were
leveled by Timaeus of Tauromenium, apparently because Aristotle had
mistreated the inhabitants of Locri (see Polybius 12.8.1), as well as other
pointless reasons. The texts are in Jacoby 1923 (*FGrHist* 566F11, 12, 152,
and 156) and in Düring 1957 (*testimonia* 9c, 12b, 58c, 60a–b, 60d).

Fortunately, there were also favorable sources, in the first place
Aristotle's nephew and collaborator, Callisthenes of Olynthus, who
wrote a book about Hermias full of praise (see section 6.1 of chapter

1). More neutral than favorable as a source is Philochorus, who gave, in his chronological work *Atthis*, the date on which Aristotle entered the Platonic Academy and the period for which he remained; see also Jacoby 1926 (*FGrHist* 328F223–224) and Düring 1957 (*testimonia* 1f and 3). Similar in nature are the reports offered by Apollodorus of Athens (second century BCE), an author generally considered to be very reliable; see Boeck 1872 (6:195+), Diels 1876 (pp. 43–47), Jacoby 1902 (pp. 318+), and Chroust 1965. The chronology provided in the so-called *Marmor Parium* (a marble stele found at Paros, on which is engraved a chronicle of all the important events that occurred in Athens from the time of its founder Cercops until 264/263 BCE) differs considerably from the one given by Apollodorus, because it states that Aristotle died in 321, at the age of fifty. This would mean that Aristotle was a student of Plato for only seven years, not twenty years, as all other sources claim. Such a chronology, despite the customary reliability of this source, is considered unacceptable precisely because it clashes with Apollodorus; see Jacoby 1904 and 1926 (commentary to *FGrHist* 239B11).[25] And for that matter, in Aristotle's works we find sufficient traces of a long period of philosophical discussion with Plato.

In the Hellenistic period, numerous legends were fabricated about Aristotle, and spurious works were created in support of them. In particular, it would seem that the attention of the Hellenistic authors was attracted by the relationship between Aristotle and Alexander the Great, the relationship between Aristotle and Hermias of Atarneus, and the trial for impiety to which Aristotle was subjected, and which may possibly have been linked to the Hermias affair. An *Apology of Aristotle* was composed (see Düring 1957, *testimonia* 22 and 45a–d and pp. 343–344). It would seem that authors such as Favorinus and Eumelus wanted to compare Aristotle to Socrates, despite the evident difference in behavior in their respective trials, since Socrates faced execution rather than disobey the laws of Athens, while the metic Aristotle preferred to flee the city (see *FGrHist* 77F1–2 of Jacoby 1923, with Gigon 1958, pp. 275–276). A certain Apellicon, a "Peripatetic" of the first century BCE, wrote a book about the relationship between Aristotle and Hermias. Another author, Artemon, published a collection of Aristotle's letters, in the same period, the first century BCE.[26] Not much later, the Epicurean

Philodemus of Gadara, in his *On Rhetoric*, gathered and recycled all of the polemical accusations of his school against Aristotle. The reports on Aristotle found in later authors such as Aulus Gellius, Aelian, Athenaeus, and Plutarch, derive largely from this Hellenistic tradition. In this period, there was also a certain interest in the relations between Aristotle and Alexander the Great, which, from this point on, gave origin to a great many legends (see especially chapters 7–8 of Plutarch's *Life of Alexander* = *testimonium* 10 of Gigon 1987).

In my opinion, the collections of letters between Aristotle and Alexander, as well as the collections of letters between Philip of Macedon and Aristotle, are to be reckoned among these literary fictions. We have, for example, a report in Aulus Gellius (9.3) about a letter in which Philip announces to Aristotle the birth of Alexander and suggests that he become his tutor (*testimonium* 30f); but it is difficult to see this as a reliable document, since Aristotle was only twenty-eight years old when Alexander was born, and was an unknown student of Plato. More credibility has been acquired by a letter from Aristotle to Philip, in which Aristotle says that he was a student of Plato for twenty years,[27] but this is also to be reckoned as the same sort of production; it is reported at *Vita Marciana* 5 (fr. 652 Rose 1886 = fr. 2a Plezia 1961 = Plezia 1977, p. 15), and at *Vita Latina* 5 (fr. 2b Plezia 1961 = Plezia 1977, p. 15). It is said here that Aristotle had been summoned by the Pythian Apollo to go to Athens, and that he had been a student of Socrates for three years, both of which are historically unreliable reports; see Gigon 1946 (pp. 17+), Gigon 1958 (p. 185), and Chroust 1973 (p. 129). Concerning the letters in general, see above, section 1.1D.

There has been a great deal of discussion concerning the issue of whether Andronicus of Rhodes wrote a biography of Aristotle prefacing his edition of the works of the philosopher. On the affirmative side are Littig 1890–1895, Brink 1940, Plezia 1946, Plezia 1961a (pp. 247–249), Gigon 1962 (p. 10), Momigliano 1971 (p. 89), and Chroust 1973 (p. 12). On the negative side stand several publications of Düring: 1957 (pp. 420–425), 1963, 1966 (pp. 50–54), 1968 (cols. 166–167). Moraux 1973 gives us the most recent and complete study of Andronicus (pp. 45–141), but takes no position on this point. Later, in Christian times, such scholars as Numenius, Atticus, and Aristocles of Messene[28] reported information on the calumnies against Aristotle and on the relations between Aristotle and Plato; see *testimonia* 40c–e, 58, and 63c Düring.

After this period begins the time of the versions of the ancient biographies of Aristotle, which we have just discussed. Concerning the Middle Ages and the modern period, references can be found in Düring 1957 (pp. 164–179),[29] and the most complete list is in Schwab 1896 (pp. 13–29). A few episodes triggered the fantasies of medieval moralists, such as the episode of Aristotle being ridden like a horse, in which the philosopher yields to the claims of a lovely courtesan without too much concern for his own dignity.[30] The legends concerning the relationship between Aristotle and and Alexander the Great (which the Arabs viewed as being on a par with the relationship between a vizier and his sultan) are examined in Brocker 1966.[31] The legends concerning Aristotle's dying in the manner of Plato's *Phaedo*, described in the *Liber de pomo* (*testimonium* 12 in Gigon 1987) have been studied in Plezia 1960, Krämer 1956, and Rousseau 1968.

2. IMAGES OF ARISTOTLE FROM THE NINETEENTH CENTURY TO THE PRESENT

In his monumental 1879 work (of which the portions on Arisotle and the earlier Peripatetics were published in English translation in 1897), Zeller summarized the studies on Aristotle's biography up to his own time, and today his reconstruction still remains one of the most balanced and reliable. Zeller does not try to fill in the gaps in the data with more or less plausible hypotheses, but tends to select those reports that are most worth relying on, so as to reconstruct a coherent picture. For instance, Zeller refuses to offer conjectures as to what Aristotle might have taught Alexander. The Aristotle of Zeller is a scholar, whose interests are limited to research; and since Aristotle was not Athenian, his philosophy was free of the political purposes of Socrates and Plato. With regard to his philosophy, the external events of Aristotle did not have any decisive significance, and, in the final analysis, they constitute nothing more than a series of events that happened to a great philosopher in the course of his human existence; if we leave aside the decision to attend Plato's school, we cannot say what effect these events had on the development of his thinking. Perhaps the biography of Aristotle in the version of Zeller is actually too thin, and for this reason the objection that can be made to it is opposite to the one that can be made against very many other scholars who have taken up this topic; today it seems to us that we know something more, even though the basic approach given by Zeller remains one of the most valid.

Substantially similar is the biography of Aristotle in Gomperz 1906, even though it is more colorful and anecdotal; Aristotle is an encyclopedic spirit, moderate to an immoderate degree, with a great love of detail and great serenity of expression, not without a certain ironic wittiness. In his reconstruction of the philosopher, Gomperz was able to make use of the research that Jaeger later published in 1912, and to give many details on the school's activities; see above, chapter 3.

Since the time of Zeller, the study of Aristotle's biography has gone through three distinct phases, separated by the publication of two crucial works: Jaeger 1923 and Düring 1957. Around and soon after Zeller's time, there was a rapid flourishing of studies of the Arabic biographical tradition, beginning with an article by Steinschneider 1869, and books by Müller 1873, Lippert 1891, and Baumstark 1898, mentioned above on pp. 129–130; on the Neoplatonic tradition, see the article of Busse 1893; on the Greek biographical tradition, see the article of Maas 1880.

At the end of the nineteenth century, there developed a distinct tendency toward a political interpretation of the activity of ancient philosophers. Bernays 1881 attributed an openly pro-Macedonian slant to the philosophical schools of Plato and Aristotle, construing them as centers of intellectual propaganda in favor of the expansionism of King Philip. This was especially true of Aristotle, who, according to Bernays (1881, p. 110), served as an observer of Athenian political events in his two Athenian periods, stayed in touch with the royal court of Macedonia, and silently influenced the chief political circles of the city, without being much hindered by his legal status as a metic. This is a reconstruction largely based on hypothesis, and yet the idea of Aristotle as a pro-Macedonian political agent reappears from time to time, including in more recent studies such as those by Chroust, Grayeff, and Maddoli. Of the same opinion as Bernays were Nissen (1892) and Wilamowitz (1881).[32]

By contrast, Wilamowitz (1893, 1:308–372) undertook a reconstruction of Aristotle's biography based entirely on a political judgment that he was hostile to the extreme democratic party, an animosity that we can find in the *Constitution of Athens*, a work that had been rediscovered and published just a few years before, in 1891. Since the style of this work is typical of an exoteric writing, that is, a work directed toward a broader audience, Wilamowitz imagines Aristotle as striving single-mindedly in favor of the preservation of a city-state in the face of a Macedonian drive for unification (p. 371), adverse to the democratic forces (whom Wilamowitz constantly refers to as demagogues), and as a friend of Isocrates. In this work there is no interest whatsoever in the reconstruction of the development of Aristotelian thought, though we already find the division of Aristotle's life into youth, travels, and teaching (*Lehrjahre, Wanderjahre,* and *Meisterjahre*) that would later be adopted by Jaeger. There is also a reference to an initial Platonism on Aristotle's part subsequently abandoned at the same time as the more general crisis of Platonism itself, a crisis that, in the view of Wilamowitz, coincided with the development of the unwritten doctrines and the *Laws*.

On the other hand, not everyone accepted such "politicized" reconstructions. Some of the best-known critiques of Bernays and Wilamowitz were those of Gomperz in 1882, 1901, and 1906 (4:25–37). Gomperz reiterated the traditional image of Aristotle as a great scientist and encyclopedic thinker, devoid of practical political interests. Gercke 1896 maintained, in support of Bernays, and against Wilamowitz 1893, the idea of a pro-Macedonian Aristotle, but he greatly limited his real, political importance and speaks ironically of his "political armchair-wisdom" (*politische Kathederweisheit*). According to Gercke in the final analysis, it was not Aristotle who educated Alexander, but the other way around; from his regular contacts with the Macedonian prince, Aristotle got used to the world of *Realpolitik,* and it added a more realistic dimension to his thinking, typical of the *Politics.* In an article that is nowadays all but completely forgotten, Waddington (1893) is more sober in ignoring the cogitations of the great German philologists, and he gives us a correct sketch of the biography of Aristotle that is not very far distant from what is generally accepted even nowadays.

We have seen the impact of the rediscovery of large parts of his *Constitution of Athens* on the reconstruction of Aristotle's biography. This major step forward took place on the basis of a papyrus codex found in

Egypt and published by F. G. Kenyon in 1891, and there were also epigraphical discoveries of the same period that had the effect of partially modifying the preceding image; in 1898 and in 1902 were published the two inscriptions on Aristotle, mentioned above, section 1.2 of chapter 4. Also published in 1902 was the critical edition of Philodemus's *Index of Academic Philosophers*, entitled by its editor S. Mekler *Academicorum philosophorum index herculanensis*; Mekler's admirable work was the first to bring into evidence the second of two charred rolls from Herculaneum that transmit fragments of the *Index*. In 1904, finally, there was published a papyrus fragment of the commentary of Didymus Chalcenterus (first century BCE) on the *Philippics* of Demosthenes, containing much information about Hermias of Atarneus.[33] These discoveries enriched the historical picture by contributing ancient documents, and to the present day there have been no others of comparable impact. The methodical analysis of the sources in this period was followed up in Mulvany 1926 and Wormell 1935.

All the same, the great change in the field of studies that we are examining did not come from these discoveries but rather from the beginning of an "evolutionary" interpretation of the work of Aristotle. Credit for this goes to Jaeger, unquestionably, despite certain precedents.[34] At the beginning of the 1920s, there was a flourishing of general interpretations of Aristotle, many of which are now forgotten (by C. Lalo, A. Goedeckemeyer, P. Kafka,[35] E. Rolfes, and Á. Pauler), but two of them, by Ross and by Jaeger, both dating from 1923, are still important.

The overview set forth in Ross 1923 is rather schematic: in Athens, Aristotle devoted himself chiefly to teaching, perhaps in a school of his own, in a rented building; the relationship with Hermias of Atarneus must have been more important than his relationship with Philip and Alexander of Macedon; Aristotle's school had some influence on the political life of the time.

The volume by Jaeger 1923 has had a decisive impact on Aristotelian studies right up to the present day.[36] As far as our limited point of view is concerned, Jaeger's work reveals its originality right away with its formal structure, given that, unlike all other monographs offering a general overview, it is not composed of a brief opening mention of Aristotle's biography and an exposition of his doctrines, but rather has a more complex structure. Jaeger mixes his exposition of Aristotle's biography with a description of the evolution of his thought, stopping from time to time to offer a panoramic overview of Aristotelian thought in a certain phase of his life. He explicitly borrows from Wilamowitz the threefold division of Aristotle's life into "youth, travels, and teaching" (*Lehrjahre, Wanderjahre, Meisterjahre*), but, in contrast with Wilamowitz, Jaeger also clearly states that he intends to oppose the political interpretation of Bernays, which he does not share (1923, p. 169). The spiritual evolution of Aristotle therefore serves as the energy source of this biographical reconstruction, and the volume thereby acquires a remarkable effect of compactness and historical concreteness.

Clearly the interest that guides Jaeger's work is not only archaeological and antiquarian but philosophical; to him, Aristotle is a classic thinker, in that he succeeded in overcoming the archaic spiritual unity of Plato and of previous philosophers without going so far as the positivism of modern science, and in knowing how to carry out an original synthesis of speculative spirit and scientific rigor, a synthesis that Jaeger considers still authoritative. Like Usener (1884), Jaeger also sees the Aristotelian Peripatos as a forerunner of modern universities[37] and, by means of his reconstruction of Aristotle's spiritual evolution, also wants to describe the birth of this form of institution that is so central to Western culture and philosophy. It is an interpretation of Aristotle's life that lines up on the side of the "philosophical" interpretations, not of the "political" interpretations of Bernays and Nissen, but it also tends just as much to give expression to the importance of the Aristotelian experience for contemporary problems.

One distinctive quality of Jaeger, and of the "compactness" of his text, as previously mentioned, is the way that it brings together the great events of Aristotle's life with the principal about-turns in his thinking: the philosopher's departure from Athens is linked to the crisis of his Platonism; his sojourns in Assos at the court of Hermias, and in Macedonia at the court of Alexander, are linked to a new phase of more original theoretical research, and not to any pro-Macedonian political engagement; and his second Athenian period is linked to the organization of the school and to his great scientific investigations. In this way, rather than seeing the historical conditioning of Aristotle's thought, Jaeger shows how the external history of Aristotle was, in the final analysis, a function of his spiritual history, and depends on it, just as one would expect in the case of a great philosopher.

This criterion allows Jaeger to rid himself of many of the hypotheses and false problems[38] of nineteenth-century critics, and to rely only on the more firm information. He establishes in a definitive manner that the crucial and essential point of departure for understanding both the philosophy and the life of Aristotle is his relationship with Plato; second in terms of importance is Aristotle's relationship with Hermias of Atarneus, and of less importance still is Aristotle's relationship with Macedonia and Alexander. In the years that followed, when the evolutionary method became the standard approach to the study of Aristotle, Jaeger's reconstruction of the philosopher's life would become the biographical vulgate, entirely overshadowing the preceding efforts of Nissen 1892, Wilamowitz 1893, Gercke 1896, and all political inter-pre-tations of the figure of Aristotle. We can see this in Bignone 1936,[39] in Burnet 1924, in Brehiér 1928 (pp. 169–171), and especially in Prächter 1926(pp. 348–353), who states that one now ought to replace Wilamo-witz's colorful biographical reconstruction with Jaeger's more sober one. See also Fuller 1931, Mure 1932, Robin 1932, Bidez 1942 (also 1943, 1943a, 1944),[40] and Robin 1944. Some scholars attempted to use the genetic method to clarify relations between Aristotle and Alexander, such as Barker 1931; Kelsen 1937–1938 tried to interpret Aristotle's *Politics* as a defense of Macedonian expansionism, but with few results; see also von Ivanka 1938, pp. 3–19.

An original intervention, immediately following the Second World War, was the one comprising three articles published by P. Merlan in 1946, 1954, and 1959.[41] Merlan reexamines the sources of the Aristotelian biographical tradition and tries in every way to show that there was no theoretical opposition at all between Plato and Aristotle, that such opposition was the fruit of subsequent interpretations, and that Aristotle, in the final analysis, is nothing more than a link in the chain that runs "from Platonism to Neoplatonism," as the title of his well-known book would have it. Essentially the same position was taken up again in Krämer 1959. Merlan claims that Aristotle and Xenocrates were the heads of two branches of the same school, separated only organizationally but not doctrinally, nor were they rivals; he believes, on the basis of the Isocratean *Letter to Alexander*,[42] that Aristotle tried to educate Alexander the Great in the same way that Plato tried to educate Dion of Syracuse, that is, by trying to convert him to philosophy, with a proper course of studies similar to that of the Academy; he claims, finally, that there were no profound disagreements between Aristotle and Speusippus, and that, therefore, when Aristotle left the Academy after Plato's death, he did not do so out of hatred for the new scholarch, as others claim; see, for example, Moraux 1951 (pp. 324–346).

A well-known article by Lee 1948 was authoritative for a long time; taking up indications from Thompson 1910 and Burnet 1924, Lee showed that many of the biological works of Aristotle had been written in Assos and in Macedonia, in the intermediate period between his first and his second stay in Athens. This hypothesis, however, had already been advanced in Zeller 1897 (1:26), and was recently questioned once again in Solmsen 1978 and Byl 1980; we have discussed this above, in section 6.1 of chapter 1. Solmsen suggested a straightforward return to Jaeger's approach, according to which Aristotle's great biological research was done in Athens, during his second stay.

The contribution that Düring 1957 brought to the study of the Aristotelian biographical tradition was so important that it could not be ignored, as was recognized even by those like Gauthier 1959 who maintain their faith in the validity of the Jaegerian schema and method, and by those like Gigon and Plezia who do not share his conclusions. Düring in general tends to eliminate the evolutionary schema that sees in Aristotle a transition from the speculative spirit of Platonism to detailed scientific investigations, and recognizes in Aristotle, right from the beginning, a plurality of tendencies, a polarity that persisted right to the end. From the biographical point of view, Düring goes on to reexamine the sources upon which Jaeger had relied and, following the traces of Foucart, Mulvany, and Wormell, tries to situate every report and every source in its time, determining whether it belonged to a tradition that was favorable, hostile, or indifferent to Aristotle. He thus makes a special effort to determine the purpose behind every report on Aristotle; for example, an anecdote written during the Hellenistic period is intended to amuse or intrigue the reader, without worrying about its historical accuracy, whereas a contemporary of Aristotle might write in order to attack him ferociously or defend him fiercely.

In the nineteenth century, there was a desire to reconstruct the life of Aristotle by picking and choosing among the various reports, often on the basis of a prefabricated picture, to which the available biographical information was fitted. After Düring, the study of Aristotle's biography became a sort of trial of circumstantial evidence, in which the few entirely reliable reports are selected out from among the extremely many reports, and what is researched is the kernel of truth underlying all the others. This latter operation is of course conjectural, and it is difficult to find agreement among scholars on every single specific point. It thus becomes impossible to provide a complete and detailed reconstruction of Aristotle's life, as the critics of the late nineteenth century attempted to do, by adding to the solid information certain hypotheses and all manner of inferences. One can, instead, describe much more easily the various images of Aristotle in the different eras and show, for instance, how the Aristotle of Cicero's time is quite different from the *dios Aristoteles* (divine Aristotle) of the Neoplatonic era.

As for the results of his research, Düring's greatest innovation has to do with Aristotle's second Athenian period: in Athens, according to Düring, he was not the political and cultural master of the Greek nation described by Wilamowitz, nor was he the great and famous encyclopedic intellectual depicted by Jaeger, or the willing political instrument of Macedon, as suggested by Bernays, Kelsen, and others; he was rather an isolated and little-known philosopher, who enjoyed little success in his lifetime, certainly much less than Plato. In fact, according to Düring, Attic comedy of the fourth century, which was happy to poke fun at Socrates and Plato, and the secure and constant tradition of the Platonic dialogues, demonstrates the popular success of Platonic thought and the continuity of the school that institutionally guaranteed the preservation and use of the master's works. In contrast, Aristotle is almost never quoted by Athenian authors; Athens seems not to have been aware of his existence, except to accuse him of impiety toward the end of his life, and the tradition of his writings is extremely confused and uncertain. In the city of Athens, according to Düring, Aristotle never had his own full-fledged school, but only a group of students who met periodically at the gymnasium located in the Lyceum grove. As a metic living in Athens, Aristotle was harmed by the rivalry between the city and the kingdom of Macedon, and he was forced to flee Athens twice by outbreaks of anti-Macedonian hatred, in 348 BCE, and upon the death of Alexander. Even the summons to the court of Pella to instruct Alexander, at that time certainly not the most important personage in the court of Philip of Macedon, was not due to the philosopher's great fame but rather to his family ties with the lordling of Atarneus, Hermias, an ally of Philip. So goes Düring's interpretation. We view this reaction against the "political" excesses of the biographies by Bernays and Wilamowitz as useful, if perhaps a bit too gloomy and pessimistic.

Much more willing to imagine a political Aristotle are Maddoli (1967), who imagines that the school of Aristotle was founded to support the spread of Macedonian hegemony,[43] and Chroust, who states that he wished to achieve an "intelligent and imaginative" use of the biographical information, but despite an impressive number of contributions[44] occupying a very large number of pages, because he often repeats his own positions as well as the *status quaestionis* of the debate, he reaches conclusions that are in the end difficult to accept. In fact, he holds that Aristotle was closely tied to Philip of Macedon, for whom he performed political missions to Hermias of Atarneus and in Athens. For Chroust, Aristotle is a Platonist philosopher who never moved away from the positions of his master, but who never had the necessary tranquillity in Athens to compose the works that bore his name. In his view, Aristotle tried in every way possible to assist in the expansionistic ambitions of Philip, and to defend the city of Athens through his powerful Macedonian friends; after the battle of Chaeronea (338 BCE), he is said to have defended Athens to Philip; in 335 he supposedly defended it to Alexander, and in 334 to Antipater. According to Chroust, Aristotle's political commitments prevented him from writing the works attributed to him, and the "works of Aristotle" are actually a collection of writings by his students, especially Theophrastus, while the true philosophy of Aristotle can be found only in the fragments of his lost works. The *corpus aristotelicum* would therefore be, as Zürcher 1952 had previously ventured, a *corpus aristotelicum peripateticorum veterum*. So much for Chroust's interpretation. Grayeff 1974 was of the same opinion, and both have been unconvincing, especially to me.

The method of source criticism took over little by little. There are no signs of the influence of Düring 1957 on either Randall 1960, Brun 1961, Moreau 1962, or Allan 1952 (not even in his revised edition of 1970). Instead they echo and discuss the previously published positions of Düring, Gigon, Gauthier, Plezia, and Chroust, on the texts we have cited several times. All of them cast doubt on the idea that Aristotle in Athens was an isolated and unknown philosopher, and they cite as proof the honorific inscription reported by Usaibia (see above, section 1.3, pp. 124–125). Many of them doubt that Aristotle, since he did not own a house in Athens because of his metic status, would have been unable to open a full-fledged school of his own, in rented or borrowed quarters, for instance (Gigon, Gauthier, Chroust). Quite close to Düring's position, on the other hand, is the short and informative volume by Zemb 1961.

Berti (1962 and 1977) applies Düring's method of source criticism with a notable equilibrium and, especially in the 1977 volume, limits himself to the best-attested biographical facts, such as the chronology and the few certainly reliable reports. Against the political interpretations of Aristotle, and basing himself primarily on the works of the philosopher, Berti rightly sees in theoretical research and the organization of the school the principal interests of Aristotle's life, for whom political events were primarily negative in their influence, distracting him from the tranquillity necessary for research. In this way, the pages of *Nicomachean Ethics* X.6–8 on the *bios theōretikos*, in which Aristole describes it as a perfect state of being, take on an exactly autobiographical flavor. The position of Zeller, from which we began, emerges again at the end of this review as one of the most reliable interpretations.

POSTSCRIPT (2012)

After an interval of twenty-one years from the original publication of the present book, it seems to me that many of its main theses still stand, such as the general picture it presents of Aristotle, the purpose of the Peripatos, and its institutional nature as a foundation. Other conclusions that I reached in this book can be considered more controversial.

It will be opportune for me to pass in review the most important scholarship published since I last worked on this book. I apologize in advance if I have neglected any important contributions, since I have worked mostly on different topics in the past twenty years.

At about the same time as the first publication of this book, the French scholar P. Louis, who had edited and translated many Aristotelian works, published a biography of Aristotle. *Vie d'Aristote: 384–322 avant Jésus-Christ* (Paris, 1990). This is a rather strange booklet. Louis writes a novelized biography of Aristotle, in which the few certain facts mix with hypotheses, uncertain elements from tradition, and speculation from passages of the works in the corpus, such as the *Meteorologica* and the *Problems* (this latter of uncertain authenticity). Louis thinks he knows what Aristotle's feelings were toward Plato (a new father to substitute for his own father, who died when Aristotle was very young); he tells us that Aristotle and Philip II of Macedon used to play together when they were children; and he thinks that Aristotle visited the zoo that, according to him, existed at the court of Macedonian kings at Pella. I suspect that all this, and much more, is a product of Louis's imagination. There are more acceptable pages in his book, for instance, his description of the departure of Aristotle from Athens in 347 BCE, or of the rivalry between Isocrates and the Platonists for the job of being Alexander's tutor in 343 BCE. But in general his book represents a step backward in scholarship on the subject, because he does not examine the bias and tendency of each of the ancient sources before accepting what they say.

More useful are the articles published in *Dictionnaire des philosophes antiques* (CRNS Paris, 1994 and onward), a large French encyclopedia edited by R. Goulet, dedicated to collecting data about the life and works of all the known ancient philosophers, major and minor, with bibliography, but without a summary of their theories. Here we find entries about most of the persons named in the present book, beginning with a large entry on Aristotle. The biographical portion of this entry, written by R. Goulet, B. Puech, and M. Aouad (1:413–443) is divided in three main sections, "Prosopography," "Chronology," and "Works." They give a select bibliography and a list of the ancient sources.

In her section on "Chronology," B. Puech discusses the evidence about the list of the victors of the Delphic games (examined in the present book on p. 60); she thinks that it contained a history of the shrine of Delphi as well as of the games. According to Puech, the inscription was a huge document, larger than has been suspected until now. She thinks also that the inscription was destroyed in 324/323 BCE, before the death of Alexander, in a period of anti-Macedonian feelings among the Delphian priests.

At the end of this portion of the article, R. Goulet discusses the destiny of Aristotle's works and rightly maintains that the treatises were known also in Hellenistic period, but he concludes that they had no influence on the Peripatetic philosophers of the second and first centuries BCE, because of the conceptual evolution of the school—and its decadence, I would add. For more contributions on the fate of Aristotle's library, see below in this postscript.

One of the ancient sources about which there is new information is the Arabic *Life of Aristotle* found in the Istanbul codex, Aya Sofya no. 4833 (mentioned above, p. 120). M. Aouad, the author of this section of the Aristotle article, says that it has been only partially edited and translated, and that, according to Plezia and Gutas, it is not by a Neoplatonist but by a Peripatetic scholar of the fourth century CE, and that the content is different from that of the Neoplatonic biographies of Aristotle. Aouad summarizes the content of the manuscript: a dedication to a certain Gallus, a biography of Aristotle, some aphorisms, and the list of his works. In fact, however, there does exist a full edition and translation of the text, by Christel Hein, on pp. 388–446 of her *Definition und Einteilung der Philosophie: Von den spätantiken Literatur zur arabischen Enzyklopädie* (Frankfurt 1985). Unfortunately, many scholars, including myself, have overlooked this publication, whose existence was made known to me by Oliver Primavesi's 2007 article (see below).

In this portion of her book, Hein gives a complete survey of the preceding literature and of the influence of this text in other compilations in Arabic. Ptolemy refers more than once to a book he has read by Andronicus of Rhodes about the works of Aristotle, but which is not in his hands when writing the present summary. Hein thinks that Ptolemy's catalog respects the division of Aristotle's works current in the Neoplatonic school in Alexandria. He modifies the ordering of the works and gives a shorter catalog of them; in fact, Ptolemy says, in Andronicus there are a thousand Aristotelian books, but he catalogs only the most important ones, one hundred in number. An edition of the preface and catalog follows (pp. 416–439), with a German translation of the preface and a back-translation of the catalog from Arabic to Greek.

In the first and subsequent volumes of the *Dictionnaire des philosophes antiques*, there are other important entries dedicated to figures relevant to the topic of this book, namely these: **Alexinos**, by R. Müller (1:149–151); **Andronicus** of Rhodes, by R. Goulet (1:200–202); **Antigonus** of Carystus, by T. Dorandi (1:209–211); **Apellicon, Artemon**, and **Athenion**, by R. Goulet (1:266–267, 615–616, 649–650); **Callisthenes** of Olynthus, by W. Spoerri (2:183–221); **Cephisodorus**, by L. Pernot (2:266–269); **Coriscus** of Scepsis, by R. Goulet (2:456–490), who thinks that Erastus and Coriscus had a good influence on Hermias's character; **Demetrius** of Phalerum, by J.-P. Schneider and F. Queyrel (2:628–635); **Diogenes Laertius**, by J. Mejer (2:824–833); **Epicurus**, by R. Goulet (3:154–181); **Eudoxos**, by J.-P. Schneider (3:293–302); **Hermias** of Atarneus, by T. Dorandi (3:650–651); **Hermippus**, by J.-P. Schneider (3:655–658); and **Isocrates**, by J. L. Lopez Cruces and P. P. Fuentes Gonzales (3:891–938). As is common for encyclopedia entries, these contributions generally present the mainstream opinion and only rarely present new perspectives or evidence; but they are very useful, because the reader can find there all the facts concerning the ancient philosophers and their works, collected in a clear and concise way.

Some of these entries deserve special mention, such as the entry by Lopez Cruces and Fuentes Gonzalez on Isocrates, with its excellent exposition of Isocrates' conception of "philosophy," and his relationship with the "real" philosophers, Sophists, Socrates, Plato, Aristotle, and so on. The treatment of Callisthenes by Spoerri is extremely detailed and complete; he doubts that Callisthenes had ever been a disciple of Aristotle, but he notes that in his historical works Callisthenes described many aspects and events of nature. In a useful part of his Cephisodorus article, L. Pernot discusses the testimony about the slander made by Cephisodorus against Aristotle (above, p. 25) and notes that the Greek text of the testimony by Athenaeus from Cephisodorus's book can be understood in two opposing ways; *epitimai tōi philosophōi ou poiēsanti logou axion to paroimiai athroisai* can mean both "he criticizes the philosopher for collecting proverbs (which are of no value)" and also "he criticizes the philosopher for not collecting proverbs (i.e., for making it of no value to collect proverbs)." He rightly observes, however, that would be strange to attack a philosopher such as Aristotle for not collecting proverbs. The former interpretation seems to me to be the right one.

In his important article "Roman Aristotle," Jonathan Barnes discusses the evidence about the editorial history of the works of Aristotle in Rome until the first century CE, in J. Barnes and M. Griffin, eds., *Philosophia togata* II (1997, pp. 1–69). He examines anew the evidence with a clear eye and makes many useful and witty remarks on each of them. He rightly thinks that Athenaeus's version of the story about the destiny of Aristotle's library is not compatible with the version of Strabo; but he prefers Strabo's account, notwithstanding the many impossibilities it contains, because he thinks that Strabo derives from Posidonius and that Posidonius wrote the truth. On the other hand, one could object that Strabo often shows a hostile attitude toward Peripatetics, as his well-known remark on Posidonius shows: **he is much too fond of imitating Aristotle's propensity for diving into causes, a subject which we** [Stoics] **scrupulously avoid, simply because of the extreme darkness in which all causes are enveloped** (*Geography* 2.3.8). As narrated by Strabo, the complicated history of the loss of Aristotle's works over many centuries is hardly neutral and has a clearly anti-Peripatetic flavor.

Barnes rightly contradicts the main point of Strabo's testimony, that copies of Aristotle's treatises were not available in the Hellenistic period before the time of Sulla. Barnes also thinks that Andronicus's work, as editor and as collector of Aristotle's *logoi* in larger units, was not so very important. His main contribution to Aristotelian scholarship was the *Pinakes,* a work in four volumes containing a *Life of Aristotle,* a catalog of the works, and a discussion about the authenticity of some of them. Barnes's conclusion is that "we have reason to believe, first, that some at least of Aristotle's major treatises were put together in something like their present form by Aristotle himself; secondly, that some of the treatises were known in something like the present form to Aristotle's immediate successors; and thirdly, that some of the treatises were available in some consolidated version in Cicero's time" (p. 65). According to him, Andronicus's work was only a single step in a complex history; in fact, the formation of the Aristotelian corpus has been a long process, and was the subject of a continuous discussion among Peripatetics, a discussion that lasted until the Renaissance and beyond.

A book with several contributors, *Demetrius of Phalerum: Text, Translation, and Discussion,* edited by W. W. Fortenbaugh and E. Schütrumpf (New Brunswick, N.J., and London, 2000), includes an interesting article by H. Gottschalk on the cultural and political activity of Demetrius. He thinks that, although Aristotle would have approved the measures taken by Demetrius when he was chief of the Athenian government, Demetrius never tried to apply Aristotle's political theory to the real world of political affairs in Athens. He tried only to achieve political stability and economic progress, and only the width and coherence of his political reforms show the influence of his philosophical training.

About the alleged "course on rhetoric" held by Aristotle in Plato's Academy (see above, pp. 26–29), the traditional interpretation has recently been defended by E. Berti, in "La polemica antiaristotelica di Filodemo a proposito della retorica," published in C. Natali and S. Maso, eds., *Antiaristotelismo* (Amsterdam, 1999, pp. 63–75), though he admits that the image of Aristotle present in Philodemus is much more similar to the mature encyclopedic scholar of later periods. Expressing the contrary opinion is a paper by D. L. Blank, who revises and discusses all the evidence and the wide bibliography connected to this episode, and presents a new edition and translation of the passage from Philodemus, in "Aristotle's 'Academic Course on Rhetoric' and the End of Philodemus' *On Rhetoric* VIII," *Cronache Ercolanesi* 37 (2007): 5–47. Blank concludes that the evidence preserved in Philodemus gives no support to the thesis that Aristotle gave a course of lectures on rhetoric in the Academy; he thinks that Philodemus's target was the *Protrepticus* and other lost popular works of Aristotle, not his teaching activities.

O. Primavesi has recently published an interesting article on the story of the fate of Aristotle's library, "Ein Blick in den Stollen von Skepsis: Vier Kapitel zur frühen Überlieferung des *Corpus aristotelicum*," *Philologus* 151 (2007): 51–77. He notes that the catalog of Aristotle's works in Diogenes Laertius distinguishes the different books by numbers (*Buchstabenziffern*), which is a practice inaugurated in Hellenistic time, whereas the treatises that constitute our corpus are numbered by letters (*Ordnungsbuchstaben*). The first way of numbering books is older than the second, and Primavesi deduces from this fact that there were two collections of Aristotle's books, one in Alexandria, whose catalog is in Diogenes Laertius, and the other in a nonprofessional library that still used the older numbering system. He also identifies this corpus with the books hidden in Skepsis by Neleus's relatives. Our corpus of Aristotle's works derives then from this second collection, which was brought to Rome by Sulla, according to Primavesi. The hypothesis is attractive, except for the idea that this second collection of books was hidden in Skepsis. As noted before, there are enough clues that some of the major Aristotelian works were known by Epicurus and by the first generation of Peripatetics. It is much more probable, in my opinion, if Primavesi is right, that this second collection of Aristotle's books never left Athens, but was neglected by later Peripatetics, to be recovered in the first century BCE by Apellicon, as we saw before.

In the first publication of this book, I quoted Wilamowitz 1893 for an optimistic description of Athens during the second stay of Aristotle (p. 56). Now this description should be superseded by Michael Scott's book, *From Democrats to Kings* (London, 2009; Italian translation, Roma-Bari, 2012), which gives a more nuanced image of the period and a very sympathetic analysis of the interventions of Isocrates. This book makes much more evident the growing influence of Macedonian kings in fourth-century Greece, and fills in details in the picture of the connections between Aristotle and Macedonian power.

Lastly, I would like to refer the reader to a couple of recent articles of mine, which could be useful for a comparison between Aristotle's school and other philosophical institutions in the ancient world: "Schools and Sites of Learning," in J. Brunschwig and G.E.R. Lloyd (eds.), *Greek Thought: A Guide to Classical Knowledge* (Cambridge, Mass., 2000), pp. 191–217; and "Philosophical Schools," in *Oxford Encyclopedia of Ancient Greece and Rome* (Oxford, 2010), pp. 250–255.

My final word is a warm thanks to Doug Hutchinson, who started and finished the project of translating my original book, and to his various friends and collaborators who helped him in the process of its development. Without his impetus, this book would never have been commissioned by Princeton University Press; and without his editorial and scholarly contributions in the final stages, it would never have seen the light of day.

CARLO NATALI
VENICE, JULY 2012

NOTES TO CHAPTER ONE
THE BIOGRAPHY OF ARISTOTLE:
FACTS, HYPOTHESES, CONJECTURES

Page 6, note 1. See Meritt, Wade-Gery, and McGregor 1939–1949, 1:412 and 2:122.

Page 6, note 2. On this story, see Wilamowitz 1881, pp. 194–197 (and the related texts, of which there is an Italian translation in Natali 1981, at pp. 32–34 and 150–152); see 1T9 Lasserre 1987 (and the related commentary on pp. 439–440) and section 4 of chapter 2, below.

Page 6, note 3. The ancient biographies say that Aristotle had Stagira rebuilt and gave laws to it after Philip destroyed it, and that the inhabitants awarded him worship similar to that of a hero cult (Diogenes Laertius 5.4; *Vita Marciana* 17–18; Mubashir 29–30; Usaibia 13 and 30; see *testimonia* 27a–k). Aristotle's *Letters* contain fragments linked to this episode (fr. 657 Rose 1886 = fr. 13 Plezia 1961 = p. 22 Plezia 1977).

Page 7, note 4. Diogenes Laertius 5.14. The Arabic versions of the will expand on the Greek version, mentioning the house "**of my ancestors.**" On this detail, see Zeller 1897 (1:25n2), Düring 1957 (p. 200), Plezia 1977 (p. 41), and Gigon 1987 (p. 38a).

Page 7, note 5. This account is repeated by Pliny, in *Natural History* 16.133. (This Pliny passage is not cited by Sollenberger in his 1985 study of the *Vita Theophrasti* in Diogenes Laertius 5.36–57.)

Page 8, note 6. In Book I of his *Aristotle*, Hermippus cited Aristotle's will in connection with Aristotle's second companion, Herpyllis, thus demonstrating that he had read this document, or was at least familiar with it in general terms. The comments of Hermippus are cited in Athenaeus 13, 589c (Hermippus fr. 26 Bollansée = fr. 46 Wehrli = Aristotle *testimonium* 12c; see Plezia 1977, p. 35).

Page 9, note 7. Diogenes Laertius 5.1, derived from Hermippus (fr. 32 Bollansée = fr. 44 Wehrli). In the *Suda* (*s.v.* "Nicomachus"), there is actually a suggestion that the works that Aristotle's father had written could be listed (six books on medicine and one on natural science). "**Nicomachus, a doctor, also from Stagira, son of the Asclepiad Machaon, from whom was descended Nicomachus the father of the philosopher Aristotle, also a doctor. He wrote six books of medicine and one of natural science**" (Aristotle *testimonium* 9b).

Page 9, note 8. This report is not quite as hostile as it seems at first, and some of the information appears accurate; see Sedley 1976, p. 127. Epicurus provides some important information about Aristotle's character and his philosophical importance; he was "**not without talent, and gradually got out of that and into the theoretical** [disposition]." According to Philodemus, *Against the Sophists* (fr. 1 Sbordone), Epicurus mentions Aristotle's *Analytics* and perhaps *Physics* as among the works that e[. . .]omen (fr. 127 Arrighetti). Usener reads this as "we have selected" (en[krin]omen), while Sbordone and Arrighetti's reading is "we prefer" (e[kleg]omen), Vogliano and Diano's is "we can find" (e[pheur]omen), and Crönert and Bignone's is "we have listed" (e[graph]omen). In any case, on the basis of any of these various supplementations and interpretations, this fragment demonstrates Epicurus's philosophical interest in Aristotle.

Page 11, note 9. Aristotle speaks of placing her statue in the temple of Demeter at Nemea or elsewhere; "**our mother's statue is to be placed in the temple of Demeter at Nemea or wherever seems more appropriate**" (Diogenes Laertius 5.16). According to the reading of the manuscripts, accepted only by Plezia and Mulvany, Aristotle wanted to place at Nemea or elsewhere a statue of his mother dressed as Demeter. Pliny states that the painter Protogenes made a portrait of Aristotle's mother (*Natural History* 35.106). In Aristotle's will, however, reference is made to a statue; therefore the two images cannot be identified.

Page 11, note 10. And not Macedonian, as reported by Epiphanius, a bishop of Cyprus in the fourth century CE, in his *Panarion* (excerpt 31 of Diels, *Doxographi Graeci*). "**Aristotle, son of Nicomachus, was said by some to be a Macedonian from Stagira, but according to some others his family was Thracian**" (Aristotle *testimonium* 9f). Some modern authors have believed the former story.

Page 11, note 11. Arimneste, a double of Arimnestus, has been added to the family in the Neoplatonic *Lives* (*Vita Marciana* 2, *Vita Latina* 2). Some scholars (Mulvany, Düring, Chroust) have given a bit of substance to this phantom figure and made her out to be the mother of Nicanor and the wife of Proxenus, to whom (Proxenus) Aristotle wished to dedicate a statue (Diogenes Laertius 5.15). Others do not believe that this Arimneste existed; see Gigon 1962 (p. 26) and Gottschalk 1972 (p. 322).

Page 11, note 12. According to the Neoplatonists, Proxenus came from Atarneus; but, according to Sextus Empiricus (*Against the Professors* 1.258), Nicanor was from Stagira, and therefore so was his father Proxenus.

Page 11, note 13. *Vita Marciana* 3; see *Vita Latina* 3, *Vita Vulgata* 2 = Plezia 1977, p. 36.

Page 12, note 14. "**Antipater is to be executor in all matters**" (Diogenes Laertius 5.11, 5.13). See below, p. 60.

Page 12, note 15. Note the proviso at Diogenes Laertius 5.12, "**until Nicanor shall arrive.**" In this period, according to Berve (1926, 2:276–277), Nicanor was with Alexander in Asia, and therefore the return here mentioned would have been the return from the expedition to Asia. This implies that Nicanor, after having read at Olympia the decree of Alexander, in 324, must have gone back to Asia, or else that Aristotle's will had been written before 324, and therefore long before the philosopher's death.

Page 12, note 16. However, others disagree with this identification, such as Mulvany 1926, Düring 1957 (p. 271), and Gottschalk 1972 (p. 322); some think it would be difficult for Aristotle to have had contact with Alexander following the death of Callisthenes. The reasoning seems fairly weak.

Page 13, note 17. See the report of Carystius of Pergamum from the third book of his *Memorabilia* (cited in Athenaeus 12, 542e) that "**his brother Himeraius had been killed by Antipater and he [Demetrius] spent his time with Nicanor, and was accused of celebrating the *epiphaneia* of his brother**" (Demetrius fr. 43a SOD). This passage is not collected in Düring 1957.

Page 13, note 18. Santoni 1988.

Page 13, note 19. According to Plutarch (*Life of Titus Flamininus* 12) and ps.-Plutarch (*The Ten Orators* 842b), it was, in fact, the democratic and anti-Macedonian orator Lycurgus, and not the pro-Macedonian Demetrius, who helped Xenocrates in this way. See Isnardi Parente 1981 (p. 144) and 1982.

Page 14, note 20. See the survey of opinions in Gottschalk 1972, p. 324; a contrary opinion is found in Düring 1957, pp. 62 and 239. This, according to some, raises the problem of Nicomachus, who would appear to be a male child, but not suited to be Aristotle's universal heir.

Page 15, note 21. A Pythia with three husbands, with the same professions as the husbands of the Pythia we are discussing here, is mentioned in a comedy by Phoenicides, of which fr. 4 is quoted by Stobaeus, in his *Anthology* 3.6.13. It is not known whether this is the same person.

Page 15, note 22. A Demaratus is mentioned in the will of Theophrastus (Diogenes Laertius 5.53). **"Let the [Peripatetic] community consist of Hipparchus, Neleus, Strato, Callinus, Demotimus, Demaratus, Callisthenes, Melanthes, Pancreon, and Nicippus."**

Page 15, note 23. In the will of Theophrastus (Diogenes Laertius 5.53), there is a particularly fond mention of **"Aristotle, son of Meidia and Pythia,"** expressing the wish that he be admitted into the Peripatetic community, once he is old enough, and if he wishes to study.

Page 15, note 24. As Cicero says at *De Finibus* 5.12 (Aristotle *testimonium* 76b).

Page 15, note 25. As Aristocles reports in his *On Philosophy* (fr. 2 Chiesara) about Nicomachus, **"it is said that Theophrastus brought him up when he was orphaned, and that he died in battle when he was still a young lad"** (excerpted in Eusebius, *Praeparatio Evangelica* 15.2.15 = Aristotle *testimonium* 58m).

Page 16, note 26. Excerpted in Eusebius, *Praeparatio Evangelica* 15.2.15 (Aristotle *testimonium* 58m).

Page 16, note 27. See Gauthier 1959 (introduction, p. 42), Taylor 1932, Düring 1957 (pp. 264 and 270), and Gottschalk 1972 (p. 327). For instance, Mulvany says that it would have been highly unseemly for Aristotle to lodge one of his former lovers in the home of his father (1926, p. 158). Nowadays we, like the ancient Greeks, would tend to view such matters in a more tolerant light.

Page 17, note 28. At *Protagoras* 315a, Plato mentions Antimoerus of Mende, who followed Protagoras in order to learn from him the *technē* and **"to become a sophist."**

Page 17, note 29. Some scholars have thought about the dynastic struggles that troubled the court of Macedonia at the time, but this would not have perturbed a citizen of the Greek *polis* of Stagira; unless, of course, his adoptive father, Proxenus of Atarneus, had taken him to live in Macedonia, as some say, including Berti 1962 (p. 133) and Chroust 1973 (pp. 135–136).

Page 18, note 30. See Berti 1962 (pp. 135–136) and Düring 1966 (pp. 9–10). Concerning the protreptic function of these dialogues, see also the anecdotes in Themistius (*Oration* 18, 356 = Aristotle, *Nerinthus*, fr. 1 Ross = *testimonium* 1 Laurenti). **"Axiothea, after having read something of the books which Plato had written on the *Republic*, left Arcadia behind and went to Athens, where she was a student of Plato's, hiding it**

a long time that she was a woman [. . .] The Corinthian farmer, when he became
conversant with the *Gorgias*—not Gorgias himself, but the book that Plato wrote
to refute the sophist—immediately abandoned his farm and his vines, mortgaged
his soul to Plato, and was seeded and planted by his views." In Neoplatonic times
an effort was made to render the story more interesting, and someone thought of a
Delphic oracle that supposedly showed Aristotle the way to the Academy (see section
1.3 of chapter 4). On these legends, see Gigon 1946.

Page 18, note 31. For example, the Megarian, Eleatic, and Eretrian schools were fixed in
a single place. Euclides taught at Megara, even though he did not establish a stable
school like the Academy. Eubulides and Alexinus also had their own personal schools.
Menedemus studied at Athens, Megara, and Elis, and taught in his own homeland of
Eretria. About Menedemus it is said that he did not organize his lessons well, that he
did not arrange the benches well, and that he did not have a precise schedule; according
to von Arnim, this criticism can be understood only if we start out from the perspective of a stable school.

Page 18, note 32. As the Neoplatonic *Lives* claim instead (*Vita Marciana* 5, *Vita Vulgata* 4,
and *Vita Latina* 5). They speak of a period of three years, in which Aristotle was supposedly a pupil of Socrates, but for chronological reasons this is impossible, since Socrates
died in 399 BCE, before Aristotle's birth. Other interpretations of the text, according
to which we should read "Isocrates" or "Socrates the Younger" instead of "Socrates,"
have not met with success; see Wilamowitz 1893 (1:320–325), Kapp 1924, Vollenhoven
1950 (1:482–486), and Chroust 1973 (pp. 97–101).

Page 19, note 33. These dates come from Apollodorus (*FGrHist* 244F38 = *testimonium*
1e) and Philochorus (*FGrHist* 328F223 = *testimonium* 1f), cited at the beginning of the
paragraph. Concerning the date of Aristotle's entry in the Academy, there has been
lengthy discussion; see, among others, Moraux 1955 (pp. 126+), Düring 1957 (pp. 249–
262), Berti 1962 (pp. 131–143), and Chroust 1965b. Certain hostile sources, such as the
Epicureans, attempted to prove that Aristotle had begun the pursuit of philosophy
late in life, and for this reason, according to Düring, right from the early period of the
Peripatos efforts were made to establish a precise chronology for this event. Neoplatonic biographies are very precise on this point.

Page 19, note 34. This is an interesting story that bears retelling. At *Vita Marciana* 11, the
narration based on Philochorus concludes that "it is therefore untrue what these
slanderers say, that Aristotle followed Plato at the age of forty, *epi Eudoxou*." This
expression is similar to ones found in preceding lines, such as *epi Philokleous*, which
make use of the names of the eponymous archons to indicate a certain Athenian
year. But there is no archon named Eudoxus in the lists of eponymous archons concerning the period when Aristotle entered the Academy, and Wilamowitz said that
he did not understand the expression *epi Eudoxou* (1893, 1:333–334). In later years,
many scholars (including Jacoby 1902 (p. 324), Düring 1957 (p. 160), Merlan 1960 (pp.
98–104), and Berti 1962, pp. 138–143) have thought that this expression meant that
Plato had left Eudoxus in charge of the school, and later the Neoplatonic biographers
had abbreviated and misunderstood the report, making Eudoxus an archon. Gigon
accepts this hypothesis as possible, along with two others: that our list of archons
is incomplete, or that Eudoxus is a mistake or a variant of a name that we know in

another form; often the ancients muddled the names of people, even in official documents, he claims, and he offers various instances (1962, *commentary* on lines 49–50). There are also chronological problems; the report is credible only if we place the *akmē* of Eudoxus around 369–367, as some scholars do, and not around 391–390, as do most ancient sources; see Lasserre 1966, pp. 137–138. [Postscript 2012: The solution to these puzzles was published in Waschkies 1977, pp. 34–58; he reasoned that the year to which Philochorus was pointing as *not* being the year that Aristotle entered the Academy was 345/344 BCE; then he scanned the list of eponymous Athenian archons, which is well established in the fourth century BCE (not incomplete or indeterminate), and found the archon name Euboulus. When this irresistible conjecture is made, the sentence resolves into a true and unproblematic report, that **"it is therefore untrue what these slanderers say, that Aristotle followed Plato at the age of forty, *epi Euboulou* [in 345/344 BCE]."** On the basis of an easily explicable scribal mistake scholars temporarily erected a scaffolding of fragile hypotheses about the imagined temporary leadership by Eudoxus of Plato's Academy. It is time for this scaffolding to be taken down.]

Page 19, note 35. See Diogenes Laertius 8.87 (Eudoxus *testimonium* 7 Lasserre 1966; see pp. 137–141). This seems excessive; there must have been relationships on the theoretical level between Eudoxus and the Academy, and the way in which the theories of Eudoxus are quoted by Aristotle in the *Metaphysics* (I.9, 991a17; XII(L).8, 1073b17+; XIII(M).5, 1079b21) and in the *Nicomachean Ethics* (I.12, 1101b28; X.2, 1172b9+) presupposes that he had been one of the participants in the Academic discussions, but it is not certain that those ideas were the content of the teaching of Eudoxus in his position as *prostatēs* of the Academy, as von Fritz 1927 claims.

Page 19, note 36. See Austin-Vidal Naquet 1972 (pp. 115–118), Whitehead 1975, and Mossé 1975.

Page 20, note 37. A recent attempt to find in the works of Aristotle reflections of his political condition appears in Romeyer-Dherbey 1986.

Page 20, note 38. At *Vita Marciana* 6 and 7 and in the *Vita Latina* 6, the following remarks are attributed to Plato: **"Let's go to the house of the reader,"** and **"The mind is absent, the audience is deaf,"** which were supposedly said when Aristotle preferred to stay home to read books. Aristotle is said to have been given the same nickname as Anaxagoras, *ho nous* (the mind). There is disagreement concerning the authenticity of these accounts; against authenticity is Maas (1958, 83n1), who doubts it, because the vocabulary is of the imperial age; in favor are Kranz (1958, pp. 81–83) and Friedländer (1960, p. 317), according to whom the vocabulary dates from the age of Plato or only slightly later. In the *Topics*, Aristotle makes various recommendations that suggest a particular focus on written sources of information, including to **"select from written sources [. . .] and also to make a note of the opinions in each of them, for example, that Empedocles said there are four elements in bodies, for one might write down the comment of some reputable person"** (I.14, 105b12–18 = Aristotle *testimonium* 56b). See chapter 3, section 1, p. 97.

Page 21, note 39. The same tone is found in a passage from *Politics* (II.6, 1265a10–12), in which Plato's dialogues are praised mostly for their ingenuity, originality, and productivity for research. **"All the *logoi* of Socrates** [the Platonic dialogues of which

Socrates was usually protagonist] **have the qualities of being striking, ingenious, innovative, and investigative; but that everything is right is perhaps hardly to be expected**." Concerning this passage, see Ross 1923 (p. 3), Düring 1957 (p. 366), and Chroust 1973 (p. 245).

Page 24, note 40. The personal observations of Aristotle continued for a long time; even in a late work like *Meteorology*, he claimed that he had personally observed (*hepheōrakamen*) that some fixed stars have a tail like a comet, and he says that this confirms the observations of the Babylonians and the Egyptians (I.6, 343b9–12). "**Some of the fixed stars too have a tail. For this reason we must not just listen to the Egyptians since they also affirm it, but we have ourselves observed it.**"

Page 25, note 41. This gives evidence against the well-known hypotheses of Jaeger (that Aristotle studied nature only during his second stay in Athens) and Thompson and Lee (that Aristotle studied nature only after his stay in Assos). See Jaeger 1923 (pp. 440–465), Thompson 1910 (p. vii), and Lee 1948.

Page 25, note 42. "**They were making distinctions about nature, giving separate definitions for the life of animals and the nature of trees and the kinds of vegetables. And while doing this they scrutinized what type** [of vegetable] **a squash was**" (Epicrates, unknown comic play, cited in Athenaeus 2, 59d–f = fr. 10 *PCG*).

Page 25, note 43. A plant that had only recently been imported into Greece and was therefore still relatively unknown; see Hehn 1902³, p. 271.

Page 25, note 44. Concerning Cephisodorus, see Gerth 1921; Blass 1868–1874 (2:419–421) and Düring 1957 (pp. 389–391). According to Düring (1957, p. 389), the text by Cephisodorus must date back to about 360 BCE, when Aristotle had already been in the Academy for years.

Page 26, note 45. Weighing against these positions is the extremely well-known polemic of Harold Cherniss: for "the German philologists of the last century, Plato was the first organizer of scientific research, and his Academy was a type of German university, with a regular program of lectures and seminars, where the best students were assigned portions of scientific fields to cultivate under the vigilant eye of the teacher" (1935, p. 72).

Page 27, note 46. The passage *dia tinas* [. . .] *aitias* refers to what goes before *eti* [. . .] *endeēs*; in this way, Philodemus takes up once again the traditional Epicurean accusations against Aristotle of having led a debauched and free-spending youth.

Page 28, note 47. For earlier and less developed editions of this important passage, see Aristotle *testimonium* 31 Düring 1957 = fr. 132 Gigon 1987, pp. 394a–398a. There are other translations, based on these earlier editions, in Düring 1957 (pp. 303–310), Natali 1981 (pp. 160–163), and Laurenti 1987 (pp. 420–423). This translation is based on the one published in Blank 2007, pp. 44–47.

Page 28, note 48. See also Quintilian 3.1.14 (Aristotle *testimonium* 32d), Strabo 14.1.48 (*testimonium* 32e), and Syrianus, *In Hermogenem commentaria*, 4.297–298 Walz = 2.95, 21 Rabe (*testimonium* 33).

Page 29, note 49. Philodemus, *Rhetoric* (col. 198: *P.Herc.*1015, 53.7–19); see Bignone 1936 (2:90+), Düring 1957 (pp. 299–311), and Laurenti 1987 (p. 423).

Page 29, note 50. If the witticism "it's a shame to be silent and allow X to speak" really was directed against Isocrates, then the episode certainly occurred during Aristotle's first stay in Athens; but that "X" is actually Isocrates seems questionable (see next note). The first observation was suggested to me by E. Berti.

Page 29, note 51. A change is noted by Diogenes Laertius (5.3) as well, but it is of a quite different nature. In this case, the "X" is Xenocrates, and the change consists not in teaching rhetoric but in abandoning the Sophistic and Platonic custom of giving lessons while walking; when he had a satisfactory number of disciples, Aristotle sat down (on a chair?) and said, "**it's a shame to be silent and let Xenocrates speak.**" It is difficult in all this to say where the truth is and where it is hidden.

Page 29, note 52. See Philodemus, *Rhetoric* VIII (above), Cicero, *On the Orator* (3.141), and Diogenes Laertius (5.3).

Page 29, note 53. Quintilian himself had evidently not read the dialogue he discusses (2.17.14 = fr. 2 Rose 1886, Ross 1955, Laurenti 1987). "**Aristotle, for the sake of discussion as usual, worked out arguments of characteristic subtlety in his *Gryllus*; but the same Aristotle also wrote three books on the art of rhetoric, in the first of which he not only admits that rhetoric is an art, but also assigns it to be a part of politics and dialectic.**" The ancient sources state that Isocrates also wrote an encomium to Gryllus (Diogenes Laertius 2.55), and on this foundation modern scholars have ventured to suppose that Aristotle wished to engage in a polemic with Isocrates. A work *For Gryllus* is, however, attributed to Speusippus (Diogenes Laertius 2.4); why should we not think that, when Aristotle says "**there are thousands who wrote encomiums and epitaphs for Gryllus, partly to win the favor of his father as well**" (Diogenes Laertius 2.55 = fr. 1 Ross), he might be alluding rather to Speusippus? Or to Isocrates and Speusippus together?

Page 31, note 54. "**Aristotle, in his *Sophist*, says that Empedocles was the first to invent rhetoric, and Zeno was the first to invent dialectic**" (Diogenes Laertius, 8.57 = fr. 1 Rose 1886, Ross 1955, Laurenti 1987).

Page 31, note 55. Some scholars read "since he was the son of Potone," *hat'ōn [Pot]ōn[ēs huios]*, of which the last two words are written *supra lineam*. Potone was Plato's sister, and many authors believe that these words indicate the reason why Speusippus received the school from Plato, that is, by hereditary right. This interlinear addition is absent from the text given as fragment 1 of Speusippus in Isnardi Parente 1980; see also Tarán 1981 (p. 203), who doubts that these words, largely the product of reconstruction, are truly part of the text, or in any case that the information provided by them is true. Buecheler instead reads it as *par'autou [Pl]atōn[os lab]ōn*, "he succeeded him as head of the school, taking it over from Plato." <Postscript 2012: Gaiser's more recent reconstruction is accepted in Dorandi's 1991 edition; the words written *supra lineam* are to be read as *[Pl]atōn[os no]sōn*, "he succeeded him, Plato, as head of the school, when he (sc. Speusippus) was sick." But none of this is solid enough to work with.>

Page 31, note 56. Philochorus (*FGrHist* 328F224) is named as his source for this account by Philodemus, in his *Index of Academic Philosophers*, col. 6.28–38 (p. 136 Dorandi = p. 37 Mekler = Aristotle *testimonium* 3). Isnardi Parente 1986 notes that here the term "museum" refers to the school and not to a sanctuary, and draws support from that fact to defend the hypothesis that Plato's Academy was organized in institutional terms as a *thiasos* of the Muses. For this discussion, see section 2 of chapter 2, pp. 78–80.

Page 31, note 57. See also Ross 1923 (p. 4) and Gauthier 1959 (p. 13). Jaeger claims that by this time only Aristotle's personal friendship with Plato kept him in the Academy; upon the death of the master, Aristotle felt free to advertise his own departure from Platonism, and went elsewhere to found a school of his own. According to Jaeger this was a full-fledged secession, that is, an explicit affirmation of a position of personal independence, which Aristotle had progressively won on a theoretical level. Jaeger also accepts the possibility of influence from the political events of the time, but he decisively subordinates those influences to the factors involved in Aristotle's philosophical evolution. Probably, Jaeger adds, neither Aristotle nor Xenocrates (who, according to Jaeger, accompanied Aristotle to Assos) found that Speusippus was a successor capable of keeping alive the spirit of Platonic philosophy.

Page 32, note 58. See Düring 1957 (pp. 276 and 388), Düring 1966 (p. 17), Düring 1968 (col. 177), Chroust 1973 (pp. 117–124 and 137), Chroust 1978 (pp. 338–341), and Grayeff 1974 (pp. 26–27). Berti wonders whether his staying away from Athens was not a product of the hostility of the Athenians toward Hermias of Atarneus, friend of Aristotle (1977, p. 28).

Page 33, note 59. See Wilamowitz 1893 (1:316), Brinkmann 1911 (p. 229), Gauthier 1959 (p. 11), Gigon 1962 (p. 31), Düring 1966 (p. 18), and Chroust 1973 (p. 119).

Page 33, note 60. Diogenes Laertius (4.3) says that Xenocrates was away from Athens toward the end of Speusippus's life, but does not say where he was, and for that matter the report is questionable, because it conflicts with what Philodemus of Gadara says in the *Index of Academic Philosophers*, cols. 6.41–8.17 = Speusippus *testimonium* 2 in Tarán 1981 = Xenocrates fr. 1 (Isnardi Parente 1980); see the comments on this in the two fragment collections.

Page 33, note 61. A brief description of the life of Hermias, hostile in approach, appears in Strabo 13.1.57. "**Hermias was a eunuch, the slave of some banker, and when he was in Athens he attended the lectures of Plato as well as Aristotle. When he went back to his city he was joint tyrant together with his master, having first attacked the districts around Assos and Atarneus, and then Hermias succeeded him and sent for both Aristotle and Xenocrates and took care of them; and he actually gave his brother's daughter in marriage to Aristotle. Memnon [= Mentor] of Rhodes, who was then serving the Persians as a general, made a pretence of friendship for Hermias and sent for him to come, out of hospitality and also for the sake of some pretended business; then he captured him and sent him to the king, where he was killed by hanging, and the philosophers escaped by fleeing the countryside, which was in the possession of the Persians.**"

Page 33, note 62. The passage, published by Diels-Schubart 1904, was republished by Pearson-Stephens 1978 (with bibliography). In this updated English version, I have used the text of the most recent edition, that of Phillip Harding (2006), which offers translation and commentary as well. Concerning the parts about Hermias, see especially Foucart 1909, Macher 1914, Wormell 1935, Düring 1957 (pp. 272–283), and the *Corpus dei Papiri filosofici e latini* 1989. Given the difficulty and unreliability of the text, I provide here only a tentative translation of it.

Page 34, note 63. This passage is extremely lacunose, and in the *Corpus dei Papiri filosofici greci e latini* 1989 (pp. 383–385), the efforts to provide a complete reconstruction of it have been abandoned. Here I have again followed the edition in Harding 2006. There have been other versions, generally more ambitiously reconstructed, not only the ones published by Pearson and Stephens and previous editors of the papyrus; see, for an example, Gaiser 1985, pp. 12–13.

Page 35, note 64. Didymus (6.18–20) states that the poem was written out of the *kēdeia* of Hermias toward Aristotle; this term may indicate "veneration," but it makes no sense to read it as "the veneration of Hermias toward Aristotle," and therefore the text is generally interpreted the other way around, as if what had been cited was "Aristotle's veneration toward Hermias," since the poem was written by the philosopher for the tyrant. On the other hand, the Greek term could also be understood as "connection through marriage" (see *Politics* II.3, 1262a11), and thus Didymus would be telling us that this poem attests to the family ties established between Aristotle and Hermias. I owe this suggestion to F. Decleva Caizzi.

Page 36, note 65. Concerning the tradition and the sources of these poems, see section 1.1C of chapter 4, pp. 121–122.

Page 37, note 66. Mulvany (1926) suggests there may have been confusion with a certain Hermotimus of Pedasa, without however having established any grounds. He refers the reader to Herodotus 8.104–106; in that passage the story is told of a certain Panionius of Chios, who earned a livelihood by castrating boys and then selling them into slavery, and who suffered the revenge of one of his victims, who was in fact named Hermotimus. This Hermotimus, having become powerful in the court of the Great King of Persia, subjected him and all his sons to the same treatment. The story seems entirely different from that of Hermias, the only point of similarity being that the bloodthirsty revenge of Hermotimus upon Panionius took place at Atarneus, where Panionius lived.

Page 37, note 67. Concerning these dates, see Körte 1905 (pp. 391–395), von der Mühl 1918 (cols. 1126–1130), Jaeger 1912 (p. 34), Jaeger 1923 (p. 153), Sordi 1959, and Bengtson 1962 (p. 299).

Page 37, note 68. Aristotle and his school, for that matter, were no strangers to the practice of fiercely defending individuals who were discredited but close to Plato or his school. Evidence for this is the use of Critias as an example in his *Rhetoric*; "**if you wish to praise Critias, you must narrate his deeds, for not many know them**" (III.16, 1416b28–29).

Page 37, note 69. Andrewes (1952) maintained that the moderate politician who is praised in *Politics* IV.11 (1296a38–40) is Hermias, but the matter is very doubtful; A. Wörle (1981, pp. 133–134) and Gaiser (1985, p. 23) are opposed to it.

Page 38, note 70. Hesychius (paragraph 2) somehow maintains both together: that Pythia was sired by Hermias, and that Hermias was a eunuch.

Page 38, note 71. According to Eubulides, however, Hermias was still alive when Aristotle married Pythia, and he claims that Aristotle made this marriage "**out of adulation**" (Aristotle *testimonium* 58f); see Gigon 1958, p. 174.

Page 39, note 72. In the nineteenth century many considered this letter to be spurious and accepted Strabo's report; see Boeckh 1853, Zeller 1897 (1:20n1), and Wilamowitz 1893 (1:334). Later it was claimed, however, that the information contained in the letter was authentic and that it was Strabo's report that was spurious; this was the position of various scholars, including von der Mühl 1918 (cols. 1126–1130), Brinkmann 1911 (pp. 226–230), Jaeger 1923 (pp. 146–147), Pasquali 1938 (pp. 233–237), and Bidez 1943 (p. 16). Following this, Stark 1954 and Düring 1957 (p. 279) attempted to find a compromise; perhaps Hermias had attended the Academy when Plato was absent, and therefore without ever having met him in person. But Düring abandoned this theory and called into question the authenticity of the *Sixth Letter* (1966, p. 18); still later, Düring said that the letter is not authentic, but that the information it contains is substantially accurate (1968, col. 177). In favor of the authenticity of the *Sixth Letter* or at least of the information it contains, the following are to be numbered: Gauthier 1959 (pp. 31–32), Weil 1960 (pp. 15–16), and Isnardi Parente 1979 (pp. 287 and 293). Against the authenticity of the *Sixth Letter*, and of the Platonic *Letters* in general, are Maddalena 1948 (pp. 394+), Edelstein 1966 (pp. 122–127), and Gaiser 1985 (p. 17).

Page 39, note 73. Hermippus is generally thought to be the author of the passage contained in Didymus Chalcenterus, *On Demosthenes* 5.51–63 = Aristotle *testimonium* 15d = Xenocrates fr. 18 in Isnardi Parente 1982 (and see p. 288) = Erastus and Coriscus, *testimonium* 10T7 in Lasserre 1987 (and see p. 541); see Pearson-Stephens 1978 (p. 17) and Harding 2006 (pp. 24–25 and 144).

Page 39, note 74. As is correctly maintained in Isnardi Parente (1979, pp. 293–294); the *hetairoi* are a typical institution of the Hellenistic tyrannies and monarchies (see Liddell-Scott 1843, *s.v. hetairoi*). Purely hypothetical as well is the theory put forth by Chroust 1972 and Grayeff 1974 (p. 28), according to which, after leaving Athens, Aristotle would have gone to Macedonia, whence he was sent as a political emissary to Hermias, in order to prepare for war against Persia; and he would have moved stealthily, as a secret agent, trying to ward off suspicion.

Page 40, note 75. It seems doubtful that Aristotle could have been the head of this school in the presence of Xenocrates, twelve years older than him, or, if Xenocrates did not accompany him, in the presence of Erastus and Coriscus, who had moved to Assos some time earlier, unless the other philosophers had found an incommensurable theoretical superiority in their younger friend. It is true, however, that according to Didymus, Hermias appreciated above all the teachings of Aristotle.

Page 40, note 76. Athenaeus 11, 508f–509a, which also cites the other speech that Demochares made against the philosophers in 306 BCE. A balanced judgment on the passage can be found in Isnardi Parente 1979, pp. 289+; see also A. Wörle 1981 and Lasserre 1987, pp. 439–440.

Page 41, note 77. Only Düring doubts its existence; he admits only that there may have been philosophical discussions (1966, p. 19). But a group of friends dedicated to regular discussion of theories such as those found in the *Metaphysics* of Aristotle would, in fact, constitute a "philosophical school." There is no need to imagine anything more highly organized, as does Jaeger 1923, p. 115.

Page 41, note 78. According to Mekler (in his commentary on this passage) this passage was derived from Dicaearchus; for the contrary opinion, see Wormell 1935 (p. 82) and Wehrli 1944 (1:50). Gaiser 1988 argued that Philochorus is the source, and the most recent editor of the text considers that Gaiser's suggestion has been proved by cogent considerations (Dorandi 1991, p. 88).

Page 41, note 79. The phase is *polin edoken oikein* "**allowed them to li**[ve in] **a city**." See Isnardi Parente (1979, p. 287), who believes that the reference here is to Erastus and

Coriscus; according to Mekler's commentary on this passage and Lasserre (1987, p. 541), the reference is instead to Aristotle and Xenocrates; but the text mentions no names, and the supplements of Mekler are not certain (see Düring 1957, p. 278). In the passage of Didymus, according to the Pearson-Stephens edition, it is said only that first Coriscus and Erastus went to Hermias, followed by Aristotle, then by others; according to the P. Harding edition, even less is legible. For Lasserre, *polin edoken oikein* should be translated rather as "gave them a city to administer," but this does not seem necessary; see also Thucydides 2.27.2 and Gaiser 1985, p. 16.

Page 41, note 80. *Index of Academic Philosophers* col. V.2–13 (p. 129, ed. Dorandi = pp. 22–23, ed. Mekler = Aristotle *testimonium* 16). [Postscript 2012: The order of columns of this papyrus is confusing, and different editors have placed columns Z–M, which had been written on the back of the roll, in different sequences relative to columns 1–36, which had been written on the front. The explanation is given in Dorandi 1991, pp. 109–115.]

Page 42, note 81. Gaiser maintains that in *On Fire* 46, when Theophrastus speaks of the stone known as *sarcophagus*, we should follow the text of the manuscripts: *ho de (en) kuklōi lithos*, and translate it as "the stone that is found in the surrounding area," and given that the stone known as *sarcophagus* was typical of Assos, he further claims that Theophrastus was actually at Assos when he wrote those lines. The other editors (Gercke, Coutant, Eichholz) instead correct it to *ho de Lukios* (or: *en Lukiai*) *lithos* since a stone with similar properties to the one described by Theophrastus is also found in Lycia. No ancient text mentions Theophrastus spending time in Assos. See also note 63.

Page 42, note 82. The hypothesis is accepted by Gauthier (1959, p. 34); others reject it, such as Lee (1948, p. 64) and Regenbogen (1940, col. 1358). Bignone argued that Epicurus found in Mytilene the remains of the school of Aristotle, a school in which special care was supposedly lavished on the teaching of rhetoric; and this can be deduced, according to Bignone, from the fact that over the centuries that followed, teachers of Aristotelian rhetoric and furious enemies of rhetoric both came from Mytilene; but these arguments are rather weak.

Page 43, note 83. Düring maintains that he undertook his monumental analysis of the entire biographical tradition about Aristotle with an investigation on the passages in which Plutarch speaks of Aristotle, in order to separate the wheat from the chaff; and he considers all this information to be very unreliable. Nonetheless, the fact that Aristotle was effectively the preceptor of Alexander is not denied by Düring (1957, pp. 5 and 468; 1966, p. 10; 1968, col. 179). Some later scholars, however, have actually called into question whether Aristotle ever really knew Alexander personally, e.g., Gigon 1962 (pp. 20 and 52–55), Chroust 1966, and Grayeff 1974 (p. 3).

Page 43, note 84. Such as for instance two historians of the fourth century BCE: Onesicritus (*FGrHist* 134F1+), a Cynic philosopher who attributed to Alexander the philosophy of Antisthenes, and Marsyas of Pella (*FGrHist* 135T1), a Macedonian nobleman. Plutarch himself, who is one of the chief sources for this event, and who recounts many reports on the relationship between Aristotle and Alexander, at a certain point (*Life of Alexander* 5) provides differing reports: the chief of Alexander's preceptors was Leonidas, a Macedonian nobleman, and, in second rank, was a certain Lysimachus of Acharnania. A rich collection of anecdotes on Alexander and Diogenes the Cynic is in Book 6 of Diogenes Laertius, at 32, 38, 44, 45, 60, 66, and 68. Concerning the scant worth of those anecdotes, see Giannantoni 1988 and 1990, 4:443–451.

Page 43, note 85. This Nicagoras was a tyrant of Zelea who liked to claim that he was the incarnation of the god Hermes; see *FGrHist* 143F4 and 268F2.

Page 44, note 86. That is Plutarch's opinion; among the moderns, it is defended only by Waddington 1893 and Radet 1931.

Page 44, note 87. This opinion is based on a report from Plutarch, according to which Aristotle made for Alexander an edition of the *Iliad*, known as "the Iliad of the Casket" because it was portable (*Life of Alexander* 8), a report adopted by Onesicritus (*FGrHist* 134F38) and by the Neoplatonic biographers (see *Vita Marciana* 4). This is the most common version among the moderns, and it is supported, among scholars of the life of Aristotle, by Wilamowitz, Moraux, Gauthier, Weil, and others, and, among scholars of Alexander the Great, by Berve 1926 (2:70–71), Kaerst 1927 (pp. 314+), Tarn 1948 (1:2 and 2:339–449), and many others. Doubts are voiced on this whole story by Wehrli 1957, 9:75–76.

Page 44, note 88. See Jaeger against its authenticity (1923, p. 311). In favor of authenticity are Mathieu and Brémond 1929 (4:177), Merlan 1954, Schachermeyer 1973 (pp. 82+), and Eucken 1983 (p. 10).

Page 45, note 89. As E. Berti has pointed out to me (personal communication).

Page 47, note 90. Of the same opinion was Isocrates (*Philip* 32 and 107), according to whom, however, the Macedonian royal family was of Greek, specifically Argive, descent.

Page 47, note 91. The legend is in Pliny (8.16.44), Aelian (14.19), and Athenaeus (9, 398e); see *testimonia* 26 a–c. Zeller had doubts about this information long ago (1897, 1:5n6); in contrast, Jaeger considered it credible (1923, p. 448).

Page 47, note 92. Bretzel claimed that Alexander had brought back to Theophrastus samples of plants for his botanical studies; but Regenbogen (1940, cols. 1462+) doubts this very much.

Page 48, note 93. There is discord concerning the dating of the text; some believe that it was written around 280 BCE (Walbank, Wehrli), but Santoni (1988), with Müller and Lorenz, proposes to move it back to circa 318 BCE, with good arguments; in fact, in 368 BCE, that is, "fifty years ago," no one could have foreseen the Macedonian success, which however was already evidently confirmed in 330 BCE. This then would be a text written in his youth.

Page 51, note 94. Sudhaus claims that Aristotle wished to provide opposition to Isocrates, who notoriously supported the unity of the Greeks against Persia under Macedonian leadership (1893, p. 559); see also Mathieu 1925, Hampl 1938 (p. 96), Zucher 1954 (pp. 226+), and Levi 1959 (pp. 117–118). However, these are fragile hypotheses built on an uncertain papyrus text; the most recent edition by Blank (2007, p. 46) reveals quite a different text, which he translates as follows: "and (third), because he virtually commended monarchy [to his students], although Philip and the Persian were then dominant" (col. 201: *P.Herc.* 1015, 56.15–20).

Page 51, note 95. Fragment 20 Isnardi Parente 1982; and see her commentary *ad loc.* The story seems favorable to Aristotle and hostile to Xenocrates. Perhaps it is an invention, but Philodemus, in his *Index of Academic Philosophers* (cols. 6.41–7.14) also speaks of a sojourn of Aristotle in Macedonia, at the time of Xenocrates' election as head of the school, that is, in 339/338 BCE (fr. 1, Isnardi Parente 1982).

Page 51, note 96. Weil has made a great deal of this fragment (1960, pp. 18+), claiming that it demonstrates that Aristotle returned to Athens before 335/334 BCE. But this report would run counter to the chronology of Apollodorus, according to which Aristotle remained away from Athens throughout the period of 348/347 to 335/334. See also Gigon 1958, p. 185.

Page 52, note 97. C. Bearzot has greatly helped me to clarify my ideas on this point, encouraging me to see the mountain of facts as a whole, which I had tended to consider separately.

Page 52, note 98. For the life of Callisthenes of Olynthus, see Jacoby 1901 and his commentary on *FGrHist* 124, Chroust 1973 (pp. 83–91), and Prandi 1985.

Page 52, note 99. According to Plutarch (*Alexander* 55.4), he was the son of Hero, a female cousin of Aristotle's.

Page 53, note 100. It is implicit in the episode narrated in Diogenes Laertius 5.39 that Theophrastus and Callisthenes had together been disciples of Aristotle; this account, however, has very questionable historic value (see Natali 1985). Other arguments in support of the hypothesis set forth here can be found in Prandi 1985, pp. 13+.

Page 53, note 101. According to Diels (1901, p. 75), Callisthenes collaborated with Aristotle also on the preparation of a catalog of the winners of the Olympic games, mentioned in the list of works by Aristotle, but of which there are no surviving fragments; Jacoby (commentary on 124F55) and Weil (1960, p. 133) question this hypothesis.

Page 53, note 102. Jacoby claims that in the library of the Peripatos there were also works by Callisthenes (1901, col. 1705); Weil finds that there are numerous similarities between the writings of Aristotle and those of Callisthenes (1960, p. 312).

Page 53, note 103. An inscription from Tauromenium, from the second century BCE, calls Callisthenes the *epistolographos* of Alexander, something similar to a "secretary"; see Prandi 1985, pp. 21–22. It is difficult to say whether the information is historically accurate.

Page 54, note 104. Anaxarchus of Abdera was a follower of Democritus, and we have very different pictures of him, depending on the source. The accounts of the death of Callisthenes present him as a perfect flatterer, while other sources emphasize his philosophical rationalism, his dignified way of life, and his heroism at the time of his death; see Diogenes Laertius 9.58–60, Diodorus Siculus 17.112.4–5, and Berve 1926, 2:33–35. The fragments and the *testimonia* are partially gathered in Diels-Kranz no. 72. The only fragment of his writing that survives (72B1) speaks of the damage that great learning can cause in those who possess it without a sense of opportunity. This seems a suitable comment on the story of Callisthenes.

Page 54, note 105. In the later biographical tradition, there remain various accounts of Aristotle's concerns over the character of Callisthenes; most probably these were invented on the basis of the disagreement we discuss here (see *testimonia* 28a–h).

Page 55, note 106. See Tarn 1948, 2:131. Often cited as proof of this are Theophrastus's work *Callisthenes* or *On Bereavement* (Diogenes Laertius 5.44), and the criticisms on the part of Dicaearchus (fr. 83 Mirhady = fr. 23 Wehrli) of Alexander's homosexuality, in his work *On the Sacrifice at Ilium* (cited in Athenaeus 13, 603a–b). But as I have noted above (see p. 54), we know very little about the text by Theophrastus, while Dicaearchus apparently felt no inhibition about stating positions contrary to those of Aristotle, and he may have been counted among a horde of enemies of Aristotle (on this issue, see note 22 to chapter 4). On the entire problem, see Badian 1958 and Bosworth 1970, pp. 407+.

Page 55, note 107. Alexander supposedly made gifts to Xenocrates and Anaximenes in order to enrage Aristotle (Diogenes Laertius 5.10–11; see also 4.18). This presupposes that Aristotle was an enemy of Xenocrates. But was he really?

Page 56, note 108. According to Gigon (1962, p. 64), Hermippus was the first to emphasize the definite contrast between the Academy and the Lyceum; this tradition later recurs in Diogenes Laertius (5.2), who clearly says that the school of Aristotle was founded as a contrast to the school of Xenocrates.

Page 58, note 109. As Zeller believed instead (1897, 1:39).

Page 59, note 110. As we shall see more clearly below, Drerup (1898) showed, by means of a comparison with similar decrees preserved in the inscriptions, that the Arabic text must have derived from a very ancient Greek source, capable of reproducing with great exactitude the forms of expression typical of the actual decrees of Athens, and all later scholars agree on this point. See also Chroust 1973a.

Page 59, note 111. The text of Usaibia, to tell the truth, uses the name "Antinoous," but this name is taken to be a corruption of "Antipater."

Page 59, note 112. This Himeraios seems to be identical with Himeraius, the brother of Demetrius of Phalerum; see above, note 17. This Himeraios, a democrat and anti-Macedonian, together with Hyperides and Aristonicus of Marathon, was killed by Antipater, after Antipater defeated the coalition led by the Athenians at the Battle of Crannon (322 BCE). According to Plutarch (*Life of Demosthenes* 28), a certain Archias, the so-called "Exile Hunter," who may have been either a stage actor or a pupil of rhetoric of Lacritus or Anaximenes, captured the three at the sanctuary of Aeacus in Aegina, where they were hiding, and sent them to Antipater, at Cleon, where they were put to death; see Lucian, *In Praise of Demosthenes* (58.38), Arrian, *Events after Alexander* (section 13 of fr. 9, cited in Photius, *Codex 92*), and the *Suda* (*s.v.* "Antipatros" = fr. 176 of Arrian, *Events after Alexander*). So it is historically true that Himeraius was killed by Antipater, and, although this may not have been due to the destruction of the inscription in Aristotle's favor, the story has a good source, well informed about the affairs of Athenian politics at the end of the fourth century BCE.

Page 60, note 113. The inscription is very fragmented, and the text has been partly reconstructed. In this place, various supplements have been proposed: by Witowski and Düring 1957 [t]ōn am[photera nen]ikēkotōn ta Puthia "of the winners of both the Pythian games"; by Pomtow and Gigon 1987 (p. 547a) tōn ap[o Gulida (?) nen]ikēkotōn ta Puthia "of those who, starting from Gulis, have won the Pythian games."

Page 60, note 114. Dittenberger 1915, no. 252, in the *commentaria*; but Pfeiffer disagrees (1973, p. 149). In the catalog of the works of Aristotle in the *Vita Hesychii*, it is said that in this work Aristotle "**defeated Menaechmus**" (no.123, p. 86 in Düring 1957), and therefore some think that there had been a public competition to win this research project, and that Aristotle came in first; see Moraux 1951 (p. 126) and Weil 1960 (pp. 133+). Others, instead, are skeptical about this hypothesis; see Gigon 1987, *ad loc.*

Page 60, note 115. See Wilamowitz 1898; later authors have many anecdotes to relate concerning the friendship between Aristotle and Antipater. We have fragments of letters from the philosopher to the general (frs. 663–666 Rose 1886 = frs. 8–12 Plezia 1961 = Plezia 1977, pp. 18–21) and, as we have seen, Plutarch actually says that, according to a certain Agnotemis, Aristotle conspired with Antipater to poison Alexander (*Life of Alexander* 77.2).

Page 60, note 116. The accounts of ancient authors concerning the later years of Aristotle's life are collected in Düring 1957, pp. 241–348 = *testimonia* 46a–48d; see also Gigon 1958 (pp. 177–181), Gigon 1962 (pp. 34 and 75–76), and Chroust 1973 (pp. 145–154 and 176–179).

Page 61, note 117. Some do not mention this event at all, or, rather, any observations they may have made on it have not reached us; for instance, Demochares does not mention it, in the parts that survive of his oration against all philosophers (mentioned on pp. 91–92). And Lyco, a contemporary of Aristotle, claims that Aristotle left Athens for Chalcis, with baggage and slaves, and therefore without concealment; see Diogenes Laertius 5.16 and Aristocles, *On Philosophy* (fr. 2 Chiesara), cited in Eusebius, *Praeparatio Evangelica* 15.2.8–9 (= *testimonia* 58i, and see 64c). A certain Eumelus, on the other hand, claimed that Aristotle drank hemlock, as Socrates did, and Diogenes Laertius adopts this invention in the epigram he dedicates to Aristotle (5.6 and 5.8); see Düring 1957 (p. 345) and Chroust 1973 (pp. 176–177). The story of Eumelus was also accepted by Hesychius and by the *Suda* (*s.v.* "Aristoteles"); see Düring 1957, pp. 82 and 345. Aristotle, on the other hand, would never have accepted dying like Socrates, as we shall see below.

Page 61, note 118. Concerning the latter, see Diogenes Laertius 2.101 = Demetrius of Phalerum fr. 48 SOD = fr. 43 Wehrli.

Page 61, note 119. That Aristotle was put on trial for his philosophy is a very late opinion; see Origen (*Against Celsus* 1.380 = Aristotle *testimonium* 45c), and Usaibia 10, tr. Düring.

Page 61, note 120. Athenaeus cites as his source (15, 696f) the first book of Hermippus's *Aristotle* (fr. 30 Bollansée = fr. 48 Wehrli).

Page 62, note 121. He was a member of the family of the Eumolpides, according to Kirchner (*Prosopographia Attica* no. 5872).

Page 62, note 122. Derenne rejects the hypothesis, put forth by Grote and Grant, that this Demophilus was the disciple of Isocrates of the same name; Davies believes that the Demophilus in question was also one of the accusers of Phocion in 348 BCE, was a member of the council, and was himself a priest (*hieropios*) of Eleusis (1971, p. 498); two of his decrees survive. This Demophilus was a politician who was always hostile to Macedonia, and was later killed by Phocion's son; see Plutarch, *Life of Phocion* 38.2, 759b.

Page 63, note 123. Düring does not believe in the existence of a school in Chalcis and therefore rejects these accounts of the ancient authors (1957, pp. 345–346), whereas Wehrli accepts the historical validity of the succession story (1955, 8:78).

Page 63, note 124. There are other examples of decrees that have first been voted on and then withdrawn, such as the one for Euphorion of Sicyon (C.I.A. IV.2, 231b).

Page 63, note 125. *Vita Marciana* 42, *Vita Vulgata* 20, *Vita Latina* 44, Usaibia 7 (tr. Düring), Diogenes Laertius 5.9, Aelian, *Varia Historia* 3.36 (*testimonium* 44a), Elias, *Commentary on Aristotle's "Categories"* (ed. Busse) 123.15+ (*testimonium* 44c), Eustathius, *Commentary on the Odyssey* VII.120 (*testimonia* 44d). For opposing views on the authenticity of this, see Düring 1957 (p. 114) and Plezia 1961 (pp. 113–116), who collects the evidence as fragment 11.

Page 63, note 126. *Vita Latina* 43, *Vita Vulgata* 19, *Vita Marciana* 41, Elias, *Commentary on Aristotle's "Categories"* 123.15+ (Aristotle *testimonium* 44c), Seneca, *On Leisure* 8.1 (*testimonium* 44e), Origen, *Against Celsus* 1.380 (*testimonium* 45c). This story is accepted not only by Düring (1957, p. 342) but also by Plezia (1961, pp. 113–116), who collects the evidence as fragment 11.

Page 64, note 127. Diogenes Laertius 5.10 (= Apollodorus *FGrHist* 244F38), Diogenes Laertius 5.16, Censorinus, *De die natali* 14 (*testimonium* 50c), Aelian, *Varia Historia* 9.23 (*testimonium* 67b), Aulus Gellius 13.5 (*testimonium* 47), Valerius Maximus 5.6, ext. 5 (*testimonium* 27b). We have already seen that Eumelus claims that Aristotle drank hemlock, and the *Vita Syriaca* II (7) and the Arabic biography of Mubashir (22–23) report that Aristotle died while studying the natural phenomenon of the tidal race in the Gulf of Euripus; concerning this issue, see Gigon 1962, pp. 76–77.

Page 64, note 128. See Diogenes Laertius 6.102, and *Suda s.v. phaios*; on this see Giannantoni 1990, 4:581–582.

Page 64, note 129. Isocrates insists on informing us, in fact, at *Panathenaicus* 7, that he is sufficiently well off to live comfortably even without the money of his pupils.

Page 64, note 130. Plato recalls with a certain aristocratic scorn the naïve boasting of Hippias on his public successes in the Greek cities (*Hippias Major* 282d–e). And even Isocrates, in *Antidosis* 93–94 and 224, says that a great many disciples come to him, from as far afield as Sicily and the Black Sea, and that many citizens (decorated with official honors of the *polis*) had been his students, such as Eunomus, Lysitheides, Callippus, Onetor, Anticles, Philonides, Philomelus, Charmantides, who were crowned with gold, as well as orators, historians, tragic poets, and men of state, such as the celebrated Timotheus son of Conon. In Aristotle, we find nothing of the sort and, although he had relations with Alexander and with the kings of Macedonia, in his works he never mentions this.

Page 65, note 131. The cost of the education offered by Aristippus is not mentioned by Xenophon at *Memoirs* 1.2.60; according to Plutarch (*On the Education of Children* 4f), it cost 1,000 drachmas; according to Diogenes Laertius (2.72), 500 drachmas; according to Alexis in his comedy *Galateia* (cited in Athenaeus 12, 544e), his course cost 1 talent (these reports are collected as Aristippus frs. 4.A.3, 5, 7, and 9 Giannantoni; see also Giannantoni 1990, 4:143–145). According to von Arnim (1898, pp. 25+), Protagoras asked 100 minai for his lessons, and Isocrates asked 1,000 drachmas for a course of three to four years; Isocrates himself, in his *Against the Sophists*, says there were those who asked only 3–4 minai for an introduction to *sophia* in general. Perhaps the reference is to Antisthenes.

Page 65, note 132. Aeschines 1.30 and 1.42; more ample documentation is available in Natali 1988a, pp. 24–29 and 211–212.

Page 66, note 133. Let us recall the witticism, mentioned above (p. 63), that Aristotle is supposed to have made upon leaving Athens at the time of his trial for impiety: "**I will not let the Athenians sin a second time against philosophy.**"

Page 66, note 134. Plato's landholdings are listed in his will, as found in Diogenes Laertius 3.41–43. In Aristotle's will, reported in Diogenes Laertius 5.12–16, it is not stated with precision how much Aristotle's estate amounted to, but the bequests are clearly those of a very well-to-do person: to Herpyllis he leaves a silver talent and three female slaves, as well as the one male and one female slave she already has; when Aristotle's daughter is married, the female slave Ambracis is to be given not only her freedom but also 500 drachmas and one female slave whom "she now has"; to a certain Thale is left 1,000 drachmas and a maidservant as well as the maidservant "whom she already has, the one who was purchased"; to a certain Simon is given a servant, or the money to buy one, as well as the money already paid to him for "another servant." Arrangements are made to free four slaves upon the marriage of Aristotle's daughter, and mention is made, in general terms, of "other slaves," aside from the twelve already mentioned (considering Thale and Simo to be slaves). Mention is also made of a house in Chalcis with a garden, and Aristotle's father's house in Stagira. The wealth of the Peripatetics became, after all, proverbial.

Page 67, note 135. Consider Aristotle's appreciation of Eudoxus, whose **"arguments (*logoi*) were convincing because of his virtuous character rather than by themselves, for he was thought to be exceptionally self-controlled"** (*Nicomachean Ethics* X.2, 1172b15–16); the arguments concerning pleasure offered by this philosopher were of little value, but he persuaded others through the moral force of his personality. This, for Aristotle, was certainly not sufficient.

Page 68, note 136. Rose linked this fragment to fr. 1 (Ross) of the dialogue *On Pleasure*, in which Athenaeus (1, 6d) cites Aristotle's deprecation of certain time-wasters who spend their time at the harbor, among sailors who come from distant lands, jugglers and such like, and **"have not read anything but the *Banquet* by Philoxenus, and not even all of it."** But nothing suggests that this polemic against the emptiness of certain ordinary people has anything to do with the judgment of Aristotle concerning the Athenian people, and, as Laurenti rightly says, "it would be wise to refrain from making worthless conjectures" (1987, p. 855).

Page 68, note 137. A very clear illustration of this point is found in the Aristotelian dialogue *On Noble Birth*, (fr. 3 Laurenti 1987 = fr. 4 Ross = fr. 94 Rose 1886).

Page 69, note 138. There is a polemical silence on this point on the part of Xenophon, who mentions, out of the whole family, only Plato's brother Glaucon, describing him as an ambitious and incompetent individual (*Memoirs of Socrates* 3.6).

Page 70, note 139. See also Laurenti 1987, p. 768.

Page 71, note 140. Concerning these differences, see also section 2 of chapter 3.

Page 71, note 141. Vegetti 1979 (pp. 84–96 and 142–147) and Cambiano 1983 (pp. 15–19). The contributions of Vegetti and Cambiano are of decisive importance, inasmuch as they allow us to go beyond the level of pure encomiastic description of a personality (as in Düring 1954, Düring 1957 (pp. 349–352 and 366–372), Plezia 1961b, and Weil 1965), and to see the problem in proper terms, viz. terms that see the invention of a new type of intellectual in this phase of Greek cultural history. But in my view their interpretation of Aristotle has some limits in the somewhat negative judgment offered of the model of intellectual that Aristotle embodied, a model of intellectual that is partly interpreted as a type of mutilated personality.

NOTES TO CHAPTER TWO
INSTITUTIONAL ASPECTS OF THE
SCHOOL OF ARISTOTLE

Page 72, note 1. On this topic, see Gauthier 1959 (2:848–866), Düring 1966 (pp. 529–534), Hardie 1968 (p. 349), and Eriksen 1976 (pp. 81–92).

Page 72, note 2. See *Nicomachean Ethics* I.8 1098b26 and 1099a32; and see Dirlmeier 1962 (p. 498), Monan 1968 (pp. 126+), and von Fragstein 1974 (pp. 380–381).

Page 72, note 3. See Dirlmeier 1962 (p. 501) and von Fragstein 1974 (p. 389). Concerning the right middle with respect to wealth, a measure is also advisable in order to have a well-organized city; see *Politics* IV.11.

Page 73, note 4. In other words, what needs to be determined has to do with the *meson pros hēmas* (*Nicomachean Ethics* II.2, 1109a30–32); the bibliography on this subject is quite vast and of widely varying worth; for my position on the subject, see Natali 1988 and 1989.

Page 73, note 5. See Eriksen 1976, p. 100.

Page 73, note 6. The work to which I refer is Tracy 1969, pp. 277–283, and, in general, all of ch. 4. The Aristotelian sage reveals the same quality of being well ordered (*kosmios*) as the philosopher in Plato's *Republic*; see VI 500c9.

Page 74, note 7. See Herodotus 1.30–32.

Page 74, note 8. See Adkins 1960 (pp. 414+ and 486+), Solmsen 1964, Dover 1974 (pp. 233–234), Adkins 1978, and Humphreys 1978 (pp. 562–563).

Page 75, note 9. See *Metaphysics* XII.7, 1072b14–26, 1073a11.

Page 75, note 10. *Metaphysics* I.1, 981b23–25.

Page 75, note 11. *Sophistical Refutations* 18, 177a 7–8; compare 7, 169a 36–b 2. Concerning this theme in general, see Mikkola 1958.

Page 75, note 12. See *Politics* VII.2, 1324a15–17 and 28; *Eudemian Ethics* I.4, 1215b6–14 and 1216a11–14.

Page 75, note 13. See Adkins 1978, p. 305.

Page 76, note 14. See Eriksen 1976, p. 104.

Page 76, note 15. See Gauthier 1959, *ad loc.*

Page 76, note 16. 1178b25; see Dirlmeier 1956, p. 358.

Page 77, note 17. See Dirlmeier 1956 (p. 561), with Isocrates, *Areopagiticus* 45 and *Panathenaicus* 27.

Page 77, note 18. *Nicomachean Ethics* VIII.1, 1155a26–28, also IX.1, 1164a8+, specifically 29–30; see also Dirlmeier 1956, p. 590.

Page 77, note 19. Eriksen 1976, pp. 81–89; for more in general, see Gomperz 1906 (4:441), Adkins 1960 (p. 488), and Hutchinson and Johnson, forthcoming.

Page 77, note 20. As is claimed in Gauthier 1959, 2:860–866. For a broader discussion of the problem, see Natali 1989, ch. 6.

Page 77, note 21. Isocrates expresses a widely held opinion when he criticizes the Platonic conception of the good life; see Isocrates *Antidosis* 285, and also the comment of Demochares in his speech *Against Philo* that Socrates was made of poor material, incapable of being fashioned into a general (Athenaeus 5, 215c and 187d = Demochares (LXII) fr. 3 Sauppe).

Page 78, note 22. See Wilamowitz 1881, pp. 181+ and 263+. Wilamowitz took into consideration all four of the major philosophical schools; here I shall consider only the school of Aristotle. For the school of Plato, the matter is different and more complex; see Boyancé 1937, Cherniss 1945, and Isnardi Parente 1980 and 1986.

Page 78, note 23. Wilamowitz relied upon Foucart 1863 and the university lectures of Bernays later published in Bernays 1881 (Wilamowitz 1881, pp. 182 and 263). The idea underlying the entire reconstruction had, however, already been put forth by Lumbroso 1873, p. 268. It was then taken up again by Dareste 1882 and 1906, 3:117–134; in 1887 Diels attempted, unsuccessfully, to extend Wilamowitz's reconstruction to the groups that had gathered around the more prominent Presocratic philosophers. Usener 1884, on the other hand, was a very successful contribution; see Usener 1907, pp. 69–102, where his article was republished. For the subsequent discussion, see Isnardi Parente 1974 and Lynch 1972, p. 109.

Page 79, note 24. Boyancé focuses especially on the organization of Plato's school and devotes a large portion to it in his work (1937, pp. 249–297), properly basing his interpretation also on the fact that in the philosophy of Plato there are themes that might lead to a "heroification" of the figure of the philosopher. Less persuasive is his position concerning the school of Aristotle (treated far more briefly than the Academy, on pp. 310–322); for the reasons set forth in the preceding paragraph, it is difficult to find in Peripatetic ethics a theoretical basis for the exaltation of the figure of the philosopher similar to what could have been given to Plato. As for the Lyceum, Boyancé basically offers two arguments: the mention of a *mouseion* in the will of Theophrastus, and the title of *epimelētēs tōn Mousōn* that is said to have been attributed to the third scholarch, Lyco, by Antigonus of Carystus (in Athenaeus 12, 547f). We shall discuss these two points in sections 3 and 4 of this chapter.

Page 79, note 25. See Haskins 1957, p. 33.

Page 79, note 26. See Gottschalk 1972, pp. 320 and 329.

Page 79, note 27. See Lynch 1972, pp. 105–134.

Page 80, note 28. Concerning this matter, see also Poland 1909, pp. 206–207; there were sanctuaries of the Muses also in an Athenian school for preparation for the *ephēbia* of young men, as well as in the foundation of Epiketas of Thera.

Page 80, note 29. The same view was expressed previously in Laum 1914.

Page 80, note 30. By Philochorus (*FGrHist* 328F224) it is said that Speusippus **"was then in control of the *Museion*"** (cited in Philodemus, *Index of Academic Philosophers*, col. 6.28+ = Aristotle *testimonium* 3). Isnardi Parente notes that here the term *Museion* refers to the school and not to a sanctuary (1988, p. 112), and she uses this to argue in favor of Wilamowitz's hypothesis. This contrasts, however, with the idea that the school had become a *thiasos* only during the time of Xenocrates; moreover, according to Liddell-Scott 1940[9], the term *mouseion* at that time had already taken on the more general meaning of "home of music or poetry." See also Aristotle, *Rhetoric* III.3, 1406a25.

Page 81, note 31. Lynch 1972, p. 100; the opposing view is held by Wehrli 1976, p. 132.

Page 83, note 32. The matter was cleared up in the best way by von Arnim (1898, pp. 64–65): educating the young people who are interested in a bit of philosophy before devoting themselves to practical life is the purpose of the Academy and of the Peripatos only by chance, even though, in their own opinion, Aristotle and Plato were capable of performing this task better than anyone else. According to von Arnim (1898, pp. 84–85), the interest in the education of young people would have been prevalent in these two schools only much later, with Lyco, when the school was devoting much of its focus to rhetoric.

Page 83, note 33. We are referring to Ziebarth 1902 (cols. 39–42), Ziebarth 1909, Laum 1914 (the broadest study on the question), Bruck 1926, which examines the question of the "foundations in perpetuity" from the point of view of the development in Greek culture of the concept of "juristic person" (a concept that Laum, in contrast, believes is extraneous to that culture), and to Ziebarth 1940 (cols. 1236–1240), which contributed various corrections and added interesting considerations to the picture already sketched out by Laum. On the cult of the dead, linked to these questions, see also Nilsson 1960, 2:107–113; concerning several important inscriptions and the title of "perpetual gymnasiarch," which we shall discuss below, see Robert 1960 and 1967. For a more recent general overview, see Veyne 1976 (pp. 241–244), in the section *L'evergetisme funéraire*. For our discussion, obviously the main sources are the wills of the Peripatetic scholarchs preserved by Diogenes Laertius (5.11–16, 51–57, 61–64, and 69–74), on which there exists a vast bibliography, including Bruns 1880, Hug 1887, and Chroust 1967, republished in Chroust 1973, pp. 183–220.

Page 84, note 34. Laum 1914, 1:221–222.

Page 85, note 35. See Robert 1960 and 1967.

Page 85, note 36. See *Life of Lyco* in Diogenes Laertius 5.71, and Laum 1914, 1:88–89. This is a custom typical of Asia Minor, more than of Greece; apparently, in fact, Lyco, who makes a bequest of this sort, is a native of the Troad.

Page 85, note 37. See Laum 1914 (1:41–42) and Ziebarth 1909 (pp. 2–9).

Page 85, note 38. These institutions have been studied in particular by Ziebarth (1909, pp. 65–66, 81, 91–94, 100).

Page 85, note 39. Concerning the relationship between these foundations and family ties, see Laum 1914 (1:41–43), Bruck 1926 (pp. 175–266), Nilsson 1960 (2:109–111), and Veyne 1976 (p. 244).

Page 85, note 40. See, for example, Wycherley 1978 (p. 227) and Gottschalk 1972 (p. 335). The presence of such a *peripatos* was an exceedingly common matter, and was not a typical characteristic of the school of Aristotle; see Poland 1909, p. 469, and section 4 of chapter 3.

Page 86, note 41. This confirms the point I made previously, concerning the relationships, sometimes personal, that were established between the master, his family, and the pupils.

Page 86, note 42. What Gottschalk observes is not sufficient to negate the distinction between the two bequests (1976, p. 71); he notes that in the section of his will transmitted by Diogenes Laertius (5.54), Theophrastus says that a certain Pompylus, who lives in the garden, should take care that Theophrastus's dispositions are implemented regarding the temple, the monument, the garden, and the promenade (*peripatos*). The fact that a single person should implement more than one disposition does not mean that the dispositions are not different from one another, and do not concern distinct objects.

Page 87, note 43. A descendant of the great Praxiteles; see Davies 1971, *ad loc.*

Page 87, note 44. According to Wehrli, as mentioned above, the expression *hōs hieron* rules it out that the property that is discussed here is identical to the *hieron* about which Theophrastus spoke above.

Page 87, note 45. See Laum 1914, 1:139, 141, and 143; for the opposing view, see Bruck 1926, pp. 256+.

Page 87, note 46. The term used is *suscholazein*, which does not seem to me to be able to indicate, in the strict sense, the act of studying together (Gigante) or studying literature (Hicks), but only the act of being together (Apelt). Concerning this question, there was a discussion among Gigante, Cambiano (1977), and Capasso (1980), a student of Gigante writing in defense of his translation.

Page 87, note 47. The term *symphilosophein* reappears later in the will of Epicurus (Diogenes Laertius 10.16) in the following sense: Epicurus bequeaths his garden to the Athenians Amynomachus and Timocrates with the provision that they make it available to Hermarchus of Mytilene and to all those who wished to engage in philosophy along with him, as well as those whom Hermarchus should designate as his successors. Epicurus establishes a preeminence of Hermarchus over the others, which makes him the scholarch, the "head" of the school, and entrusts him with the selection of his successors (*diadochoi*). Moreover, an express provision of the bequest is to follow the doctrines of Epicurus; the garden is bequeathed "to those who follow our philosophical ideas" (*apo hemōn philosophountes*). These characteristics suggest a stronger dogmatism of the Epicurean school, as well as a more rigid structure, compared with the more liberal Peripatetic school.

Page 88, note 48. This can be compared with similar cases described in Veyne 1976, pp. 233+.

Page 88, note 49. See Biscardi 1955, pp. 105–143.

Page 89, note 50. See Bruck 1926, p. 266.

Page 89, note 51. Against von Arnim (1928, pp. 101–107), who thought instead that with this act Theophrastus had implicitly decided to name Neleus scholarch of the Peripatetic school. Gottschalk disagrees (1972, p. 336); and, in fact, both in the will of Theophrastus and in the will of Strato (Diogenes Laertius 5.62) we can clearly see that the library and the school are the subjects of two different bequests, clearly distinguished in the text: *kataleipō . . . tēn diatribēn . . . kataleipō . . . ta biblia.*

Page 89, note 52. See Wilamowitz (1881, p. 265) and Bruck (1926, p. 258).

Page 90, note 53. The first opinion is held by Usener (1884, p. 76), the second by Nilsson (1960, 2:109).

Page 90, note 54. See Laum 1914 (1:88–89), Biscardi 1955 (pp. 108–110), and Veyne 1976 (pp. 243–244).

Page 90, note 55. See Bruns 1880, pp. 36–41.

Page 90, note 56. Diogenes Laertius (5.37) recalls also an accusation of impiety that was supposedly brought by the democrat Agnonides against Theophrastus, a charge from which Theophrastus is said to have easily defended himself. Not much is known about this; see Derenne 1930 (pp. 198+) and Boyancé 1937 (pp. 310+).

Page 91, note 57. Nephew, in fact.

Page 92, note 58. Plato greatly insists on the valor of Socrates, which must have been the subject of whisperings and gossip among the Athenians, in his *Apology* 29e, *Charmides* 153b, and *Symposium* 220e.

Page 92, note 59. Athenaeus 5, 215c–216a (see also 187d) = fr. 3 Baiter-Sauppe = *testimonium* 1.C.39 Giannantoni 1990, in which the issue of the prowess of Socrates is discussed at length.

Page 92, note 60. According to the hypothesis of Meineke and Edmonds, the words in the passage by Alexis must have been spoken by an old man, angry with the philosophers who had corrupted his son by making him disobedient.

Page 92, note 61. The array of opinions is collected in Gottschalk 1972, pp. 30–33. A variability in the procedures for the election of the chief is not entirely strange; jurists have compared this characteristic to what took place in the monasteries of the sixth and tenth centuries CE, where the head of the monastic community could be named by the preceding abbot, or else elected by a vote; see Steinweter 1931, pp. 405–407.

Page 93, note 62. For the opinion that the schools closed in the first century BCE, see Lynch 1972, pp. 154+ and 192–207; for a reconsideration of this opinion, see Natali 1996 (English translation 2000, pp. 206–207 = English translation 2003, pp. 55–56).

Page 94, note 63. *tōn Mousōn epimelētēn genesthai*, according to the text of Wilamowitz 1881, pp. 194+. The expression does not refer to Lyco in person, as Lynch and Isnardi Parente maintain, but rather to the holder of the monthly liturgy described here, as Wilamowitz and Gottschalk understand it.

Page 95, note 64. We do not find a precise distinction between *presbuteroi* and *neaniskoi* (this latter term is used by Wilamowitz, but it does not appear in the texts), even in the part of the will of Theophrastus in which he establishes the foundation dedicated to the philosophers (Diogenes Laertius 5.52–53); in that passage it says only that the grandson of Aristotle (his namesake) can be part of the community, and that the older members should take affectionate care of him. In my view, this is a provision for that individual, and not the establishment of two fixed categories of disciples, distinguished by their levels of advancement in knowledge.

NOTES TO CHAPTER THREE
INTERNAL ORGANIZATION
OF THE SCHOOL OF ARISTOTLE

Page 100, note 1. This passage seems to entail a silent reading, like that which we do today, while it is often said that the ancients always read aloud.

Page 101, note 2. Aristophanes was already making fun of him for his bibliophilia; see *Frogs* 943.

Page 101, note 3. See the will of Theophrastus (Diogenes Laertius 5.52), concerning which see section 3 of chapter 2. The Peripatetics took great care of the fate of their libraries; Strato left his library to Lyco (Diogenes Laertius 5.62), and Lyco left his own published works to his slave Chares and his unpublished works to the philosopher Callinus, "**for an accurate edition**" (Diogenes Laertius 5.73).

Page 101, note 4. Concerning Demetrius of Phalerum and the Library of Alexandria, see frs. 38–40 SOD (= frs. 63–65 Wehrli). [Postscript 2012: That the Alexandrian Library possessed the manuscripts of Aristotle is attested also by a quotation from Al-Farabi's *On the Appearance of Philosophy*, cited by Usaibia. "**The Roman Emperor Augustus defeated her** [Cleopatra], **put her to death, and took over the rule. When he had secured it, he inspected the libraries and the (dates of) production of books, and found there manuscripts of Aristotle's works, written in his lifetime and in that of Theophrastus**" (= Theophrastus fr. 41 FHSG).]

Page 102, note 5. For the problem of the relationship between Aristotle and the Stoics, there is an extensive discussion in Sandbach 1985; on the diffusion of Aristotle's biological works in the Hellenistic age, see Düring 1950, which claims that the citations of Aristotle's biological works in Athenaeus reflect the state of these works in the Hellenistic age, before the edition of Andronicus of Rhodes.

Page 105, note 6. For a balanced evaluation of the discussion, and a detached judgment of Plato's value as a scientist, see Lloyd 1968 and Lloyd 1970, pp. 65–78.

Page 106, note 7. On this point, there is the classic essay by G.E.L. Owen (1961, reprinted in 1986, pp. 83–103; see also Berti 1966 (pp. 61–88), Berti 1972 (pp. 109–133), and Nussbaum 1986 (pp. 240–258, with additional bibliography).

Page 107, note 8. Its manuscripts ascribe *Weather Signs* to Aristotle, but no modern scholar accepts this attribution, and questions have arisen about its status; in its present form, it cannot be attributed to Theophrastus, but its content is Theophrastean (see book title no. 17 (p. 282) and fr. 194 FHSG, and see Regenbogen 1940, cols. 1412–1413). The latest view on the issue holds it to be an abridgment of the *Weather Signs* that Theophrastus is known to have written (which is lost in its original complete version), a shorter version that preserves the data but strips the work of its discussions of the underlying causes (Sider and Brunschön 2007, pp. 40–43).

Page 108, note 9. See Krämer 1968, Lanza and Vegetti 1971 (pp. 88+ and 102+), and P. Pellegrin 1982. The most recent scholars, on the basis of the criticisms directed against

Aristotelian classification by nineteenth-century biologists, such as G. Pouchet (1884–1885), have underlined that this work is not a simple repository of information but that the use of such Platonic dialectical techniques, such as the *diairesis*, makes the text a full-fledged scientific study, in which the facts are already steeped in theorization, an integral part of the research on causes. Some present a contrast between this study and the biological works that followed; for example, "the *Research on Animals* is perfectly autonomous and its scientific structure by itself does not require any completion" (Lanza and Vegetti 1971, p. 86). But others consider this work in a line of continuity with the works *Parts of Animals* and *Generation of Animals*, such as Pellegrin (1982, p. 172), who sees "a division of labor between the three great biological treatises." I shall not venture into this debate, even if it seems to me that Aristotle's explicit statements give greater support to Pellegrin (see, for instance, *Parts of Animals* II.1, 646a8). My position is the following: the *historiai* of Aristotle and Theophrastus are the writings that bring us closest to the phase of the collection of data and the research activity of the Peripatos. In my opinion, it is useless to think that these facts were grouped in an even simpler manner, for instance, in some type of index, and then were organized in a more theoretical manner, according to the form of *diairesis*, and were then studied, in an even more theoretical manner, in the writings devoted to the research on causes. It is simpler to imagine that the facts, taken from personal observation, from the accounts of experts and reliable persons, and from the reading of Homer and the poets, were inserted directly into these *historiai*, with a view to a subsequent reworking.

Page 108, note 10. Concerning the similarity of composition of the two works, see Wörle 1985, pp. 3+.

Page 108, note 11. Putting into practice Aristotle's advice in *Politics* I.11, 1259a3–5 that **"we must collect (*sullegein*) the scattered things said about how some people were fortunate at making money."**

Page 108, note 12. A typical example of this interpretation is Oncken 1870, pp. 4–12; for Oncken, Aristotle was the son of an Asclepian physician, and as such he must have learned anatomy and the scientific method from his family, and he was the first to apply the scientific method to the entire body of Greek knowledge. He was the father of the inductive method and of empirical observation, and, for that reason, he had neither masters nor pupils. His position therefore would be opposed to the pure contemplation of ideas practiced in the Academy.

Page 111, note 13. Concerning the interpretation of the letter, see Gigante 1962 (pp. 515–516) and Sollenberger 1985 (pp. 12 and 45–46). [Postscript 2012: According to the Greek text printed in the recent Teubner edition, Theophrastus is speaking about *tou deiktēriou*, a rare word (transmitted by some but not all manuscripts) meaning "the proof stage" or perhaps "the showroom." Other editions of Diogenes Laertius, such as the Loeb and the OCT, print the other reading presented by the manuscripts *dikastēriou* or "jury room," without however even reporting in the apparatus the alternative transmitted reading *deiktēriou*. Also worth considering perhaps is a conjectural emendation such as Apelt's suggestion *didaktēriou* or "teaching room."]

Page 112, note 14. Concerning the interpretation of *Parts of Animals* I.5, see Kullmann 1974, pp. 79–85.

Page 113, note 15. On the range of senses that Aristotle gives to the term *diagōgē*, see Bonitz 1870, *s.v.*; the passages cited focus on the value of intellectual pastimes.

NOTES TO CHAPTER FOUR
STUDIES OF ARISTOTLE'S BIOGRAPHY
FROM ZELLER TO THE PRESENT DAY

Page 120, note 1. A comparable case is that of the relations between Isocrates and Nicocles of Cyprus. Scholars of Isocrates such as Mathieu and Brémond claim that Nicocles came to Athens and was a disciple of Isocrates (1942a, 2:92), a claim taken up again by Eucken (1983, p. 212); from his works it is clear that Isocrates received lavish gifts from Nicocles (*Antidosis* 40). In the case of Themison and Aristotle, however, we have no report comparable to this.

Page 121, note 2. Düring (1957) offers a comparison of the various texts in English translation.

Page 121, note 3. Plezia (1961) reports the Greek version, with the principal variants of the Arab texts translated into Latin, in the critical apparatus.

Page 121, note 4. Chroust gives a complete translation of both texts, arranging them in parallel columns (1973, pp. 185–189).

Page 121, note 5. The *testimonia* basically amount to the sum of the passages that in the ancient biographies of Aristotle introduce the text of the will, plus Athenaeus 13, 589c (Hermippus fr. 26 Bollansée = fr. 46 Wehrli).

Page 121, note 6. Diels-Schubart edition 1904; Pearson-Stephens edition 1983; latest edition P. Harding 2006.

Page 121, note 7. Plezia 1977 also publishes the related *testimonia* on pp. 1–3.

Page 121, note 8. Diehl-Beutler edition, 1925 and 1949[3].

Page 123, note 9. He states that the picture of Aristotle that we can draw from the letters has little to do with the picture of Aristotle that we can draw from the authentic fragments and the surviving treatises; he claims, furthermore, that it is only beginning with Epicurus that we are certainly dealing with an authentic private correspondence, whose preservation can be explained both on the basis of the importance that friendship has in Epicurus's system, and by the fact that Epicurus entrusted to his friends the publication of the correspondence.

Page 125, note 10. There is an Italian translation in Natali 1981, pp. 69–96, of a relevant part of Wehrli 1959, his *Ruckblick: Der Peripatos in Vorchristlicher Zeit*.

Page 126, note 11. In this way, Wehrli takes up the traditional opinion represented by many scholars; see, e.g., Gercke 1896, Moraux 1951 (p. 244, with bibliography), Moraux 1955, Düring 1956 (p. 13), Düring 1957 (pp. 346 and 464), and Gigon 1958 (p. 149, no. 5 with some doubts). The hypothesis, however, has been subjected to criticism in Plezia 1951a (p. 272), Plezia 1961a (pp. 246–247), Gauthier 1959 (introduction, p. 6), and Düring 1968 (col. 163).

Page 126, note 12. Hermippus quotes Aristotle's will, which he may have taken from the collection of documents on the Peripatetic scholarchs assembled by Ariston; see Aristotle *testimonium* 12c.

Page 126, note 13. Some think instead that in his love for anecdotes Hermippus also gathered reports and inventions that were hostile to Aristotle; see Foucart 1909 and Wormell 1935.

Page 126, note 14. Plezia 1951a seems willing to lend Hermippus a certain credence, and makes him the main source for Diogenes Laertius, Didymus, and Athenaeus.

Page 126, note 15. Even if it is true, as some say, that Diogenes Laertius relies more on Ariston than on Hermippus, in either case these are sources from the late Peripatos, as is rightly observed in Berti 1962, pp. 125–126. [Postscript 2012: For Hermippus, see also Plezia 1951a, Düring 1957 (pp. 57–61, 263, 269, 278–279, 313, 346, 352, 406, and 464–467), and Chroust 1964. The fragments of Hermippus are now collected in Bollansée 1999, with ample commentary.]

Page 130, note 16. The concluding chapter of this can be found, in a partial Italian translation, in Natali 1981, pp. 97–105.

Page 130, note 17. About Aristocles of Messene, see Heiland 1925, Moraux 1967, and Moraux 1984, pp. 399–401. The authors cited, eight in total (Epicurus, Timaeus of Tauromenium, Aristoxenus, Alexinus, Eubulides, Cephisodorus, Lyco, Theocritus of Chios), are all contemporaries of Aristotle, except for Epicurus, who was only slightly later. There is an Italian translation in Natali 1981, pp. 157–160.

Page 130, note 18. In Eusebius, *Praeparatio Evangelica* 15.2.9.

Page 131, note 19. See Radermacher 1951, pp. 197–199. Apparently the work comprised four books (Athenaeus 2, 60d = fr. 3 Radermacher), in which Cephisodorus engaged in a polemic against Aristotle, attacking the Platonic doctrine of ideas, according to Numenius (excerpted in Eusebius, *Praeparatio Evangelica* 14.6.9 = fr. 2). The passage was used extensively by Jaeger (1923, pp. 37–38) and by all those who had theorized an initial adherence on Aristotle's part to the Platonic doctrine of ideas; see the review in Berti 1962, pp. 184+. But this may be a generic polemic against the Academics, since it is unlikely that an orator would make subtle distinctions between philosophical theories and positions that from the outside might well appear quite similar. For that matter, even for the comedians the doctrine of ideas is that part of Plato's philosophy that was easiest to ridicule. Cephisodorus also admitted that Isocrates had written judicial speeches, which the master denied, but, added Cephisodorus, he wrote only a few (fr. 4 = Dionysius of Halicarnassus, *Isocrates* 18). Lastly, he repeated the usual personal accusations: lover of pleasure, glutton, and things of that sort (fr. 5 = Aristocles, *On Philosophy* (fr. 2 Chiesara), excerpted in Eusebius, *Praeparatio Evangelica* 15.2.7).

Page 131, note 20. This testimony about the *Life of Plato* by Aristoxenus (fr. 64 Wehrli) comes from Aristocles, *On Philosophy* (fr. 2 Chiesara), excerpted in Eusebius, *Praeparatio Evangelica* 15.2.3 (= Aristotle *testimonium* 58d). To judge from the evidence preserved in *Vita Marciana* 9, Philochorus interprets the testimony about the book of Aristoxenus precisely in the way that Aristocles of Messene says that it should not be interpreted. "**Aristotle did not erect the Lyceum to oppose Plato, as Aristoxenus was the first to accuse him of doing**" (*FGrHist* 328F223–224, Aristoxenus fr. 66 Wehrli). In his *Against the Four* (249.10), Aelius Aristides says that during the third trip to Sicily some disciples of Plato rebelled, but he names no names, while a scholion *ad loc.* applies the report to Aristotle (*testimonium* 61a). In the *Suda* (*s.v.* "Aristoxenus" = fr. 1 Wehrli), Aristoxenus is called "**a student of his father and of Lamprus of Eretria, then of Xenophilus the Pythagorean, and lastly of Aristotle; he insulted him on** his deathbed, because he left Theophrastus as successor in the school, who had greater fame than he did among the students of Aristotle" (*testimonium* 61b Düring; see Wehrli 1945, 3:48). The story is very doubtful, because it presupposes the existence of a fully organized philosophical school at the time of Aristotle's death.

Page 131, note 21. Döring claims to be able to date the book of Eubulides to between 340 and 335 BCE (1972, pp. 102–104), that is, after the presumed date of Aristotle's marriage to Pythia (which is certain) and prior to the date of Philip's death (but this is more questionable).

Page 131, note 22. The most important passage is from Aristocles, *On Philosophy* (fr. 2 Chiesara), excerpted in Eusebius, *Praeparatio Evangelica* 15.2.5. "And Eubulides too, in his book against him [Aristotle], is clearly lying, first because he proffers as though they were by Aristotle some frigid poems written by others, concerning his marriage and the familiarity he had developed with Hermias, next by saying that he offended Philip, and that he didn't visit Plato when he was dying, and he destroyed his books." The mention of the poems to Hermias is not slander, but is historically correct. As for the other fragments, including Athenaeus 8 (354b–c), see section 3 of chapter 1. Diogenes Laertius 2.109 recalls only the controversy between Aristotle and Eubulides. Finally, in *Oration* 23 (285a–c), Themistius cites the "whole horde" of those who wrote against Aristotle, "the Cephisidoruses, the Eubulideses, the Timaeuses, the Dicaearchuses," whose writings have come down to his time, "displaying their animosity and their competitiveness" (= Aristotle *testimonium* 63e). [Postscript 2012: The presence of the name of Dicaearchus in this list has occasioned surprise; Luzac proposed emending the text so as to refer to Demochares, a known enemy of Aristotle; Düring accepted the emendation (1957, p. 388), as did P. Huby (2001, 312n2), the effect of which is to remove this report from the Dicaearchus evidence base, where it has been collected as fr. 6 Mirhady = fr. 26 Wehrli.]

Page 132, note 23. See also *testimonia* 64a–c in Düring 1957, and pp. 65 and 391. [Postscript 2012: What was alleged is the discovery of a ridiculous quantity of *lopadia*, a cooking utensil corresponding to the modern Italian *pentolino* or saucepan; the *lopadion* is distinct from the larger *chutra* or stockpot and the wider *tēganon* or frying pan. To have one's *batterie de cuisine* not earthenware but bronze is a sign of considerable wealth (Aristophanes, *Wealth* 812).]

Page 132, note 24. There are Italian translations in Natali 1981 (pp. 160–162) and in Laurenti 1987 (pp. 420–423).

Page 133, note 25. An attempt in the opposite direction in Cardona 1966 has not met with success.

Page 133, note 26. Chronology according to Düring 1957 (pp. 235–236 and 467) and Düring 1968 (col. 164), while Plezia 1961 thinks that this Artemon was a contemporary of Theophrastus, and therefore places great value on the fragments of the surviving letters of Aristotle that are presumed to have come from this collection.

Page 134, note 27. It is quoted, for instance, by Jaeger 1923 (p. 11), who opens his account with this letter, by Moraux 1951 (p. 134), and by Plezia 1961 (pp. 100–101). They believe that Aristotle meant to argue with Theopompus and Isocrates, and to show his credentials as a philosopher to Philip, in order to earn the position of tutor, much as a modern professor might present his own curriculum in an application for a permanent position in a university or in a research institute.

Page 134, note 28. About this, see Heiland 1925 and Moraux 1967.

Page 135, note 29. He translates or describes the biographies of Johannes Valensis, of Walter Burleigh, of an anonymous master of Cornelius Agrippa, and of Leonardo Bruni, Giambattista Guarini, J. J. Beurer, P. J. Nuñez, and A. Schottus. See also the observations of Mansion 1958.

Page 135, note 30. See De Cesare 1956, with bibliography.

Page 136, note 31. See the summary in Philips 1970.

Page 138, note 32. There is an Italian translation of the relevant parts of Wilamowitz 1881 in Natali 1981, pp. 29–46.

Page 138, note 33. Published by H. Diels and W. Schubart (Berlin 1904, *editio minor* Leipzig 1904). See Foucart 1909. For the most recent edition, see Dorandi 1991.

Page 138, note 34. Case referred to this idea in Case 1910 and defended its primacy in Case 1925, against the dismissive judgment of Taylor 1924.

Page 138, note 35. This title has been recently reprinted; see Kafka 1922.

Page 138, note 36. See the reviews of Berti 1962 (pp. 9–122), and of Lanza and Vegetti 1971.

Page 139, note 37. This theme is even more heavily emphasized in Jaeger 1938, pp. 220–236; the philosophy of Aristotle is said to have greatly encouraged the development of medical studies.

Page 140, note 38. Such as wondering whether Aristotle was Greek or half barbarian, or whether the fact that he was the son of a physician had decisively influenced his thinking; see Gomperz 1906, 4:81+.

Page 140, note 39. Bignone's only original idea with respect to Jaeger, an idea for that matter already present in Wilamowitz 1893 (p. 334), was that Aristotle had supposedly already opened a philosophical school in Mytilene prior to his second stay in Athens. This hypothesis is not now very widely accepted among scholars.

Page 140, note 40. Bidez has some peculiar ideas; apparently he applies to Alexander the *Führerprinzip*, and sees the Alexander educated by Aristotle as a commander who, when "facing the menace of chaotic revolutionary politics," imposed his will on Greece, establishing "a new world order" in place of the old political institutions (see pp. 20–21). The desire to be up-to-date sometimes leads to very risky claims.

Page 140, note 41. Now all assembled in Merlan 1976 (pp. 127–143, 144–152, and 167–188).

Page 141, note 42. Considered spurious by Jaeger 1938, p. 280.

Page 143, note 43. Justified criticism of Maddoli by Isnardi Parente 1974, p. 874.

Page 143, note 44. Aside from the ones already mentioned, I make note of Chroust 1971, 1972, 1972a, and various chapters in Chroust 1973.

INDEX OF SOURCES

Page numbers given are for pages in this book. Bold numbers indicate that the occurrence is a citation.

[1972, ed. O. Stählin, with L. Früchtel and U. Treu, *Clemens Alexandrinus*, 4 vols., Berlin]

Demetrius of Phalerum (c.350–c.280 BCE)

On Fortune, fragment (fr.82a SOD = fr.81 Wehrli) cited in **Polybius**, *Histories* 29.21.3–6, and in **Diodorus** of Sicily, *Library of History* 31.10.1–2 – **48**

Other works: fragment (fr.33a SOD = fr.58b Wehrli), citing Sosicrates, *Successions*, cited in **Athenaeus** 10, 422c–d – 14; fragment (fr.48 SOD = fr.43 Wehrli), cited in **Diogenes Laertius** 2.101 – 13, 167n118; fragment (fr.49 SOD = fr.44 Wehrli), citing Myronianus, *Historical Parallels*, cited in **Diogenes Laertius** 4.14 – 13; fragment (fr.104 SOD = fr.96 Wehrli), cited in **Plutarch**, *Life of Aristides* 27.3–5 – 14; fragment (missing in SOD), cited in **Diogenes Laertius** 5.39 – 13

[2000, ed. SOD = "Demetrius of Phalerum: The Sources, Text, and Translation," ed. P. Stork, J. M. von Ophuijsen, and T. Dorandi, in *Demetrius of Phalerum: Text, Translation, and Discussion*, ed. W. W. Fortenbaugh and W. Schütrumpf (New Jersey and London); see also *Demetrius von Phaleron* = vol. 4 of *Die Schule des Aristoteles*, ed. F. Wehrli, Basel 1949]

[Demetrius]

Elocution: 28, mentioning **Aristotle**, *On Justice* – **68**; 29 and 154, citing a letter of **Aristotle** to an unknown addressee – **51**, 165n96

[1902, W. Rhys Roberts, Cambridge]

Demochares of Athens (c.355–c.275 BCE)

Against Philo: fragment (fr.3 Sauppe) cited in **Athenaeus** 5, 187d and 215c – **92**, 171n21, 174n59; fragment cited in **Aristocles**, *On Philosophy* (cited in **Eusebius**, *P. E.*, 15.2.6) – **92**; comment against Theophrastus, cited in **Aelian**, *Miscellaneous Research* 8.12 – 62

[1850, *Fragmenta Oratorum Atticorum* (LXII = Demochares), ed. H. Sauppe, in vol. 2 of *Oratores Attici*, ed. G. Baiter and H. Sauppe, Zurich]

Demosthenes of Athens (384–322 BCE)

Third Philippic 26 – 6

Fourth Philippic 32 – **33**, **52**

[2002, ed. M. R. Dilts, OCT]

Dicaearchus of Messana (c.350–285 BCE)

On the Sacrifice at Ilium, cited in **Athenaeus** 13, 603a–b – 165n106

Tripolitikos: book title (fr.11B Mirhady) mentioned in **Cicero**, *Letters to Atticus* 13.32.2 – 23; a view (fr.33 Mirhady = Theophrastus fr.481 FHSG), reported in **Cicero**, *Letters to Atticus* 2.16.3 – 23

Unknown work: fragment (fr.6 Mirhady = fr.26 Wehrli) – 179n22; fragment (fr.43 Mirhady = fr.29 Wehrli) cited in **Plutarch**, *Should Old Men Be Politicians?* 26, 796d – **117**, 131; fragment (fr.83 Mirhady = fr.23 Wehrli) – 165n106

[2001, ed. D. Mirhady, in *Dicaearchus of Messana*, ed. W. Fortenbaugh and E. Schütrumpf, New Brunswick (NJ); see also *Dikaiarchos* = vol. 2 of *Die Schule des Aristoteles*, ed. F. Wehrli, Basel 1944]

Didymus of Alexandria (Didymus "Chalcenterus") (1st c. BCE–1st c. CE)

On Demosthenes (in columns 4–6 of P.Berol.9780): 4.59–65 – **33–34**; 4.66–5.21 (citing **Theopompus**) – 34; 5.19–21 – 36; 5.24–63 (citing **Theopompus**) – **34**; 5.51–63 – 162n73; 5.66–6.18 (citing **Callisthenes**, *Encomium to Hermias* – **34–35**; 6.22–36 (citing **Aristotle's** hymn to Hermias) – **35**, 121; 6.39–43 (citing **Aristotle's** inscription to Hermias) – **36**, 121; 6.44–49 (citing **Bryon**) – 36; 6.50–59 (referring to **Hermippus**, *Aristotle*) – 36

[2006, ed. P. Harding, Oxford]

L. **Dio Cassius** (Cassius Dio "Cocceianus") (c.150–235 CE)

Roman History 77.7 – **55**

BIBLIOGRAPHICAL INDEX

Abbrevations

R.-E. = *Real-Encyclopädie der classischen Altertumswissenschaft*, eds. A. F. Pauly and G. Wissowa

n. s. = new series

Adkins, A.W.H., *Merit and Responsibility: A Study in Greek Values*, Oxford 1960 – 170n8

Adkins, A.W.H., "*Theoria* versus *Praxis* in the *Nicomachean Ethics* and the *Politics*," *Classical Philology* 73 (1978), 297–313 – 170nn8, 13, and 19

Alfonsi, L., "Su una vita di Aristotele scritta da Lascaris," *Giornale di Metafisica* 4 (1949), 381–383 – 129

Allan, D. J., *The Philosophy of Aristotle*, London 1952, 2nd (revised) ed, 1970 – 144

Andrewes, P., "Aristotle, *Politics* IV.11, 1296a 38–40," *Classical Review*, n. s. 2 (1952), 141–144 – 161n69

Aouad, M. *See* Goulet, R., with B. Puech and M. Aouad

Arnim, H. von, *Leben und Werke des Dion von Prusa*, Berlin 1898 – 18, 26, 65, 156n31, 168n31, 172n32

Arnim, H. von, "Neleus von Skepsis," *Hermes* 62 (1928), 101–107 – 173n51

Austin, M., and P. Vidal-Naquet, *Économies et societies en Grèce ancienne*, Paris 1972, English translation *Economic and Social History of Ancient Greece: An Introduction*, Berkeley 1977, Italian translation *Economia e società nella Grecia antica*, Turin 1982 – 157n36

Badian, E., "The Eunuch Bagoas: A Study on Method," *Classical Quarterly* n. s. 8 (1958), 144–157 – 166n106

Barker, E., "The Life of Aristotle and the Composition and the Structure of the *Politics*," *Classical Review* 45 (1931), 162–172; reprinted in *Schriften zu den "Politika" des Aristoteles*, ed. P. Steinmetz, Berlin and New York 1973 – 140

Barnes, J., *The Presocratic Philosophers*, 2 vols., London 1979; 2nd ed., London 1982 – 1

Barnes, J., "Roman Aristotle," in *Philosophia Togata* II, ed. J. Barnes and M. Griffin, Oxford 1997, 1–69 – 148–149

Baumstark, A., *Syrisch-arabisch Biographien des Aristoteles*, Leipzig 1898, 3rd ed. Aalen 1975 – 59, 129, 130, 136

Bearzot, C., "Platone; e i 'moderati' ateniesi," *Memorie dell'Istituto Lombardo: Classe di Lettere; Scienze morali e storiche* 37:1 (1981) – 154n97

Bélis, A., *Aristoxène de Tarente et Aristote: "Le Traité d'Harmonique*," Paris 1986 – 131

Bénatouïl, T., "Théophraste: Les limites éthiques, psychologiques, et cosmologiques de la contemplation," in *"Theoria," "Praxis," and the Contemplative Life after Plato and Aristotle*, eds. T. Bénatouïl and M. Bonazzi, Leiden and Boston 2012 – xix

Bengtson, H., *Die Staatsverträge des Altertums*, Munich and Berlin 1962 – 161n67

Bergk, T., *Griechische Literaturgeshcichte*, vol. 4, Berlin 1887 – 50

Bernays, J., *Phokion und seine neueren Beurteilers*, Berlin 1881 – 57–58, 136, 137, 139, 142, 143, 171n23

Berti, E., *La filosofia del primo Aristotele*, Padua 1962, 2nd ed. Milan 1997 – 144, 155n29, 155n30, 155n33, 155n34, 178nn15 and 19, 180n36

Berti, E., "Il principio di non-contraddizione come criterio supremo di significanza nella metafisica aristotelica," first published in *Accademia dei lincei: Rendiconti della classe di Scienze Morali, Storiche e Filologiche*, series 8, vol. 21 (1966), 224–252; reprinted in E. Berti, *Studi aristotelici*, L'Aquila 1975, 61–88 – 175n7

Berti, E., "La dialettica in Aristotele," first published in *L'attualità della problematica aristotelica: Atti del convegno franco-italiano su Aristotele*, Padua 1972, 33–80; reprinted in E. Berti, *Studi aristotelici*, L'Aquila 1975, 109–133 – 175n7

Berti, E., *Aristotele: Dalla dialettica alla filosofia prima*, Padua 1977 – 22, 31, 42, 45, 56, 123, 144, 160n58

Berti, E., "Note sulla tradizione dei primi due libri della *Metafisica* di Aristotele," *Elenchos* 3 (1982), 5–37 – 102

Berti, E., *Le ragioni di Aristotele*, Rome and Bari 1989 – 3

Berti, E., "La polemica antiaristotelica di Filodemo a proposito della retorica," in *Antiaristotelismo*, eds. C. Natali and S. Maso (Amsterdam 1999) – 149

Berve, H., *Das Alexanderreich auf prosopographischen Gründlage*, Munich 1926 – 12, 154n15, 164n87, 165n104

Bidez, J., "À propos d'un fragment retrouvé de l'Aristote perdu," *Bulletin de la Classe des lettres et des sciences morales et politiques et de la Classe des beaux-arts: L'Académie Royale de Belgique*, series 5, 28 (1942), 201–230 – 140

Bidez, J., *Un singulier naufrage littéraire dans l'antiquité*, Brussels 1943 – 140, 162n72

Bidez, J., "Hermias d'Atarnée," *Bulletin de la Classe des lettres et des sciences morales et politiques et de la Classe des beaux-arts: L'Académie Royale de Belgique*, series 5, 29 (1943), 133–146 – 40, 140, 180n40

Bidez, J., "À propos d'une manière nouvelle de lire Aristote," *Bulletin de la Classe des lettres et des sciences morales et politiques et de la Classe des beaux-arts: L'Académie Royale de Belgique*, series 5, 30 (1944), 43–55 – 140

Bielawski, J., and M. Plezia (eds.), *Lettre d'Aristote à Alexandre sur la politique envers les cités*, Wroclaw, Warsaw, and Cracow 1970 – 46, 123

Bignone, E., *L'Aristotele perduto e la formazione filosofica di Epicuro*, Florence 1936, 2nd ed. 1973 – 40, 42, 132, 140, 154n8, 158n49, 163n82, 180n39

Biscardi, A., "Sul regime della comproprietà nel diritto attico," in *Studi in onore di U. E. Paoli*, Florence 1955, 105–143 – 88, 173nn49 and 54

Blank, D., "Aristotle's 'Academic Course on Rhetoric' and the end of Philodemus, *On Rhetoric VIII*," *Cronache Ercolanesi* 37 (2007), 5–48 – xv, 27, 149–150, 158n47, 164n94

Blass, F, *Die attische Beredsamkeit*, Leipzig 1868–1874 – 158n44

Boeckh, A., "Hermias von Atarneus und Bündniss desselben mit den Erythräern," *Abhandlung der Akademie der Wissenschaften: Historisch-philosophische Classe*, Berlin 1858, 133–157; repr. in *Gesammelte Kleine Schriften*, Leipzig 1872, 6:183+ – 161n72

Boer, W. W. (ed.), *Epistula Alexandri ad Aristotelem*, Meisenheim a/G 1973 – 124

Bosworth, A. B., "Aristotle and Callisthenes," *Historia* 19 (1970), 407–413 – 53, 166n106

Bourgey, L., *Observation et expérience chez Aristote*, Paris 1955 – 107

Bowra, C.M., "Aristotle's Hymn to Virtue," *Classical Quarterly* 32 (1938), 182–189; reprinted in *Problems in Greek Poetry*, Oxford 1953, 139–150 – 37

Boyancé, P., *Le culte des Muses chez les philosophes grecs*, Paris 1937 – 62, 79, 90, 171nn22 and 24, 174n56

Brehier, É., *Histoire de la philosophie*, vol. I, Paris 1928 – 140

Brémond, E. See Mathieu, G., and E. Brémond

Brink, K. O., *s.v.* "Peripatos," *R.-E.* Suppl. VII (1940), coll. 899–949 – 58, 119, 122, 134

Brinkmann, A., "Ein Brief Platons," *Rheinisches Museum* 66 (1911), 226–230 – 160n59, 162n72

Bruck, E. F., *Totenteil und Seelgeräte im griechischen Recht*, Munich 1926 – 172nn33 and 39, 173nn45, 50, and 52

Brun, J., *Aristote et le Lycée*, Paris 1961 – 144

Bruns, G. B., "Die Testamente der griechischen Philosophen," *Zeitschrift der Savigny-Stiftung für Rechtsgeschichte*, Römanistische Abteilung 1 (1880), 1–52 – 172nn33 and 55

Brunschön, C. W. See Sider, D., and C. W. Brunschön

Brunschwig, J., and G.E.R. Lloyd (eds.), *Le savoir grec: Dictionnaire critique*, Paris 1996; English translation *Greek Thought: A Guide to Classical Knowledge*, Cambridge (Mass.) 2000; reprinted as *The Greek Pursuit of Knowledge*, Cambridge (Mass.) and London 2003 – 151, 174n62

Buhle, J. T. (ed.), *Aristotelis opera omnia*, Biponti (Zweibrücken) 1791 – 127

Burnet, J., *Aristotle*, London 1924 – 140–141

Busse, A., "Die neuplatonische Lebensbeschreibungen des Aristoteles," *Hermes* 28 (1893), 252–276 – 119, 128–129, 136, 168n125

Byl, S., "Recherches sur les grands traités biologiques d'Aristote, sources écrites et préjugés," *Académie Royale de Belgique: Mémoires de la Classe de Lettres*, 2nd series 64/3 (1980) — 42, 141

Bywater, I., *Aristotelis Vita Scriptore Laertio*, Oxford 1879 – 127

Cambiano, G., "Il problema dell'esistenza di una scuola megarica," in *Scuole socratiche minori*, ed. G. Giannantoni, Bologna 1977 – 173n46

Cambiano, G., *La filosofia in Grecia e a Roma*, Rome and Bari 1983 – 169n141

Capasso, M., "Note laerziane," *Elenchos* 1 (1980), 161–163 – 173n46

Cardona, G., "Ricerche sulla biografia aristotelica," *Nuova Rivista Storica* 50 (1966), 86–115 – 179n25

Case, T., *s.v.* "Aristotle," *Encyclopaedia Britannica*, 11th ed., 1910 – 180n34

Case, T., "The Development of Aristotle," *Mind* 34 (1925), 192–198 – 180n34

Chatzis, A., *Der Philosopher und Grammatiker Ptolemaios Chennos*, I, Paderborn 1914 – 128

Cherniss, H., *Aristotle's Criticism of Plato and the Academy*, vol. 1 (2nd vol. never published) Baltimore 1935; reprinted New York 1944 and 1962 – 22, 158n45

Cherniss, H., *The Riddle of the Early Academy*, Berkeley and Los Angeles 1945 – 79, 99, 171n22

Christ, W. von, W. Schmid, and O. Stählin, *Geschichte der Griechischen Literatur*, Munich 1912–1924 – 128

Chroust, A.-H., "A Brief Account of the (Lost) *Vita Aristotelis* of Hermippus and of the (Lost) *Vita Aristotelis* of Ptolemy el-Garib," *Revue d'Études Grecques* 77 (1964), 50–69; reprinted in Chroust 1973 – 128, 178n15

Chroust, A.-H., "Aristotle's Earliest 'Course of Lectures on Rhetoric'," *Antiquité Classique* 32 (1964), 58–72; reprinted in Chroust; 1973 – 126

Chroust, A.-H., "The *Vita Aristotelis* of Dionysius of Halicarnassus," *Acta Antiqua Academiae Scientarum Hungaricae* 13 (1965), 369–377; reprinted in Chroust 1973 – 133

Chroust, A.-H., "An Analysis of the *Vita Aristotelis* of Diogenes Laertius," *Antiquité Classique* 34 (1965), 97–129; reprinted in Chroust 1973, 25–53 – 127

Chroust, A.-H., "Was Aristotle Actually the Chief Praeceptor of Alexander the Great?," *Classical Folia* 18 (1966), 26–33; reprinted in Chroust; 1973, 125–132 – 43, 50, 163n83

Chroust, A.-H., "Aristotle Leaves the Academy," *Greece and Rome* 14 (1967), 39–43; reprinted in Chroust; 1973, 117–124 – 160n58

Chroust, A.-H., "Aristotle Enters the Academy," *Classical Folia* 19 (1967), 21–29; reprinted in Chroust; 1973, 92–104 – 11, 19–20, 154n11

Chroust, A.-H., "Aristotle's Last Will and Testament," *Wiener Studien* 80 (1967), 90–114; reprinted in Chroust; 1973, 183–220 – 121, 172n33

Chroust, A.-H., "Aristotle's Return to Athens in the Year 335/4 B.C.," *Laval Théologique et Philosophique* 23 (1967), 244–254; reprinted in Chroust; 1973, 133–144. – 59

Chroust, A.-H., "Speusippus Succeeds Plato in the Scholarcate of the Academy," *Revue d'Études Grecques* 84 (1971), 338–341 – 172n33, 180n44

Chroust, A.-H., "Aristotle's Sojourn in Assos," *Historia* 21 (1972), 170–176 – 162n74, 180n44

Chroust, A.-H., "Did Aristotle Own a School at Athens?," *Rheinisches Museum* 115 (1972), 310–318 – 58, 113, 180n44

Chroust, A.-H., *Aristotle: New Light on His Life and on Some of His Lost Works*, London 1973, 2 vols. – 53, 58, 59, 121, 123, 127, 130, 134, 136, 143, 144, 156nn29 and 32–33, 158n39, 160nn58 and 59, 165n82, 167nn116–117, 177n4

Chroust, A.-H., "Athens Bestows the Decree of Proxenia on Aristotle," *Hermes* 101 (1973), 187–194 – 59, 166n110

Cobet, C. G. (ed.), *Diogenis Laertii de clarorum philosophorum vitis, dogmatibus*, Paris 1850 – 127

Dareste, R., "Les testaments des philosophes Grecs," *Annuaire pour l'incouragement des études grecques* 16 (1882), 1–21 – 171n23

Dareste, R., *Nouvelles Études d'Histoire du Droit*, Paris 1906 – 171n23

Davies, J. K., *Athenian Propertied Families 600–300 BC*, Oxford 1971 – 167n122, 173n43

De Cesare, R., "Di nuovo sulla leggenda di Aristotele cavalcato," *Miscellanea del Centro di Studi Medievali* 1 (1956), 181–215 – 180n30

Derenne, E., *Les procès d'impiété intentés aux philosophes à Athènes aux Vième et IVième siècles avant J.C.*, Liège and Paris 1930 – 61, 167n122, 174n56

Diels, H., "Chronologische Untersuchungen über Apollodors Chronika," *Rheinisches Museum* 31 (1876), 45–47 – 133

Diels, H. (ed.), *Doxographi graeci*, Berlin 1879, 3rd ed. 1958 – 97, 154n10

Diels, H., "Über die ältesten Philosophenschulen der Griechen," in *Philosophische Aufsätze: Eduard Zeller zu seinem fünfzigjährigen Doctor-Jubiläum gewidmet*, Leipzig 1887, 241–260 – 171n23

Diels, H., "Die Olympionikenliste aus Oxyrhynchos," *Hermes* 36 (1901), 72–80 – 165n101

Diels, H., and W. Schubart (eds.), *Didymi de Demosthene commenta*, Berlin 1904 – 160n62, 177n6, 180n33

Dihle, A., "Studien zur griechischen Biographie," *Abhandlungen der Akademie der Wissenschaften zu Göttingen: Philologisch-historische Klasse* 3rd series, 37 (1956), 2nd ed., 1970 – 125

Dihle, A., "Der platoniker Ptolemaios," *Hermes* 85 (1957), 314–325; reprinted in A. Dihle, *Antike und Orient*, Heidelberg 1984, 9–20 – 128

Dirlmeier, F., *Aristoteles: "Nikomachische Ethik"*, Berlin 1956 – 170nn16–18

Dirlmeier, F., *Aristoteles: "Eudemische Ethik"*, Berlin 1962 – 170nn2–3

Dirlmeier, F., *Merkwürdige Zitate in der "Eudemischen Ethik" des Aristoteles*, Heidelberg 1962 – 113, 116

Dittenberger, G. (ed.), *Sylloge inscriptionum graecorum*, 3rd ed., Leipzig 1915 – 39, 60, 63, 124, 166n52

Dorandi, T., *s.v.* "Antigonus of Carystus," *Dictionnaires des Philosophes Antiques*, ed. R. Goulet, vol. 1 (1989), 209–211 – 147

Dorandi, T., *Filodemo, Storia dei Filosofi: Platone e l'Academia (PHerc. 1021 e 164)*, Napoli 1991 – 180n33

Dorandi, T., *s.v.* "Hermias of Atarneus," *Dictionnaires des Philosophes Antiques*, ed. R. Goulet, vol. 3 (2000), 650–651 – 147

Döring, K. (ed.), *Die Megariker*, Amsterdam 1972 – 131, 179n2

Dover, K. J., *Greek Popular Morality in the Time of Plato and Aristotle*, Oxford 1974 – 170n8

Dover, K. J., "The Freedom of the Intellectual in Greek Society," *Talanta* 7 (1976), 24–54 – 61

Drerup, E., "Ein athenisches Proxeniendekret für Aristoteles," *Mitteilungen des Deutschen Archäologischen Instituts: Athenische Abteilung* 23 (1898), 369–381 – 59, 125, 166n110

Düring, I., "Notes on the History of Transmission of Aristotle's Writings," *Göteborgs Högskolas Årsskrift* 56 (1950), 37–70 – 175n5

Düring, I., "Aristotle the Scholar," *Arctos* n. s. 1 (1954), 61–77 – 169n141

Düring, I., "Ariston or Hermippus?," *Classica et Mediaevalia* 17 (1956), 11–21 – 177n11

Düring, I., *Aristotle in the Ancient Biographical Tradition*, Göteborg 1957. [Separately indexed on pp. 194–195.]

Düring, I., Review of Gigon 1962, *Gnomon* 25 (1963), 342–346 – 134

Düring, I., *Aristoteles*, Heidelberg 1966 – 20, 57, 60, 134, 155n30, 170n1, 160nn58–59, 162nn72 and 77, 163nn58 and 83, 170n1

Düring, I., *s.v.* "Aristoteles," *R.-E.* Suppl. XI (1968), coll. 159–336 – 122, 129, 134, 160n58, 162n72, 163n83, 177n11, 179n26

Düring, I., "Ptolemy's *Vita Aristotelis* Rediscovered," in *Philomathes: Studies and Essays in the Humanities in Memory of Philip Merlan*, The Hague 1971, 264–269 – 128

Edelstein, L., *Plato's "Seventh Letter"*, Leiden 1966 – 162n72

Ehrenberg, V., *Alexander and the Greeks*, Oxford 1938 – 47

Eriksen, T. B., *"Bios Theoretikos": Notes on Aristotle's "E.N."* X 6-8, Oslo 1976 – 170nn1, 5, 14, and 19

Eucken, C., *Isokrates: Seine Position in der Auseinandersetzung mit dem zeitgenössischen Philosophen*, Berlin and New York 1983 – 44, 164n88, 177n1

Festa, N., "Un epinicio per Alcibiade e l'ode di Aristotele; in onore di Ermia," *Rendiconti: Atti dell'Academia nazionale dei Lincei, Classe scienze morali, storiche e filologiche*, series 5 (1923), 198–211 – 37

Flach, J. von, *Hesychii Milesii onomatologi quae supersunt omnia*, Leipzig 1882 – 127, 129

Flügel, G., and Rödiger, J. (eds.), *Ibn-al-Nadim: Kitab-al-Fihrist*, Leipzig 1871–1872 – 29

Ford, A. *Aristotle as Poet: The Song for Hermias and Its Contexts*, Oxford and New York 2011 – xviii

Fortenbaugh, W. W., with P. Huby and A. A. Long (eds.), *Theophrastus of Eresus: On His Life and Work*, New Brunswick (N.J.) and Oxford 1985, 1–62 – 153n5, 176n13

Fortenbaugh, W. W., with P. Huby, R. Sharples, and D. Gutas (eds.), *Theophrastus of Eresus: Sources for His Life, Writings, Thought, and Influence*, 8 vols., Leiden 1991+ – xiv

Fortenbaugh, W. W., and W. Schütrumpf (eds.), *Demetrius of Phalerum: Text, Translation, and Discussion*, New Brunswick (N. J.) and London 2000 – xiv, 149

Fortenbaugh, W. W., and W. Schütrumpf, *Dicaearchus of Messana: Text, Translation, and Discussion*, New Brunswick (N. J.) and London 2001 – xiv

Foucart, P., *Des associations réligieuses chez les Grecs*, Paris 1863 – 171n23

Foucart, P., "Étude sur Didymos d'après un papyrus de Berlin," *Mémoires de l'Académie des Inscriptions et Belles-Lettres* 38 (1909), 27–128 – 130, 141, 160n62, 178n13, 180n33

Fragstein, A. von, *Studien zur "Ethik" des Aristoteles*, Amsterdam 1974 – 170nn2–3

Friedländer, P., "Akademische Randglossen," in *Die Gegenwart der Griechen im neueren Denken: Festschrift für Hans-Georg Gadamer zum 60. Geburtstag*, Tübingen 1960, 327+ – 157n38

Fritz, K. von, "Die Ideenlehre des Eudoxos von Knidos und ihr Verhältnis zur Platonischen Ideenlehre," *Philologus* 82 (1927), 1–28 – 157n35

Fritz, K. von, Review of J. Bielawski and M. Plezia 1970, *Gnomon* 44 (1972), 442–450 – 124

Fuentes, Gonzalez, P. P. *See* Lopez Cruces, J. L., and P. P. Fuentes Gonzalez

Fuller, B.A.G., *History of Greek Philosophy III: Aristotle*, New York 1931 – 140

Gaiser, K., *Theophrast in Assos*, Heidelberg 1985 – 39, 42, 161nn63 and 69, 162n70, 163nn79 and 81

Gaiser, K. (ed.), *Supplementum Platonicum: Die Texte der indirekten Platonüberlieferung*, Stuttgart and Bad Cannstatt 1988 – 159n55, 162n78

Gauthier, R.-A. and J.-Y. Jolif, (eds.), *Aristote: "L'Étique à Nicomaque"*, Louvain and Paris 1959, 2nd ed. 1970. – 40, 58, 125, 128, 130, 141, 144, 155n27, 160nn57 and 59, 162n72, 163n82, 164n87, 170nn1, 15, and 20, 177n11

Gercke, A., *s.v.* "Aristoteles," *R.-E.* 2 (1896), coll. 1012–1054 – 137, 140

Gercke, A., *s.v.* "Andronikos 25," *R.-E.* 2 (1896), coll. 2164–2167 – 177n11

Gerth, A., *s.v.* "Kephisodoros," *R.-E.* 11 (1921), coll. 227–229 – 131, 158n44

Giannantoni, G. (ed.), *I Cirenaici: Raccolta delle fonti antiche*, Florence 1958 – 168n131

Giannantoni, G. (ed.), *Socraticorum reliquiae*, 4 vols., Naples 1983–1985, 2nd ed., revised as *Socratis et Socraticorum reliquiae*, Naples 1990 – 69, 131, 164n84, 168nn128 and 131, 174n59

Giannantoni, G., "Cinici e Stoici su Alessandro; Magno," in *I filosofi e il potere nella società e nella cultura antiche*, ed. G. Casertano, Naples 1988, 75–87 – 164n84

Gigante, M. (ed.), *Diogene Laerzio: "Vite dei filosofi"*, Rome and Bari 1962, 2nd ed. 1976 – 127, 173n46, 176n13

Gigon, O., "Antike Erzälungen über die Berufung zur Philosophie," *Museum Helveticum* 3 (1946), 1–21 – 68, 134, 156n30

Gigon, O., "Interpretationen zu den antiken Aristoteles-Viten," *Museum Helveticum* 15 (1958), 146–193 – 21, 53, 59, 61, 62, 113, 123, 127, 133, 134, 161n71, 165n96, 167n116, 177n11

Gigon, O., "Das Leben des Aristoteles," in *Aristoteles: Einführungschriften*, ed. O. Gigon, Zurich and Stuttgart 1961 – 6, 123

Gigon, O. (ed.), *Vita Aristotelis Marciana*, Berlin 1962 – xvii, 11, 21, 56, 59, 62, 97, 118, 123, 129, 134, 154n11, 156n34, 160n59, 163n83, 166n108, 167n116, 168n127

Gigon, O., *s.v.* "Biographie," in *Lexicon der alten Welt*, ed. K. Bartels and L. Huber, Zurich 1965 – 125, 128

Gigon, O. (ed.), *Aristotelis opera, vol. III: Librorum deperditorum fragmenta*, Berlin and New York 1987 – xiii, 121–122, 123, 125, 127, 129, 130, 153n4, 166n114

Goedeckemeyer A., *Aristoteles' praktische Philosophie (Ethik und Politik)*, Leipzig 1922 – 138

Gomperz, T., "Die Akademie und ihr vermeintlicher Philomakedonismus," *Wiener Studien* 4 (1882), 102–120 – 137

Gomperz, T., "Platonische Aufsätze II," *Sitzungs-Berichte der Akadamie der Wissenschaften in Wien: Philologisch-historische Klasse* 141 (1901), 1–11 – 78–80, 137

Gomperz, T., *Griechische Denker*, Leipzig 1906, 3rd ed. 1911 – 136, 137, 170n19, 180n38

Gottschalk, H. B., "Notes on the Wills of Peripatetic Scholarchs," *Hermes* 100 (1972), 314–342 – 15, 104, 154nn11 and 16, 155nn20 and 27, 171n26, 172n40, 173n51, 174n61

Gottschalk, H. B., Review of Lynch 1972, *Classical Review* 90 (1976), 70–72 – 79, 172n42, 174n63

Gottschalk, H. B., "Demetrius of Phalerum: A Politician among Philosophers and a Philosopher among Politicians," in *Demetrius of Phalerum: Text, Translation, and Discussion*, ed. W. W. Fortenbaugh and W. Schütrumpf, New Brunswick (N. J.) and London 2000, 367–380. – 149

Lanza, D., and M. Vegetti (eds.), "W. Jaeger e il neoumanesimo," *Il Pensiero* 18.1–3 (1972) – 180n36

Lasserre, F., *Die Fragmente des Eudoxos von Knidos*, Berlin 1966 – 24, 157nn34–35

Lasserre, F., *De Léodamas de Thasos à Philippe d'Oponte*, Naples 1987 – 38, 153n2, 162nn73, 76, and 79

Laum, B., *Stiftungen in der griechischen und römischen Antike*, Berlin 1914, 2 vols. – 171n29, 172nn33–34, 36–37, and 39, 173nn45 and 54

Laurenti, R. (ed.), *Aristotele: I frammenti dei dialoghi*, Naples 1987, 2 vols. – 45, 46, 68, 124, 169nn136 and 139

Lee, H.D.P., "Place-names and the Date of Aristotle's Biological Works," *Classical Quarterly* 42 (1948), 61–67 – 41, 42, 51, 141, 158n41, 163n82

Leo, F., *Die griechisch-römischen Biographie nach ihrer literarischen Form*, Leipzig 1901 – 125

Levi, M. A., *Isocrate: Saggio critico*, Milan 1959 – 164n94

Lewis, A., "An Aristotle Publication-Date," *Classical Review* n. s. 8 (1958), 108 – 60

Lippert, J., *De epistula pseudaristotelica "peri basileias" commentatio*, Berlin 1891 – 123, 136

Lippert, J., *Studien auf den Gebiete der griechische-arabische Überlieferungsliteratur*, Braunschweig 1894 – 130

Littig, F., *Andronikos von Rhodos*, Munich and Erlangen 1890–1895 – 128, 134

Lloyd, G.E.R., "Plato as a Natural Scientist," *Journal of Hellenic Studies* 88 (1968), 78–92 – 175n6

Lloyd, G.E.R., *Early Greek Science: Thales to Aristotle*, London 1970 – 175n6

Lloyd, G.E.R. *See* Brunschwig, J., and G. E. R. Lloyd

Long, A. A. *See* Fortenbaugh, W. W., P. Huby, and A. A. Long

Long, H. S. (ed.), *Diogenis Laertii vitae philosophorum*, Oxford 1964, 2 vols. – 127

Lopez Cruces, J. L., and P. P. Fuentes Gonzalez, *s.v.* "Isocrates," *Dictionnaires des Philosophes Antiques*, ed. R. Goulet, vol. 3 (2000), 891–938 – 147, 148

Losev, A. and A. Takho-Godi, *Aristotel*, Moscow 1982, English translation *Aristotle*, Moscow 1990 – 2

Louis, P., *Vie d'Aristote: 384–322 avant Jésus-Christ*, Paris 1990 – 145

Lumbroso, G., "Ricerche alessandrine," *Memorie della Reale Accademia delle Scienze di Torino* Series 2, 27 (1873), 179–273 – 171n23

Luzac, J., *Lectiones atticae*, Leiden 1809 – 130

Lynch, J. P., *Aristotle's School. A Study of a Greek Educational Institution*, Berkeley 1972 – 79–81, 83, 85, 126, 171nn23 and 27, 172n31, 174nn62–63

Maas, P., Letter to Kranz, cited in Kranz 1958, at 83n1 – 157n38

Maas, E., *De biographis Graecis questiones selectae*, Berlin 1880 – 136

Macher, E., *Die Hermiasepisode im Demostheneskommentar des Didymos*, Gymn. Programm, Lundenburg 1914 – 160n62

Maddalena, A., *Le lettere di Platone*, Bari 1948 – 162n72

Maddoli, G., "Senocrate; nel clima politico del suo tempo," *Dialoghi di Archeologia* 1 (1967), 304–327 – 136, 143, 180n43

Mansion, A., Review of Düring; 1957, *Revue Philosophique de Louvain* 56 (1958), 624–629 – 180n29

Marasco, G., "I processi d'empietà nella democrazia ateniese," *Atene e Roma* n. s. 21 (1976), 113–131 – 65, 193

Marcovich, M. (ed.), *Diogenis Laertii Vitae philosophorum*, 3 vols., Stuttgart 1999–2002 – xvi, 127

Maso, S. *See* Natali, C., and S. Maso

Mathieu, G., *Les idées politiques d'Isocrate*, Paris 1925 – 86, 171, 193

Mathieu, G., and E. Brémond, *Isocrate: "Discours"*, 4 vols., Paris 1929–1962 – 86, 171, 193

McGregor, M. F. *See* Meritt, B. D., H. T. Wade-Gery, and M. F. McGregor

Mejer, J., *s.v.* "Diogenes Laertius," *Dictionnaires des Philosophes Antiques,* ed. R. Goulet, vol. 2 (1994), 824–833 – 147

Merkelbach, R., *Die Quellen der griechischen Alexanderromans,* Munich 1954 – 151, 193

Merlan, P., "The Successor of Speusippos," *Transactions of the American Philological Association* 77 (1946), 103–111 – 140

Merlan, P., "Isocrates, Aristotle and Alexander the Great," *Historia* 3 (1954), 60–81 – 140, 164n88

Merlan, P., "Zur Biographie des Speusippos', *Philologus* 103 (1959), 60–81. – 140

Merlan, P., *Studies in Epicurus and Aristotle,* Wiesbaden 1960. – 156n34

Merlan, P., *Kleine philologische Schriften,* ed. F. Merlan, Hildesheim and New York 1976. – 180n41

Meritt, B. D., Wade-Gery, H. T. and M. F. McGregor, *The Athenian Tribute Lists,* Cambridge (Mass.) 1939–1953. – 153n1

Mejer, J., s.v. 'Diogenes Laertius', *Dictionnaires des Philosophes Antiques,* ed. R. Goulet, vol. 2 (1994), 824-833. – 147

Mikkola, E., 'Scholē', *Arctos,* 2 (1958), 68–87 – 170n11

Misch, G., *Geschichte der Autobiographie,* vol. 1, Leipzig and Berlin 1907, 2nd ed., Frankfurt 1949 – 125

Momigliano, A., *The Development of Greek Biography,* Cambridge (Mass.) 1971 – 125, 134

Monan, J. D., *Moral Knowledge and Its Methodology in Aristotle,* Oxford 1968 – 170n2

Moraux, P., "L'exposé de la philosophie d'Aristote chez Diogène Laerce," *Revue Philosophique de Louvain* 47 (1949), 5–43 – 127

Moraux, P., *Les listes anciennes des ouvrages d'Aristote,* Louvain 1951 – 26, 50, 122, 127, 128, 141, 164n87, 166n114, 177n11, 179n27

Moraux, P., "Le reveille-matin d'Aristote," *Études Classiques* 19 (1951), 305–315 – 127

Moraux, P., "La composition de la vie d'Aristote chez Diogène Laerce," *Revue d'Études Grecques* 68 (1955), 124–163 – 55, 127, 158n33

Moraux, P., "Aristoteles der Lehrer Alexanders von Aphrodisias," *Archiv für Geschichte der Philosophie* 49 (1967), 169–182 – 178n17, 180n28

Moraux, P., *Der Aristotelismus bei den Griechen von Andronikos bis Alexander von Aphrodisias,* vol. 1, Berlin and New York 1973 – 101, 134

Moraux, P., *Der Aristotelismus bei den Griechen von Andronikos bis Alexander von Aphrodisias,* vol. 2, Berlin and New York 1984 – 178n17

Moraux, P., "Diogène Laerce et le *Peripatos*," *Elenchos* 7 (1986), 245–294 – 127

Moreau, J., *Aristote et son école,* Paris 1962 – 170, 194

Mossé, C., "Methéques et étrangers à Athènes aux IV–III siècles avant notre ère," in *Symposion 1971: Vorträge über Hellenistisches Rechtgeschichte,* ed. H. Wolf, Köln 1975, 205–213 – 79, 194

Mühl, P. von der, *s.v.* "Hermias 11," *R.-E.* Suppl. III (1918), coll. 1126–1130 – 83, 84, 194

Müller, F. A., *Die griechischen Philosophen in der arabischen Überlieferung,* Halle 1873 – 129, 136

Müller, F. A., *Ibn abi Usaibia: 'Uyun al-anba fi tabaqat al-stibba,* Königsberg and Cairo 1884 – 130

Müller, K. O., *Geschichte der griechischen Literatur bis auf das Zeitalter Alexanders,* ed. E. Müller, reslaus 1941 – 132

Müller, R., *s.v.* "Alexinos," in *Dictionnaire des Philosophes Antiques,* ed. R. Goulet, vol. 1 (1989), 149–151 – 147

Mulvany, C. M., "Notes on the Legend of Aristotle," *Classical Quarterly* 20 (1926), 155–167 – 7, 16, 37, 38, 58, 138, 141, 154nn9, 11, and 16, 155n27, 161n66

206 · Bibliographical Index ·

Mure, G.R.G., *Aristotle*, London 1932 – 140

Natali, C., "La teoria aristotelica delle catastrofi: Metodi di razionalizzazione di un mito," *Rivista di Filologia e Istruzione Classica* 105 (1977), 403–424 – 26

Natali, C., "Una data nella vita di Aristotele," *Quaderni di Storia* 8 (1978), 359–363 – 24

Natali, C. (ed.), *La scuola dei filosofi: Scienza ed organizzazione istituzionale della scuola di Aristotele*, L'Aquila 1981 – 153n2, 158n47, 177n10, 178nn16–17, 179n24, 180n32,

Natali, C., "Aspetti organizzativi di alcune scuole filosofiche ateniesi," *Hermes* 111 (1983), 52–69 – 130

Natali, C., "L'immagine di Isocrate nelle opere di Cicerone," *Rhetorica* 3 (1985), 233–243 – 29, 165n100

Natali, C., "*Adoleschia, Leptologia*, and the Philosophers in Athens," *Phronesis* 32 (1987), 232–241 – 57

Natali, C., "Les fins et les moyens, un puzzle aristotélicien," *Revue de philosophie ancienne* 6 (1988), 107–146 – 170n4

Natali, C. (ed.), *Senofonte: L'Amministrazione della Casa ("Economico")*, Venice 1988 – 168n32

Natali, C., "Lieux et écoles du savoir," in *Le savoir grec: Dictionnaire critique*, eds. J. Brunschwig and G.E.R. Lloyd, Paris 1996, 229–249; English translation "Schools and Sites of Learning," in *Greek Thought: A Guide to Classical Knowledge*, eds. J. Brunschwig and G.E.R. Lloyd, Cambridge (Mass.) 2000, 191–217; reprinted as *The Greek Pursuit of Knowledge*, Cambridge (Mass.) and London 2003, 40–66 – 151, 174n62

Natali, C., *La Saggezza di Aristotele*, Naples 1989; English translation *The Wisdom of Aristotle*, tr. G. Parks, Albany (NY) 2001 – 170n4, 170n20

Natali, C., "Philosophical Schools," in *Oxford Encyclopedia of Ancient Greece and Rome*, eds. M. Gagarin and E. Fantham, Oxford 2010, 250–255 – 151

Natali, C., and S. Maso (eds.), *Antiaristotelismo*, Amsterdam 1999 – 149

Nilsson, M. P., *Geschichte der griechischen Religion*, Munich 1960, 2 vols. – 172nn33 and 39, 173n53

Nissen, H., "Die Staatschriften des Aristoteles," *Rheinisches Museum* 42 (1892), 161–206 – 50, 123, 136, 139, 140

Nock, A. D., *Conversion: The Old and the New in Religion from Alexander the Great to Augustine of Hippo*, Oxford 1933 – 68

Nussbaum, M. C., *The Fragility of Goodness: Luck and Ethics in Greek Tragedy and Philosophy*, Cambridge 1986 – 175n7

Oncken, W., *Die Staatslehre des Aristoteles im historisch-politischen Umrissen*, 2 vols., Leipzig 1870–1875 – 176n12

Owen, G.E.L., "Tithenai ta phainomena," in *Aristote et les problèmes de méthode*, ed. S. Mansion, Louvain 1961, 83–103; reprinted in G.E.L. Owen, *Logic, Science and Dialectic: Collected Papers on Ancient Greek Philosophy*, ed. M. C. Nussbaum, London 1986 – 175n7

Pasquali, G., *Le lettere di Platone*, Florence 1938 – 162n72

Pavese, C., "Aristotele e i filosofi ad Asso," *Parola del Passato* 16 (1961), 113–119 – 39

Pauler, Á., *Aristoteles*, Paderborn 1933 – 138

Pearson, L., "The Diary and the Letters of Alexander the Great," *Historia* 3 (1954), 443–450 – 123, 124

Pearson, L., and S. Stephens (eds.), *Didymi in Demosthenis commenta*, Stuttgart 1983 – xv, 160nn62 and 63, 162n73, 163n79, 177n6

Pellegrin, P., *La classification des animaux chez Aristote*, Paris 1982 – 175n9

Pernot, L., *s.v.* "Cephisodorus," *Dictionnaires des Philosophes Antiques*, ed. R. Goulet, vol. 2 (1994), 266–269 – xviii, 147, 148

Robbe, L., *Vita Aristotelis ex codice marciano nunc primum edita*, Leiden 1861 – 129

Robert, L., "Recherches epigraphiques," *Revue des Études Anciennes* 62 (1960), 276–361, at 294 – 172nn33 and 35

Robert, L., "Sur des inscriptions d'Éphèse: Fêtes, athlètes, empereurs, épigrammes," *Revue de philologie, de littérature, et d'histoire anciennes* 93 (= 3. sér. 46) (1967), 7–84, at 42–43 – 172nn33 and 35

Robin, L., "Projet d'article pour le dictionnaire historique des sciences . . . Aristote I: vie, oeuvre, doctrine," *Revue de Synthèse Historique* 4 (1932), 65–96 – 140

Robin, L., *Aristote*, Paris 1944 – 45, 140

Rödiger, J. *See* Flügel, G., and J. Rödiger

Rolfes, E., *Die Philosophie des Aristoteles als Naturklärung und Weltschauung*, Leipzig 1923 – 138

Romeyer-Dherbey, G., "Le statut social d'Aristote à Athènes," *Revue de Métaphysique et de Morale* 91 (1986), 365–378 – 157n37

Rose, V., *De Aristotelis librorum ordine et autoritate commentatio*, Berlin 1854 – 45, 128

Rose, V. (ed.), *Aristotelis fragmenta*, Leipzig 1886 – 121–122, 127, 129

Ross, W. D., *Aristotle*, London 1923 – 58, 138, 158n39, 160n57

Ross, W. D. (ed.), *Aristotelis fragmenta selecta*, Oxford 1955 – 46, 121

Rossitto, C., *Aristotele; e altri: Divisioni*, Padua 1984 – 107

Rousseau, M. F., *The Apple, or Aristotle's Death*, Milwaukee 1968 – 135

Sandbach, F. H., *Aristotle and the Stoics*, Cambridge 1985 – 175n5

Santoni, A., *Demetrio; di Falero*, unpublished typescript 1988 – 154n18

Savoie, D., "Problemes de datation d'une occultation observé par Aristote," *Revue d'histoire des sciences* 56 (2003), 493–504 – xvii

Schachermeyer, F., *Alexander der Große*, Vienna 1973 – 164n88

Schmid, W. *See* Christ, W. von, W. Schmid, and O. Stählin

Schneider, J.-P., *s.v.* "Eudoxus," *Dictionnaires des Philosophes Antiques*, ed. R. Goulet, vol. 3 (2000), 293–302 – 147

Schneider, J.-P., *s.v.* "Hermippus," *Dictionnaires des Philosophes Antiques*, ed. R. Goulet, vol. 3 (2000), 655–658 – 147

Schneider, J.-P., and F. Queryel, *s.v.* "Demetrius of Phalerum," *Dictionnaires des Philosophes Antiques*, ed. R. Goulet, vol. 2 (1994), 628–635 – 147

Schubart, W. *See* Diels, H. , and W. Schubart

Schultz, H., *s.v.* "Hesychios 10," *R.-E.* 8 (1913), coll. 1322–1327 – 127

Schütrumpf, W. *See* Fortenbaugh, W. W., and W. Schütrumpf

Schwab, M., *Bibliographie d'Aristote*, Paris 1896; reprinted New York 1967 – 135

Schwartz, E., *s.v.* "Curtius Rufus 30," *R.-E.* 4 (1901), coll. 1870–1891 – 54

Schwartz, E., *s.v.* 'Diogenes von Kyzikos', *R.-E.* 5 (1905), coll. 738–763 – 127

Scott, M., *From Democrats to Kings*, London 2009 – 150–151

Sedley, D., "Epicurus and His Professional Rivals," in *Études sur l'Epicurisme antique*, eds. J. Bollack and A. Laks, Lille 1976, 119–160 – 11, 130, 132, 153n8

Sharples, R. W., "Editor's Notes," *Phronesis* 38 (1993), 111+ – xvi

Sharples, R. W., *Peripatetic Philosophy 200 BC to AD 200: An Introduction and Collection of Sources in Translation*, Cambridge 2010 – xviii

Sharples, R. W. *See* Fortenbaugh, W. W., P. Huby, R. Sharples, and D. Gutas

Sider, D., and C. W. Brunschön (eds.), *Theophrastus of Eresus: "On Weather Signs"*, Leiden and Boston 2007 – xiv, 175n8

Sollenberger, M. G., "Diogenes Laertius 5.36–57: The *Vita Theophrasti*," in *Theophrastus of Eresus: On His Life and Work*, eds. W. W. Fortenbaugh, P. Huby, and A. A. Long, New Brunswick and Oxford 1985, 1–62 – 153n5, 176n13

Solmsen, F., "Leisure and Play in Aristotle's Ideal State," *Rheinisches Museum* 107 (1964), 193–210 – 170n8

Solmsen, F., "The Fishes of Lesbos and Their Alleged Significance for the Development of Aristotle," *Hermes* 106 (1978), 467–484 – 42, 141

Sorabji, R., "The Ancient Commentators on Aristotle," in *Aristotle Transformed: The Ancient Commentators and Their Influence*, ed. R. Sorabji, London 1990, 1–30 – 90

Sordi, M., "La cronologia delle vittorie persiane e la caduta di Ermia di Atarneo," *Kokalos* 5 (1959), 107–118 – 161

Sordi, M., "La lettera di Aristotele a Alessandro e i rapporti tra Greci e barbari," *Aevum* 58 (1984), 3–12 – 124

Spoerri, W., *s.v.* "Callisthenes of Olynthus," *Dictionnaires des Philosophes Antiques*, ed. R. Goulet, vol. 2 (1994), 183–221 – 147, 148

Stählin, O. See Christ, W. von, W. Schmid, and O. Stählin

Stahr, A., *Aristotelia: Leben, Schriften und Schüler des Aristoteles*, 2 vols., Halle 1830–1832 – 130

Stark, R., *Aristotelesstudien*, Munich 1954 – 162n72

Steiner, G., "Whereof One Cannot Speak," *London Review of Books* 10:12 (1988), 15–16 – viii–ix, 1–3, 125

Steinmetz, P., *Die Physik des Theophrast*, Bad Homburg 1964 – 108

Steinschneider, M., "Al-Farabi: Des arabischen Philosophen Leben und Schriften," *Mémoires de l'Académie Imperiale des sciences de Saint-Petersbourg* 7th series, 13/4 (1869), 187–207 – 59, 136

Steinweter, A., *Zeitschrift der Savigny-Stiftung für Rechtsgeschichte*, Romanistische Abteilung 51 (1931), 405–407 – 174n61

Stephens, S. See Pearson, L., and S. Stephens

Stern, S. M., *Aristotle and the World-State*, London 1968 – 123

Stroux, J., "Die stoische Beurteilung Alexanders des Grossens," *Philologus* 88 (1933), 222–240 – 43

Sudhaus, S., "Aristoteles in der Beurteilung des Epikur und Philodem," *Rheinisches Museum* 48 (1893), 552–564 – 132, 164n94

Susemihl, F., *Geschichte der Litteratur in der Alexandrinischer Zeit*, Leipzig 1891–1892 – 122

Takho-Godi, A. See Losev, A., and A. Takho-Godi

Taormina, D. P., *Plutarco di Atene: L'Uno, l'Anima, le Forme*, Catania 1989 – 90

Tarán, L., *Speusippus of Athens*, Leiden 1981 – 105, 159n55, 160n60

Tarn, W. W., *Alexander the Great*, 2 vols., Cambridge 1948 – 164n87, 165n106

Taylor, A. E. Review of Ross 1923, *Mind* 33 (1924), 316–321 – 138n34

Taylor, A. E. Review of Mure 1932, *Mind* 41 (1932), 501–505 – 155n27

Thillet, P., "Aristote conseilleur politique d'Alexandre vainqueur des Perses?," *Revue d'Études Grecques* 85 (1972), 527–542 – 124

Thompson, D. W., *Aristotle: History of Animals*, Oxford 1910 – 41, 141, 158n41

Tovar, A., "Para la formación de la *Vita Marciana* de Aristoteles," *Emerita* 11 (1943), 180–200 – 50, 129

Tracy, T., *Physiological Theory and the Doctrine of the Mean in Aristotle*, The Hague 1969 – 73, 170n6

Usener, H., "Organisation der wissenschaftlichen Arbeit; Bilder aus der Geschichte der Wissenschaft," *Preussische Jahrbücher* 53 (1884), 1–25; reprinted in *Vorträge und Aufsätze*, Leipzig and Berlin 1907, 67–102 – 139, 153n8, 171n23

Van Groningen, B. A., *Aristote: Le Second Livre de l'Économique*, Leiden 1933 – 40, 108

Vegetti, M., *Il coltello e lo stilo*, Milan 1979 – 96, 169n141

Vegetti, M. See Lanza, D. and M. Vegetti

Veyne, P., *Le Pain and le Cirque: Sociologie historique d'un pluralisme politique*, Paris 1976, English translation *Bread and Circuses*, tr. B Pearce, London 1990 – 172nn33 and 39, 173nn48 and 54

Vidal-Naquet, P. *See* Austin, M. and P. Vidal-Naquet

Vollenhoven, D.H.T., *Geschiedenis der Wijsbegeerte*, Wever 1950 – 156n32

Waddington, C., "Quelques points à éclaircir dans la vie d'Aristote," *Annales de Philosophie Chrétienne* n. s. 28 (1893); reprinted in *La philosophie ancienne et la critique historique*, Paris 1904 – 137, 164n86

Wade-Gery, H. T. *See* Meritt, B. D., H. T. Wade-Gery, and M. F. McGregor

Waschkies, H.-J., *Von Eudoxos zu Aristoteles: Das Fortwirken der Eudoxischen Proportionentheorie in der Aristotelischen Lehre vom Kontinuum*, Amsterdam 1977 – xvii, 157n34

Wehrli, F., *Die Schule des Aristoteles*, Texte u. Komm., Basel and Stuttgart 1944–1978, 10 volumes + 2 supplements – 79, 80, 100, 117, 125, 126, 162n78, 164nn87 and 93, 167n123, 172n31, 173n44, 177nn10–11, 178n20

Wehrli, F., Review of Lynch 1972, *Gnomon* 48 (1976), 129–130 – 80

Weil, R., *Aristote et l'histoire*, Paris 1960 – 38, 47, 162n72, 164n87, 165nn96 and 101–102, 166n114

Weil, R., "Aristote le professeur," *L'Information Littéraire* 1 (1965), 17–29 – 169n141

Wes, M. A., "Quelques remarques à propos d'une lettre d'Aristote à Alexandre," *Mnemosyne* 25 (1972), 261–295 – 124

Westermann, A., *Biographoi: Vitarum Scriptores graeci minores*, Brunsvigae (Braunschweig) 1845 – 127

Whitehead, P., "Aristotle the Metic," *Proceedings of the Cambridge Philological Society* 21 (1975), 94–99 – 20, 157n36

Wilamowitz-Moellendorff, U. von, *Antigonos von Karystos*, Berlin and Zurich 1965 (2nd ed., first published 1881). – 57, 78–81, 90, 92, 94–95, 119. 122, 123, 125, 136, 153n2, 171nn22–23, and 30, 173n52, 174nn63–64, 180n32

Wilamowitz-Moellendorff, U. von, *Aristoteles und Athen*, Berlin 1966 (2nd ed., first published 1893). – 12, 40, 46, 47, 50, 56, 136–137, 139, 140, 142, 143, 150, 156nn32 and 34, 160n59, 161n72, 164n87, 180n39

Wilamowitz-Moellendorff, U. von, "Lesefrüchte 22," *Hermes* 33 (1898), 531–532 – 167n115

Will, W., *Athen und Alexander: Untersuchungen zur Geschichte der Stadt von 338 bis 322 v. Chr.*, Munich 1983 – 46

Wörle, A., *Die politische Tätigkeit der Schuler Platons*, Lauterburg 1981 – 161n69, 162n76

Wörle, G., *Theophrasts Methode in seinen Botanischen Schriften*, Amsterdam 1985 – 109, 176n10

Wormell, D.E.W., "The Literary Tradition Concerning Hermias of Atarneus," *Yale Classical Studies* 5 (1935), 57–92 – 53, 130, 138, 141, 160n62, 162n78, 178n13

Wycherley, R. E., *The Stones of Athens*, Princeton (N.J.) 1978 – 172n40

Zadro A., *Aristotele, "I Topici"*, Naples 1974 – 97

Zeller, E., *Die Philosophie der Griechen in ihrer geschichtlichen Entwicklung*, Leipzig 1879, 4th ed. 1921; reprinted Hildesheim 1963. – 4, 12, 26, 31, 42, 51, 122, 135–136, 141, 144, 153n4, 161n72, 164n91, 166n109

Zemb, J. M., *Aristoteles im Selbstzeugnissen und Bilddokumenten*, Hamburg 1961 – 144

Ziebarth, E., s.v. "diathēke," *R.-E.* 9 (1902), coll. 39–42 – 172n33

Ziebarth, E., *Aus dem griechischen Schuhlwesen*, Berlin-Leipzig 1909 – 172nn33 and 37–38

Ziebarth, E., s.v. "Stiftungen," *R.-E.* Suppl. VII (1940), coll. 1236–1240 – 172n33

Zucher, F., "Isokrates' *Panathenaikos*," in *Isokrates*, ed. F. Seck, Darmstadt 1976, 226–252 (first published 1954) – 164n94

Zürcher, J., *Aristoteles' Werk und Geist*, Paderborn 1952 – 143

INDEX OF ANCIENT
PERSONS AND PLACES

Persons. All those ancient persons who are historically significant are indexed here; those whose only significance is historiographical (e.g. Apollodorus, Diogenes Laertius) are excluded, and indexed instead in the index of sources. Those persons who are historically significant and are also authors of works that are sources of evidence (e.g. Plato, Isocrates, Theophrastus) are indexed in both indexes.

Places. Place names that indicate locations of events are indexed (e.g. Athens, Zereia). To each geographical entry are appended cross-references to all persons from that place, e.g. from Athens, Macedonia, or Stagira. Place names that occur only as parts of personal names, e.g. Abdera (home of Anaxarchus) and Zelea (home of Nicagoras), are entirely excluded.

Abbreviation: A = Aristotle

Callinus, literary executor of Lyco, 175n3
Callinus, member of Peripatetic community, mentioned in will of Theophrastus, 7, 86, 87, 155n22
Callippus, student of Isocrates, 168n130
Callisthenes, member of Peripatetic community, mentioned in will of Theophrastus, 87, 155n22
Callisthenes of Olynthus, nephew of A, 16, 45, 49, 52–55, 90, 147–148, 154n16, 165nn98–106; accompanied Alexander to Asia, 51, 52–53; collaborated with A on Pythian chronology, 53, 60, 124, 165n101; heroic portrait of Hermias by, 34, 36, 37, 132–133
Caracalla, expelled "Aristotelian" philosophers from Alexandria, 55
Cassander of Macedonia, son of Antipater, 13, 48
Cephalus, metic respected in Athens, 20
Cephisodorus, eponymous Athenian archon of 323/322 BCE, 61
Cephisodorus, student of Isocrates, wrote a work attacking A, xvii, xviii, 9, 25, 26, 131, 147–148, 158n44, 178nn17 and 19
Cercops, founder of Athens, 153
Chalcedon (Bithynia), city near Assos, home of Xenocrates, 33. See also Xenocrates
Chalcidian peninsula (Thrace), 6, 7, 17. See also Methone; Olynthus; Stagira
Chalcis (Euboea), last residence of A, xiv–xv, 15, 60–64, 132, 167n117, 169n134; school of A in?, 63, 81, 85, 167n123; settlement of Stagira by colonists from, 8, 11
Chares, slave and beneficiary of Lyco, 175n3
Charmantides, student of Isocrates, 168n130
Charmides, uncle of Plato, 69
Chios (Aegean island), animosity of Chians toward A, 132. See also Bryon; Panionius; Theocritus
Chrysippus of Cnidus, teacher of Metrodorus (husband of A's daughter Pythia), 15
Cilicia (southern Asia Minor), site of battles with Persians, 10

Citium (Cyprus), location of astronomical observations of Eudoxus, 24. See also Zeno
Clearchus of Soli: commentaries on Plato by, 100; dialogue between A and a Jew recounted by, 126
Cnidus (Caria), location of astronomical observations of Eudoxus, 24. See also Chrysippus; Eudoxus
Conon of Athens, father of Timotheus, 168n130
Conon of Athens, rented fancy room to Lyco, 94
Coriscus of Scepsis, Academic philosopher, colleague of A at Assos, father of Neleus, 38–39, 41, 89, 102, 118, 147, 162nn75 and 79
Crates, Cynic philosopher, 13, 65; wife and brother-in-law also philosophers, 69
Critias of Athens, Plato's uncle, 69, 161n68

Damotimus of Olynthus, father of Callisthenes, 53, 60
Delphi (central Greece): location of A's monument to Hermias, 36; location of monument honoring A for his work on Pythian victors, 59–60, 63, 124, 146; oracle advising A to study with Plato, 11, 128, 156n30
Demaratus, member of Peripatetic community, mentioned in will of Theophrastus, 87
Demetrius of Phalerum, Peripatetic philosopher, xiv, 13, 51–52, 91, 147, 149, 166n112; comments on fate of empires by, 48–49; favorable treatment of philosophers by, 13, 91, 155n19; friend of Nicanor 13, 17, 154n17; and library of Alexandria, 101, 103, 175n4; and Theophrastus, 17, 58, 85, 90
Demetrius I "Poliorcetes" of Macedonia, expelled philosophers from Athens, 91
Demochares of Athens, politician, nephew of Demosthenes, attacked A, 6–7, 32, 50, 91–92, 162n76, 167n117, 171n21, 179n22
Democritus of Abdera, philosopher, teacher of Anaxarchus, 43, 165n104